Managing a Consumer Lending Business

DAVID LAWRENCE
ARLENE SOLOMON

SOLOMON LAWRENCE PARTNERS

NEW YORK   2002

Published by Solomon Lawrence Partners
119 West 57th Street, Suite 200
New York, New York 10019
http://solomon-lawrence.com

ISBN-13: 978-0-9717537-0-9

ISBN-10: 0-9717537-0-9

Book design and type formatting by Bernard Schleifer
Manufactured in the United States of America
FIRST EDITION
9 8 7 6 5 4

Contents

Preface

T HIS IS MY THIRD and, I daresay, final attempt to write about a business I have participated in and learned a great deal about over the past twenty-five years, namely, the consumer lending business. I have found the business a fascinating challenge, one that some institutions have been able to deliver brilliantly (and very profitably) and others have failed at. In this book, and my two earlier books,[1] I have tried to define some of the processes which helped the winners to win and the lack of which contributed to the losers' losing. This time, I have a partner, Arlene Solomon, who has been a full participant in helping me write this book. More about Arlene below.

What I find fascinating is that, on the whole, the banks and other types of consumer lending institutions all started from about the same point in mid-1970, when the business began to change. At that time, the traditional banker was conservative and dedicated primarily to servicing his corporate clients (note how I can safely say *he* because almost all bankers were men in those days). Retail banking, as it was then called, consisted of offering home mortgage, automobile, and some revolving loans to the bank's customers, primarily through their main office or branch locations. The senior bankers may have started in the branch system, but as they moved up the ladder, their main goal was to get to know the corporate clients and service their needs. Retail bankers were well down the ladder in the organization.

All this began to change in the mid-1970s with the explosive growth of the credit card business. Citicorp led the way with a massive, national mailing of credit card offers that was bold, ingenious and, initially, a disaster. But the chairman of Citicorp, the visionary Walter Wriston, allowed the consumer banking "boys" under John Reed enough time and financial support to truly learn the business, and they did. Every few months new consumer lending businesses were bought or expanded around the world, and new people joined every month, bringing their expertise from such diverse businesses as Lever Bros., Procter & Gamble (marketing expertise), Ford Motor Company (finance expertise), and the top business schools. John Reed then led Citicorp through many years of extraordinary growth as he became chairman after Walter Wriston retired.

---

1. *Risk and Reward: The Craft of Consumer Lending* (New York: Citicorp, 1984); *The Handbook of Consumer Lending* (New York: Simon & Schuster, 1992).

Far from being an "orphan" of the business, consumer lending today at many financial institutions is often the most profitable and fastest growing part of the business.

The traditional concept of risk management—to minimize losses—went out the window, along with the concept that you had to know your customers through face-to-face contact at the branch. Fortunately, just at this time, the practice of scoring, that is, managing a high-volume business with statistical tools, was beginning to be widely accepted. The use of scoring techniques allowed Citicorp and other financial institutions to expand with some confidence. Many regional and smaller banks, however, never bothered to change or adapt to the new world of consumer lending and were absorbed or faded away over the years.

In my earlier books, I tried to document the changes that were taking place and to describe the tools that successful lenders were using. Rereading those books today, I find that what I wrote wasn't bad; it's just out-of-date. Things have changed so rapidly in the business, including the growth of the Internet as a sales and distribution system, the explosion of data-mining (the technique of gathering and analyzing vast amounts of information from different sources on your customers and potential customers), and the worldwide growth of credit cards and consumer lending, that I thought it was time to redo the earlier books.

This time I have help from my partner, Arlene Solomon. Arlene is the co-author of this book, and it really is true that two heads are better than one. She also suggested including many of the charts from our training program, *Consumer Credit: Managing Risk and Reward.* I'm sure the reader will find them helpful.

I have also incorporated material from the training program initially prepared for us by Alan Schiffres and Joe DeBellis of Portfolio Management Associates, a New York City–based management consulting company. We have used their expertise in the field of consumer lending throughout this book, particularly in the areas of account acquisition, scoring, and account maintenance. Another vital source of information has been Don Griffin, president of The Center for Business Solutions, a Colorado-based consulting group specializing in collections. He drafted the two chapters on collections and has been a proponent of many of the concepts driving collection organizations today that we have incorporated in this book.

We have also asked friends with many years' experience in the business to review various chapters before we sent them off to the printers. The comments from Jeff Fread, John Holder, Don Kumka, Mark Lieberman, Ray Romano, Alan Schiffres, and Larry Sussman were very helpful in keeping us on track with the industry of today. We have enjoyed working with them and with all the many wonderful people who have made a difference in the way consumers are treated by lenders today.

We are also both in awe of the work done by Carol Shookhoff, who was to be our editor, but who turned out to be our taskmaster, our conscience, as well as our editor. By constantly prodding us ("this contradicts previous material"; "give example"), she has made this a better book. Thank you, Carol. Finally, we thank Bernie Schleifer for his design of the book and Kelly Holohan who came up with the glorious cover. If this book is attractive and readable, it is due to their good work.

David Lawrence
Arlene Solomon

Introduction

A T A RETIREMENT PARTY in the late 1950s, a senior banker was asked to name the most important change in banking during his forty years in the business. After a moment's reflection, he replied, "Air conditioning." While the introduction of office air conditioning may have meant a great deal to bankers who wilted in hot offices in those days, no one at Jim Bailey's retirement party at Citigroup in June 2000 would ever consider their physical comfort a significant factor in banking. Jim had played a key risk management role at the Citicorp (as it was then called) credit card business during the 1980s and then moved up to run its domestic consumer business during the early 1990s. Many of the people who had changed the industry were there to wish Jim farewell.

These guests could have talked from firsthand experience about the dazzling changes in banking, and indeed, the whole financial services industry, over the last twenty-five years: the growth of the global economy, the development of the Internet and electronic banking, the introduction of new products and services. Forget air conditioning! In particular, the growth of the worldwide credit card business had literally revolutionized the way goods and services are purchased, and even more important, the profits generated by the business contributed significantly to the banking system's current financial strength.

This financial revolution wouldn't have worked unless the fundamentals of the business, in particular the way people behave, were sound:

- *Most people use credit wisely and repay their debts on time.*
- *Most people reduce their spending during periods of hardship.*
- *Most lenders extend credit responsibly and prudently.*

In other words, the credit system works. If it didn't, this book would be unnecessary because we would be living in an all-cash society. Anyone who has tried to rent a car, buy an airline ticket, or check into a hotel knows that in many situations, a credit card is not merely convenient . . . it is essential. In addition, mortgages, automobile loans, and other forms of financing give consumers the freedom to buy a home or to purchase items they would otherwise never be able to afford without years of saving.

A few people abuse the system: they have no intention of ever repaying the debts they incur and consider bankruptcy a financial planning tool. Others simply rationalize their inability to meet their obligations as the fault of the "system" that has encouraged them to accept credit they didn't ask for (remember, in recent years three to four billion offers for credit cards have been mailed annually in the United States). Certainly some lenders do not understand the business, and some bend the rules of common sense by extending credit carelessly. Some even offer services to help those wishing to exploit the system. Their advertisements tell people they can "Wipe out bad credit" or "Get 20 credit cards through the mail." Today the Internet is full of offers for credit cards to people with poor credit records (one offer reads "$5000 Major International Credit Card, guaranteed, unsecured, regardless of Credit History, Even Bankruptcy"). But these are the exceptions, and this book was not written to moralize about the use or misuse of credit by either consumers or lenders.

The purpose of this book is to describe for legitimate financial institutions the tools available to manage a consumer loan business and to outline a process for intelligent risk-taking that is commensurate with achieving an appropriate return.

CONSUMER DEBT PATTERNS

Consumer credit has been an explosive growth product in the past century. Consumers have demonstrated an increasing willingness, indeed eagerness, to take on debt, and financial institutions have been keen to help them. Total consumer debt has grown from $3 trillion in 1990 to more than $7 trillion in 2001, with home mortgages accounting by far for the largest increase in dollars. Growth, however, has occurred in all product lines—home mortgages, credit cards, auto financing, and personal loans—but revolving products have overwhelmingly experienced the fastest *rate* of growth (typically around 15–20% per year in the U.S. as opposed to 10% or less for mortgages and other consumer products).

Although inflation has played some role, growth can also be attributed to several obvious, as well as some not-so-obvious, factors:

- *Credit cards have been given greater utility. In addition to their traditional role in clothing, hardware, and other retail shops, credit cards are also being used at grocery stores, at the movies, for taxis, at gas stations, to buy a burger at McDonald's, or even cover the $1.50 charge for an airport luggage cart. Catalog and Internet purchases are continually growing in number, and these are frequently charged on a credit card. As electronic processing has lowered handling costs, using credit cards for even small purchases has become cost-effective. Consumers have become accus-*

tomed to charging "everything" (usually with the intention of paying the entire balance monthly, although in reality they do not manage this most of the time).

There is still enormous potential for growth: credit cards are used in less than 25% of potential card transaction situations in the U.S. and even less than that in the rest of the world.

- *As a rule, repayment terms have been liberalized. Lower minimum repayments on credit cards are available (e.g., 2% or less of the outstanding balance per month compared to the early rates of 3–5% per month). In addition, interest-only terms on home equity loans are more common for longer and longer terms.*

- *Down payments on secured products are being lowered. For instance, no-down-payment auto loans were widely advertised in the late 1990s, as are "Equity Stretcher Loans" today on homes ("Borrow up to 125% of the value of your home") as competition increases to gain customers at any price.*

- *An entirely new market of lending to less-creditworthy customers has sprung up. Lenders are expanding their market share by making loans to those with little or no credit record, or with some previous poor credit history (the "C&D" or subprime market, as it is commonly called).[1]*

All these factors have contributed to the increasing dollar volume of debt outstanding. Has all this growth in debt put an unbearable burden on the U.S. consumer? Some doomsayers say yes. One widely publicized Federal Reserve statistic (debt service as a percentage of disposable personal income) shows that consumers were spending about 13–14% of their income to service their debt in recent years, but this is about the same as it was in the mid-1980s, and up only slightly from the level of around 12% in the mid-1990s. Not much change.

Overall then, and in absolute dollars, consumer credit has been a booming business, and the boom has not gone unnoticed at the major financial services companies and banks. A whole group of new entrants came into the credit card market in the 1980s and 1990s: the "monoline" companies such as Capital One, Advanta, Providian, First USA, among others. The term *monoline* comes from the fact that these institutions typically started with only one product, usually a credit card, offered nationally. Rather than develop branches, the monolines invested heavily in "data mining" and mail solicitations to build a business (some shareholders were rewarded as stock prices rose). By early 2002, however, at least three monolines (Advanta, Providian, and First USA) had encountered severe financial difficulties.

---

1. The term *C&D* lending comes from the practice of some lenders ranking their loans by risk, ranging from "A" loans, those with the lowest risk, to "D" loans, those with the highest risk.

Consolidations have also occurred in the industry; mid-size banks have merged and the larger banks have swallowed up both the mid-size and the smaller institutions. In the United States, the top ten credit card issuers (Citibank, MBNA, First USA, Discover, Chase, American Express, Capital One, Providian, Bank of America, and Household) had card receivables totaling $489 billion by year end 2001, representing 78% of the current domestic United States credit card business. At the beginning of the 1990s, the top ten controlled less than 50% of the credit card market.

Mortgage lenders are also consolidating, and the largest originating banks, such as Wells Fargo, Countrywide, and Chase, control more than 25% of the business. This trend of consolidation, however, does not signify a lack of room for the regional or local banks. The smart, strong-willed smaller institutions will continue to survive and thrive as long as they cover their own markets and serve their customers well. Nonetheless, they will still need to know what they are doing. Most of the techniques discussed in this book apply most effectively to large portfolios where thousands, hundreds of thousands, or even millions of credit decisions are made in a year. The same *principles,* however, apply to smaller portfolios where only a few hundred decisions are made.

Overseas, the markets also are changing, but in the opposite direction—the markets are becoming more competitive. The days when five or six banks controlled the financial markets in such countries as the U.K., Germany, France, Australia, or Canada are over. Newcomers are entering the business, and some multinational banks are aggressively expanding their consumer lending operations worldwide. Citigroup, for instance, is the leading consumer lender not only in the United States, but in country after country, issuing credit cards, mortgages, automobile loans, and every other form of consumer lending product conceived thus far. Competition thrives as these newcomers expand their services.

Enough background on this growth business. What are the principles of good management that we cover in this book? What will the winners do to differentiate themselves from the stodgy old banks of the past? The consumer lending business is governed by five underlying principles.

THE FIVE PRINCIPLES OF GOOD MANAGEMENT

- *Balance Risk and Reward—There is an appropriate balance between risk and reward, and optimizing profits is better than merely minimizing losses.*

- *Plan Ahead—Good planning at the front end (acquiring and managing accounts) prevents problems at the back end (i.e., collections and writeoffs).*

- *Manage by the Odds—Statistical control techniques allow risks to be managed predictably.*

- *Develop and Analyze Management Information—Good management information must be available, read, and used.*
- *Assign Responsibility for Managing Risk—There are different ways to manage risk, but the responsibility should be clearly defined.*

These five principles are the core of this book. Let's examine each one in some detail.

Balance Risk and Reward

The overall objective of a business is to make a profit, a profit that meets management's goals and rewards its shareholders appropriately. The goal in consumer credit is *not* to minimize bad loans, but rather to make every effort to balance the risk (the losses or writeoffs) with the reward (optimal profits). One indicator of general understanding of this concept across an organization is that writeoff levels are never discussed without a reference to how much profit (or loss) the product is generating. And, remember, the risk/reward of each product varies widely—some products are just inherently riskier than others. For instance, the typical rate of writeoffs on major credit products in the United States currently varies from 5.5–6.5% on credit cards, while home mortgage products range from 0.2–0.4% (20 to 40 basis points); however, the return on assets of credit cards is well above that on mortgages.

EXHIBIT 1-1
Typical Loss Ratios—By Product

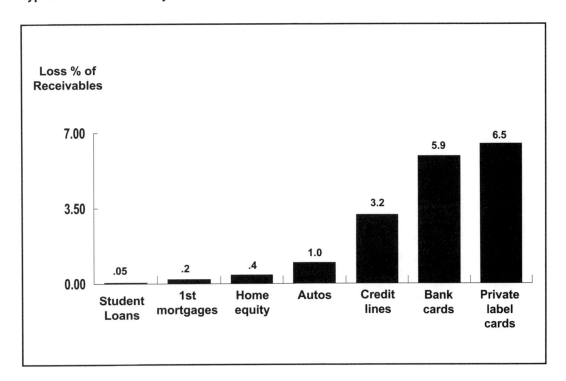

While these loss rates are based on historical performance in the USA, they can change over time, and they will certainly vary from country to country. But losses are only half of the equation; as we have said, you cannot talk about write-offs without relating them to the inherent rate of profit in each product. Each product has an underlying rate of profitability based on the price that can be charged for the product, its inherent cost structure, and the cost of writeoffs. In the following exhibit, each of the major consumer credit products is placed in the quarter of the box that reflects its usual risk/reward ratio:

EXHIBIT 1-2
Risk/Reward Ratios

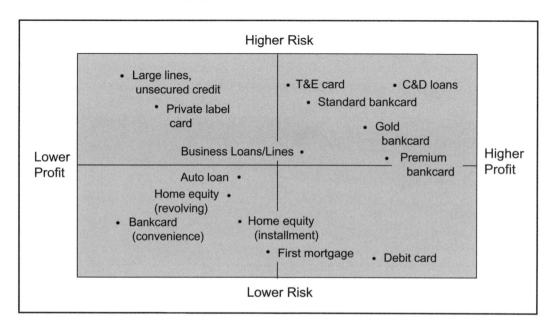

In theory, a line could be drawn from the lower left of the chart to the top right-hand side, with all products spread along this line. The question is, are you making enough profit—that is to say, is there a sufficient spread between your revenue and your costs, particularly the level of writeoffs, to justify the inherent risk of the product? Sometimes, but not always, the reward justifies the level of risk taken; for instance, the credit card, mortgage, and other key products fall along this theoretical line (in the appropriate risk/reward sector), and the high-risk/high-reward subprime or C&D products *should* be where I have placed them (in the upper right-hand sector); however, they often have been unprofitable/very high risk for many lenders and end up "off the chart"; that is, they are so far to the left that they don't show on this chart at all. The only product I placed in the low-risk/high-reward category is the debit card, where relatively high interchange fees and the inherent low risk of the product (remember, no credit is advanced) justify the product's position here. Will this always be true? Only time can tell.

A couple of problem products have been placed in the chart's top left-hand corner (not the most desirable place to be, the low-profit/high-risk quartile), namely the private label or department store cards and large lines of unsecured credit. Private label cards are issued by department stores and other retailers, and their low profitability may be acceptable to these card issuers because the seller of the goods, typically a retailer or department store, is earning sufficient profit on the sale of merchandise generated by the card to justify the lack of profitability on the card itself. Large lines of unsecured credit have been on the decline in the U.S. because of the flexibility of the standard credit card offerings and the growth of lines of credit secured by a home where there are tax advantages; the risk on large lines of consumer credit typically has not been rewarded by the pricing for this product.

This book will teach consumer lenders the analytical techniques they need to manage whatever type of loan portfolio they may have and to decide whether they can afford to compete aggressively with the riskier products (i.e., does the reward offset the risk?) or be content to stay with the traditional low-risk ones.

Many financial institutions *are* risk-averse. The people who approve consumer credit are often told to err on the side of conservatism. The message is that putting even a few bad customers on the books is a firing offense. If the corporate goal is to minimize writeoffs, regardless of lost volume and potential profit, management doesn't take long to get the message. After all, in the short term, lost volume is hard to quantify (although it becomes clearer over the long term), but writeoffs are very visible.

The one time being risk-averse makes sense is when an organization is facing a disastrous drain on capital from bad loans, whether from heavy commercial loan losses, trading losses, or a geographic/product concentration that went sour. If the regulators are at the door, bank managers should minimize writeoffs, expenses, or whatever is necessary until operations can be brought under control again.

Plan Ahead

A good planning process is essential to managing a business. Planning begins with determining where/how you will make a profit; but good planning must also articulate the step-by-step processes needed to achieve that goal and to avoid potential pitfalls. For instance, when in a hurry to grow a business, senior managers sometimes pressure the organization to enter or expand operations without fully understanding the importance of good up-front planning. The planning can be as simple as determining if the collection staff can handle hundreds or thousands more calls a month, or as complicated as setting up control and test cells to thoroughly understand the ramifications of a potential mass mailing to a new target market. Operating system failures (including out-of-date scoring systems, insufficient computer power, untrained/inadequate staff, etc.) are notorious for ruining an expanding business, especially when operating managers are unable to get the correct data to even determine where the problem exists. Planning to avoid disaster is not a discipline in which many bankers are trained, but it is one of the keys to the business. We will cover the steps in the planning process in the next chapter.

Manage by the Odds

Because it makes large numbers of relatively small loans, the consumer lending industry is able to spread its risk statistically; that is, with the powerful mathematical tools and computers available today, lenders can predict behavior with a substantial degree of confidence. The generic term applied to the method of computing the odds in the consumer business is *scoring*. If lenders can get enough information on their customers or potential customers, they can *score* them and calculate their odds of behaving in a particular fashion. By controlling the risks, lenders can control one key part of their business.

The consumer lending business shares significant similarities with two different major businesses: gambling and insurance. All of these are industries that control risk through statistics. Although the gambling industry is delighted to point to individual winners ("Factory Worker Wins $35 Million"), the business succeeds on the principle that the more people bet, the more they will lose. The odds always favor the "house." If they did not, Atlantic City, Monte Carlo, and Las Vegas would still be small villages trying to sell the virtues of relaxing in the sun. The house wins because the odds on each game are carefully calculated to be in its favor.

Likewise, the insurance industry can always be hit by a natural disaster (a hurricane, a $10 million life insurance payout, an earthquake), but the odds are still in the industry's favor as a result of careful analysis of the laws of probability. In the world of probabilities, almost all 30-year-olds reach the age of 31; far fewer 95-year-olds live to be 96.

With scoring today, the same probability process can be applied to the consumer lending business. No system in the world, however, can select *which* individual account will act as predicted; scoring systems predict only the odds that one in ten or one in thirty will do so. Similarly, in gambling there is always someone who, despite the odds, literally breaks the bank—for one day at least.

This ability to predict the performance of a large number of accounts (i.e., a portfolio) with a degree of certainty is what makes the consumer business so exciting today and such a management challenge. Knowing that these tools are available is not enough; they must be managed intelligently and applied diligently and, most important, you must have the appropriate management information to be able to read and act on the results.

Develop and Analyze Management Information

Controlling a consumer lending business depends on the ability to design, develop, and read the management information—the operating numbers, the revenue and expense numbers—needed to understand the business. Management information should both predict what is *going* to happen to the business and report what *actually* happened. An examination of the management information systems (the MIS), or metrics or management information—these terms are used interchangeably—in a well-managed portfolio usually identifies quickly where the problems are/where they are not. For instance, a well-run organization will have the means to immediately identify a change in the quality of the loans being booked (e.g., the Western Region booked 27% very-high-risk, D-rated loans in September vs. a planned rate of 8%). In badly managed portfolios, no one will have the answer to the most elementary questions, such as why the cost per unit booked was $156 in August vs. a planned cost of $75. Management won't even know what information to look at until the accountants tell them that "expenses sure were high last month."

Outlining the MIS required to run a high-volume consumer business, however, is only one part of the challenge. The hardest part may be getting operational and computer support to deliver it, so managers must focus on that capability before expanding the business.

There is also the problem of functional managers providing too much detail to senior management. For instance, a scoring manager may provide reports on portfolio performance by every score range (620, 625, 650, etc.), by month, by vintage, by product, and subproduct. While these may be important indicators of whether the scoring system is working (and should be available to be read by *someone* in authority), it is too much detail to be called management information. (I call it data.) I always like to show key information visually, to be able to really see what is going on in a business. For instance, one glance at a visual chart (Exhibit 1-3) can tell a manager if scoring is working or not:

EXHIBIT 1-3
Charge-Offs by Score Range

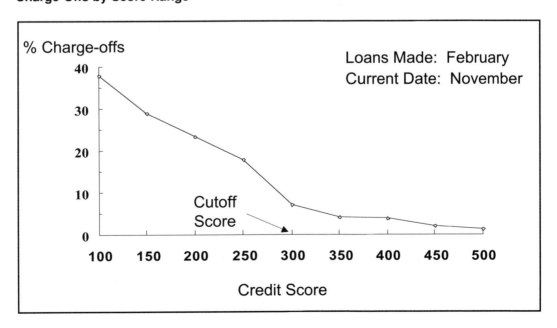

In this chart, the high-risk, low-score accounts indeed have a high rate of charge-offs and the rate of charge-offs goes down smoothly, as predicted, as the score increases. If there were an upturn in the line, say, on the higher-scoring accounts, it would be easy to know to ask the question, Why? Good MIS organizes information into significant patterns, including the major trends of the business versus earlier forecasts, so that management can understand and act upon it and not waste time searching through piles of data. If you can't see the forest for the trees, you have lousy MIS.

The trick is to manage by relying on a few key reports of the really significant information, which is backed up with enough detail to research and identify the real problems. At times, therefore, less MIS is better than too much. In the consumer lending business, you cannot succeed without good MIS (examples appear throughout this book), and we describe MIS more completely in Chapter 12.

Assign Responsibility for Managing Risk

There should be a clear understanding as to who is responsible for the management of risk in a consumer lending business. Responsibility can be assigned in several ways. The two extremes are when (1) *everyone* is a manager of risk, or (2) a professional risk manager provides the check and balance to an organization in which everyone is striving to achieve individual goals: increasing the volume of business, reducing costs, or some other objective. Because each person's goal can be narrow, some balanced oversight is required to make the organization work.

Both types of organization work, but the first requires extraordinarily professional and experienced management and a lot of good will. The second type is more likely to be seen in the really high-volume organizations. In this case, the ideal is for balanced professionals to work out their differences openly and aboveboard . . . hopefully using the same well-developed, concise management information.

The important thing is to remember that there is no easy answer to risk management. Whatever style an organization chooses, that organization will run into trouble without a balance of professionals who understand the nuances of risk and reward.

These five principles of good management are the basis of understanding and controlling the credit cycle. Now let us take a look at the conceptual model we use to describe and define the consumer lending business.

Exhibit 1-4 illustrates the five interrelated steps in managing the credit cycle: planning consumer lending products, acquiring accounts, maintaining accounts, collecting funds due, and finally, writing off a certain portion of accounts. At the center of the model, management oversees every step of the process, with the aid of extensive, well-organized MIS. (Each step is covered in detail in the succeeding chapters.) The results of one step in the process flow into the next steps of the credit cycle. For instance, knowing the number and type of accounts in collections

EXHIBIT 1-4
The Credit Cycle

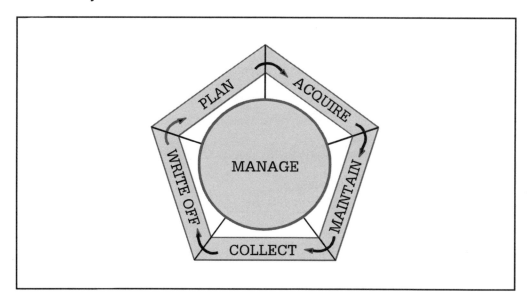

and those written off is essential to planning new products or revising existing ones. Similarly, the performance of accounts given line increases or changes in acquisition policies is information fed back to the front-end planning process.

Managing a Consumer Lending Business summarizes the lore and knowledge of the business as the new century begins. It covers many subjects a good manager should know—the importance of attracting enough good accounts to offset the inevitable bad accounts that every lender will get, controlling line sizes, encouraging use by good customers/discouraging or controlling bad customers, managing profitability with predictability—if she is to run a high-volume consumer business effectively.

We try to avoid overly mystifying a business that has become heavily statistical and technical. As a former boss of mine once noted, "The consumer lending business isn't so complicated: you borrow money at one rate and lend it out at another and make a profit." This definition, while oversimplified, does make a point. Some consumer lenders get so analytical that they lose sight of the underlying principles of the business.

The worst thing a manager can do is to leave the business decisions to the pure technicians. Instead, he should take advantage of the available technical information but be able to distill it down to the basic, underlying facts that should go into making a well-informed decision. The manager must have enough knowledge to ask the right questions and to be confident that he is not being conned by a fast-talking "expert" who lacks sufficient knowledge of the overall business, the background, or the judgment to make the proper decision.

This book hopes to provide you, the reader, with enough knowledge to at least ask the right questions and to navigate your way around the business.

Planning Consumer Products 2

G OOD PLANNING—researching what products to offer, understanding how to attract good customers and screen out bad ones, and managing the entire credit cycle while returning an appropriate profit to the organization—is the key to managing a consumer lending business. This chapter covers the major steps needed for an institution to plan its consumer lending business successfully.

A process should be in place to:

- *Introduce new products.*
- *Evaluate and modify existing products.*
- *Eliminate products when necessary.*

We rarely see a formal product-planning function within consumer financial institutions; planning, typically, is carried out by committees (sometimes ad hoc) made up of representatives from all areas of the company, including marketing, operations, branch management, finance, and risk management, all working together under the direction of senior management. This approach requires good leadership and cooperation among all parties.

Businesses can get into trouble, even fail completely, because of poor or inadequate planning. Poor planning typically occurs when an organization decides to grow an existing business rapidly or to expand into a new, untried area where its managers have only a superficial understanding of the likely or potential consequences. The industry is changing so rapidly that often the old rules no longer apply; if no one in the organization has the ability or knowledge to respond to significant changes, the results can be painful. Some of the events of the mid- and late 1990s that dramatically affected the consumer lending business include

A MONOLINE COMPANY

Disasters can take many forms. Let's examine the numbers for one institution that grew its credit card business rapidly in the mid-1990s. Wall Street considered this company a very well-managed business, and the company's stock price reflected that favorable opinion.

These charts show the spectacular growth of this institution's credit card business. During 1994–96, receivables were growing at more than 60% per year; the company gained an advantage over its competition through highly targeted mass mailings, competitive balance transfer programs, and good products (featuring carefully crafted premium card offers). Wall Street rewarded the company with favorable write-ups and the stock soared . . . at least until early 1997. Financial analysts, the professionals who follow individual companies on behalf of the stock brokerage houses, predicted continuing growth in earnings. For instance, the original earnings consensus estimate for 1997 was $4.85 per share—up 27% from the previous year—but it was not to be.

EXHIBIT 2-1a Credit Card Receivables

2-1b: Earnings per share

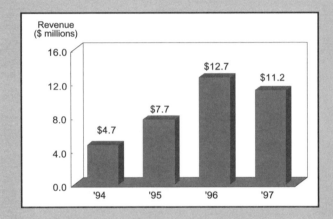

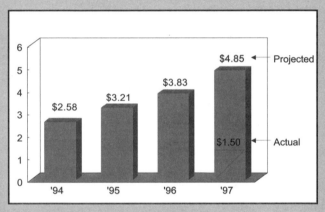

the growth in personal bankruptcies, loss rates rising to new highs (although both turned around in 1999), growth of Internet-sourced customers, and lending to high-risk customers (the subprime market). Moreover, intense competition fostered balance-transfer programs and low introductory rates on credit cards, raising risk and reducing profitability. Some lenders thrived in this atmosphere, others wilted.

Although the typical planning failure occurs with the introduction of new products or the rapid growth of existing ones from a very small base, disasters have also occurred with seemingly small changes in product terms and conditions, such as financing more used cars than new ones, lowering the down payment or documentation requirements on collateralized products, implementing what seemed to be a modest credit line increase program. The ensuing crises typically occur when the financial institution changes the fundamental way it does business without going through the appropriate planning and test/review processes to understand the real risks it is undertaking as it moves into uncharted territory.

The bad news came in the first quarter of 1997. The company announced that it would take a special writeoff for credit card losses and would report a large loss for the quarter. Overnight the stock dropped in half as the financial analysts sharply cut their earnings projections.

What happened? While the details may never be known outside the company, it is obvious in retrospect that credit card writeoffs must have been climbing for a while. Furthermore, receivables flattened as the company retrenched and cut back on new mailings. Writeoffs ultimately climbed to 7.8%, up from the 3–4% range of prior years.

A key lesson here: rapid growth conceals problems. New accounts take time to build up balances, become delinquent, and go to writeoff, and the volume of newer, current receivables helps to conceal the true rate of writeoff (we cover this more in Chapter 7, Collection Strategies). But portfolios can be tracked separately by vintage (the time period when booked), so management could have determined early on if later portfolios were performing much more poorly than earlier ones. It appears that management did not follow the common-sense rule to get bad news out quickly. Both management and the shareholders paid the price with a disastrous slide in the value of their stock.

2-2a: Writeoffs

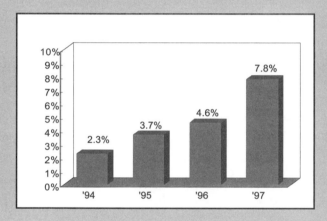

2-2b: Year-End Stock Price

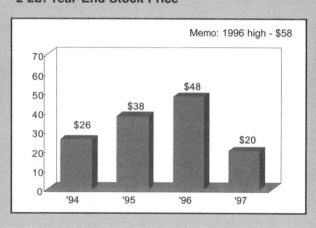

OVERALL STRATEGY OF THE ORGANIZATION

Good planning starts with an understanding of the underlying strategy of an organization, its Board of Directors, and senior management in terms of the overall business plan. Broad approaches to the business can range from:

- *Expansionist. A highly aggressive management intends to grow a business rapidly. It accepts and understands risk and is willing to invest in the necessary resources (people and technology) to do the job right. It accepts that profitability may require a long-term commitment to every detail of the business.*

- *Controlling. Management is content to do the best job it can with existing resources. It is always looking for ways to improve current product offerings and profitability but has no plans to grow. Stability and reliability are rewarded.*

- **Minimalist.** *Management is defensive and unwilling to take risks. It makes little attempt to change the existing way of doing business, and it is willing to sell assets or cut product offerings in the face of aggressive competition.*

There are many variations within these broad categories. Additionally, some parts of the business may be growing, while others may be in a controlling phase and some may be cutting back. But the key is for management to have a clear idea of where it is going and to allocate the resources it is willing to devote to achieving such a goal.

BACKGROUND ANALYSIS

After the institution's strategic direction has been decided, including its willingness to absorb risk, the next steps in the planning process are to review the *external* forces and *internal* factors that will influence its ability to carry out the decision.

External Forces

External forces, such as the state of the economy, the competence and effectiveness of the competition, and the types of products available in the marketplace, all must be analyzed.

The following questions should be asked regarding the economy:

- *Is it a propitious time to expand, or a time to be cautious?*
- *Are certain geographic areas to be avoided, or to be sought out?*
- *Are housing prices going up, down, or are they stable?*
- *Are regulatory controls increasing or decreasing?*
- *Are consumers feeling confident or cautious?*

Seasoned professionals will always find opportunities to bring good products to the market—in good times or bad—but they sometimes must be prepared to stay the course when conditions are less than perfect.

Internal Factors

After addressing the external forces and determining whether conditions are appropriate for implementing a growth plan, the financial institution must next determine whether it has the internal resources necessary to do so.

- *Are there enough capable and knowledgeable managers within the organization who can actually run the business?*
- *Can outside hires fill any gaps, or is it possible to outsource the work?*

- *If a move to a new location is necessary, will the key members of existing management be willing to transfer?*
- *Can new hires be trained and indoctrinated quickly in the organization's style of customer service, collections, and so forth?*

Operational support should also be examined:

- *Do you have the necessary computer, systems, and programming support to meet all the booking, payment, billing, and processing requirements of an expanding operation?*
- *Will enough office space be available for all the people and required equipment, and will all be ready before rollout?*

Finally, does the organization have the funding and financial strength to grow?

- *Is there a reliable deposit/borrowing base and sufficient capital to support the required levels of borrowing?*
- *Do you have the financial strength to survive if the plan does not work as well as it should—if operating losses or writeoffs occur at a higher rate than forecasted, and for longer than planned?*

If the background analysis indicates that the business can be expanded and if the growth plans conform with the overall corporate strategy as recorded in the mission statement, the organization can proceed to the next step.

PRODUCT DEVELOPMENT

Once the preliminary analysis of the business's goals and internal and external factors are analyzed, product development can begin.

However, the basic control and analytical techniques for consumer lending described in this book must be used on a large number of loans that perform similarly over time. That is, they are applied by product. Therefore, before examining the planning process in more detail, we need to define the term *product*.

Product Definition

A *product* is a collection of loans or lines of credit governed by *standard terms and conditions*. For example, a *new* auto loan typically has one set of lending terms, a *used* car loan has another. A new auto loan in Hong Kong would be different from one offered in the USA or Germany. Similarly, a gold credit card would be one product, a classic credit card would be another, and a first-time credit card offered to students would be yet a third product. Each product has its own approval requirements; each is tracked separately from other products; each has its profit dynamics.

Exhibit 2-3 shows the major products currently available in the market-place. There are inherent differences between the major categories of loans—term/installment vs. revolving loans, direct vs. indirect products, and secured vs. unsecured products.

EXHIBIT 2-3
Major Consumer Credit Products

Credit Product	Security		Payments		Source	
	Secured	Unsecured	Installment/Term	Revolving	Direct	Indirect
Bankcards (classic, gold, platinum, etc.)	✓	✓		✓	✓	✓ affinity
Travel & Entertainment cards (e.g., American Express)		✓		✓ *	✓	
Department store/Private label card		✓		✓	✓	✓
Oil company cards		✓		✓	✓	
Lines of credit		✓		✓	✓	
Personal loans		✓	✓		✓	
Home mortgages • First mortgage	✓		✓		✓	✓
• Home equity/second mortgage check and card access	✓		✓	✓	✓	✓
Automobile	✓		✓		✓	✓
Mobile home	✓		✓		✓	✓
Boat	✓		✓		✓	✓
Recreational vehicle	✓		✓		✓	✓

*due in full each month.

Term/Installment vs. Revolving Products

Term or installment are closed-end loans, requiring the borrower to repay a fixed amount (the amount borrowed plus interest) over a predetermined period of time. Although payments of principal and interest may vary, installment or term loans are contractually predefined in terms of when/how any changes will occur. Term loans typically are made for a specific use (such as to purchase a home or an automobile), although funds from a second mortgage may be unrestricted as to purpose.

Revolving lines are open ended and the customer can draw down/repay the funds at will, subject only to a cap or limit on the total credit extended. The terms of the agreement may require a minimum monthly repayment of principal, or they may allow interest-only payments for a period of time. Revolving lines typically have an expiration date.

Direct vs. Indirect Products

Direct loan products are offered through an institution's own distribution system such as branch offices or through the Internet, advertising, direct mail, or "take-one" campaigns. Indirect products are marketed through independent distributors or agents, such as automobile or boat dealers, department store retailers, or mortgage brokers. The livelihood of the broker/dealer usually depends on someone else's ability to finance their sales, so they have a vital interest in how their customers are handled.

Secured vs. Unsecured

The final major identifying characteristic is whether or not the loan is secured. With a secured product, the lender will lend money only by taking a lien on an asset of the borrower (e.g., house or auto) or will lend against specific deposits (e.g., certificates of deposit [CDs] or marketable stock). With unsecured lending, a lender has no access to specific assets of the borrower, although it may be able to obtain a judgment after default to go after an unencumbered asset.

Selecting the Target Market

A critical part of the planning process is selecting which customers to target; to a great extent, the target market defines the degree of risk in a product. By selecting the right customers, a business starts the process of controlling two key elements in the product's profitability: usage and rate of writeoffs.

Major considerations in defining the target market are the geographic area(s) in which you will operate, the profile of the customers, and the sources (e.g., magazine lists, automobile registrations, etc.) of the customers.

The first decision is how far from your home office and existing customer base you are willing to go to solicit customers in the future. With the ability today to share information regionally, nationally, or even worldwide at the speed of light, there is little problem expanding operationally way beyond your regional base. But what will you know about your potential customers in these new regions? For instance, one important factor is the economic health of the targeted area. Obviously, there are national economic recessions, but of more significance are regional recessions and booms. The "rust belt" (the heavy manufacturing states) was in trouble for a while; the "farm belt" states go in and out of hard times; if orders for Boeing aircraft drop sharply, Seattle could face a recession (unless Bill Gates decides to go on a shopping spree). Regional recessions and booms must be tracked if your institution is to avoid sending the only mail solicitation to arrive while hard times are hitting, or conversely, sending the last one to arrive when good times return.

What type of customers do you seek? Very sophisticated data-mining[1] tools allow organizations to target specific customer groups with great accuracy.

Many organizations fail to take advantage of a cross-sell opportunity—targeting their *own* customers first (customers about whom they already know a great deal) before spending hundreds of thousands or millions of dollars in search of new ones.

Although hundreds of potential target markets exist (e.g., geographic, demographic), for illustrative purposes, the target market can be divided into three broad categories

- ***High-usage, high-risk***—*Those who need credit badly, have limited opportunity to obtain it, and expect to pay a high price.*
- ***Moderate-usage, moderate-risk***—*Those who use credit regularly, have ample offers for credit products, and are not too fussy about pricing; this group is interested in convenience, product features, enhancements, and good service.*
- ***Low-usage, low-risk***—*Those who pride themselves on paying their bills on time, try to keep their debts at a minimum, and always look for the lowest price; they are constantly bombarded with offers of credit.*

Research the Market (Know the Competition)

Planning successful products begins with effective research and analysis. Once the overall strategy and target market have been determined, the next steps involve researching the competition. Knowing what products are available in the marketplace, and how well they are succeeding, is absolutely essential to developing your own products successfully. Some questions to answer are:

- *How intense is the competition in the particular product that the institution is trying to market?*
- *How many really strong competitors are there?*
- *Does it make sense to match the most liberal terms of the competition, or are these terms encouraging the wrong people to borrow excessively?*
- *Does your institution have some unique advantage (e.g., a large number of branches, better locations, or unique brand recognition) to help it succeed without matching the competition? Conversely, is having few branches and low overhead an advantage in a particular case?*

---

1. *Data mining* is the term used to describe the process of sifting through vast amounts of information to learn as much about your potential target market as possible. For instance, a credit card offer could be targeted to single working females who earn more than $25,000, use credit heavily, own an automobile, respond to direct mail offers at a higher than average rate. Other targets could include "Dinks"—a family with a double income, no kids, earning in excess of $50,000; "Yuppies"—young urban professionals, and so forth. These data may be derived from many different sources, and the challenge is to cross-reference the data as accurately as possible to meet your goals.

Further, to deliver a competitive product, planners must understand competitors' product terms and conditions in detail. The following exhibit illustrates some of the information that is publicly available to study what the competition is offering—in this case, a premium credit card.

EXHIBIT 2-4
Bankcard Survey

PRICING	Bank A (Gold)	Bank B (Gold)	Bank C (Gold)	Bank D (Platinum)	Bank E (Titanium)
Introductory Rate	3.9% (3 months)	2.9% (6 months)	none	5.9% (1 year)	2.9% (3 months)
On-going Rate	Prime + 4.9%	9.9%	CD rate + 9.9%	10.9% (9.9% for balances over $3,500)	9.9%
Minimum Penalty Rate (2 x late)	20.9%	21.4%	22.4%	Prime +12.4%	19.8%
Annual fee	$40 (1ˢᵗ year free)	None	None	None	None
Ancillary fees:					
late fee	$29	$16/1% of balance	$21	$29	$21
over-limit fee	$29	$21	$25	$29	$21
bad check fee	$20	$25	$25	$20	$25
Cash Advance:					
fee	2.5% ($2 min, $20 max)	free	2% ($2 min, $10 max)	1%	0% ($3,000 min.)
APR	20.9%	21.4%	22.4%	Prime +12.4%	19.8%
FEATURES					
Grace period (days)	21	21	20	21	None
Convenience checks	yes/free	yes/free	yes/$.95 per check used	yes/free	yes/free
Additional cards	yes/free	yes/free	yes/free	yes/free	yes/free
Min. monthly payment	3% highest balance/$20	3% declining balance/$25	4% highest balance/$25	3% highest balance/$20	2% declining balance/$25
ENHANCEMENTS					
Rebate on purchases	None	1%	1%	None	None
Airline miles	yes/ConAir	no	no	no	yes/selected carriers
Travel accident insurance	$250,000	$350,000	$1,000,000	$1,000,000	$500,000
Rental car insurance	yes	yes	no	no	yes

A good competitive survey for a credit product gathers information about:

- *The basic interest rate charged*
- *The fees (including the not-so-obvious ones)*
- *Minimum monthly payment requirements*
- *Product features (e.g., grace period)*
- *Enhancements (e.g., airline miles, travel insurance)*

Details can also be gathered about even finer points of differentiation, such as customer service hours and the competitors' ability to deliver the services promised. All this information will help determine whether the product being planned by your organization compares favorably to the competition's products; it may also help you determine whether their products are profitable or not.

Designing the Terms and Conditions

Once you know what is available in the marketplace, the next step is to set the terms and conditions of your product (pricing, features, enhancements). These ultimately determine the quality and profitability of the business being established. The objective is to design a product that will attract your target customers, that can survive and be profitable in the marketplace, and will be accepted by your institution's management. A high-rate credit card aimed at top-quality customers won't succeed; a low-rate card aimed at subprime lenders won't be profitable. Each target market must be examined separately.

At this point, some of the planning steps we will cover, e.g., features and enhancements, will emphasize unsecured consumer revolving products (primarily credit cards). Later chapters cover the unique terms and conditions that apply to secured products, such as loan-to-value ratios, down payments, the appraisal process, and so forth.

1. PRICING

Pricing the product and designing the product features most visible to the customer are obviously the most critical factors in the planning process. These factors generate the most heat (and emotion) for the customer as well as for the lending organization's management. Understanding the details of your competitors' products and pricing helps you avoid incorrect pricing. While customers may not always be aware of the *exact* rate being charged, they will certainly be aware if the interest rate is high; and they most assuredly will know if they have a low introductory rate (say, 2.9% for a few months), just as they will know when the rate returns to "normal." One item they will always know: the annual fee. Somehow the annual fee rouses great emotion. Customers happily go out and spend $20 on a bottle of wine for dinner, but spending $20 for an annual fee is out of the question!

The three basic approaches to pricing are:

1) *Undercutting the competition*
2) *Matching the competition*
3) *Pricing above the competition.*

Each option has its own problems and opportunities.

Pricing below the Market

Pricing below the competition can be justified for new entrants in the marketplace that are attempting to build market share, and for truly low-cost producers. Typically, businesses that have successfully priced below the market have done it only for a limited time period. Note that always being the low pricer is an invitation for retaliation.

The most dangerous competitors are those who cut prices because they are ignorant of their own costs and do not understand profitability. It is easy to give away credit, and new, low-ball competitors, sometimes with an inferior product, often try to undercut the market. Before starting or abetting a price war, analyze what is really happening in the market. Is it likely to be a long-term or short-term problem? Only then make a carefully crafted response.

Pricing at the Market

The second approach to pricing—the conventional one—is to match the competition. Although it is uncontroversial, managers should choose this approach with a full understanding of their true costs (obviously if your costs are substantially above the competition's, pricing at the market may not be profitable). The appropriateness of this strategy also depends on whether the products are comparable.

Pricing above the Market

An opportunity to price above the competition should not be avoided if your service or product is truly superior. For instance, American Express charges a $300 annual fee for its Platinum card, way above the norm. They also, however, provide excellent services and enhancements for this fee (such as a concierge service that books tickets for shows or trips). The lesson: not everyone drives a Ford Escort; some people are more than willing to pay for a Jaguar.

Pricing entails more than simply meeting the one, well-publicized, basic interest rate flaunted on the envelope mailed to prospective customers. Prices can be adjusted in numerous, less publicized ways. These include:

- *Risk-adjusted pricing. Pricing is calculated to match risk with reward by offering lower prices to active, prompt payers, and selectively higher prices to the rest. One caveat: the terms and conditions must be carefully spelled out to avoid customer confusion and legal problems.*

- *Special introductory rates to attract new customers. These rates are usually offered for a short time and can be part of a balance transfer program ("transfer all your credit card balances to us and you'll receive a 3.9% introductory rate"). One caveat: if your product has nothing going for it other than the special introductory rate, assume that the people you attract will move on when you raise it. You can't make a profit on transient, "professional" rate chasers; identify these customers ahead of time and exclude them before the mailing.*

- *Additional fees for late payments, over-limit conditions, and returned or NSF checks. Fees can be added for items such as too many inquiries (when not caused by administrative errors). Fees have grown rapidly as a source of income since standard interest rates have become highly competitive. Late fees now are around $35 per every late payment (vs. $10 to $11 in the early 1990s), and fees in total account* *for 13% of the revenue for credit card issuers. While fees can be a viable source of income and an excellent way to remind your customers to pay attention to your bills, sometimes they can be excessive. Some suggestions on late fees:*

= *Make sure the customer understands when the payment is due in order to avoid incurring a penalty fee. Most issuers grant cardholders 25 days to pay (some have been cutting this to 20 days), and the actual due date should be obvious and easy for the customer to find. In the event of a late payment, there should be no argument as to when it was due.*

= *Establish a policy on how much the late fee will be in the event of a small balance owing. For many years lenders charged a standard, flat fee (currently $35) regardless of the balance due. This policy obviously annoyed customers owing very small balances (e.g., $1.65, $9.15 or $25.60), particularly when these small balances may have been merely overlooked by otherwise good customers. A $35*

PREDATORY PRICING TACTICS—ONE OF THE WORST CASES I HAVE EVER SEEN

In planning a product, remember that you need not follow the competition's worst practices. Some competitors are truly bad, offering very high-priced, low-utility products to unwary consumers. There is a difference between pricing reasonably for risk and predatory pricing. In November 2000 I received one of the worst examples of a predatory product offering from a mid-western bank.

The basic offer was for a MasterCard with a credit line up to $1,000 ($250 minimum). Reading the details, I learned that I would have to send a $19 check for processing ($25 for express processing) along with some minimum documentation (pay stub, etc.). If approved, my first bill would contain the following charges:

- A $119 one-time acceptance fee
- A $50 annual fee
- A $6 monthly participation fee (= $72/year)
- A $20 fee for a second card (if requested).

Just to open the account, I could be billed for as much as $220 after one month. If I were approved for a minimum $250 line of credit, my open-to-buy amount would be $30!! For the privilege of applying for this card and being approved, I would owe $220 for virtually nothing. Oh yes, and if I failed to pay in full within the grace period, I would be charged interest at the rate of 18.9%; if my payments were late, there would be a late payment fee of $20 (and an over-limit fee if I ran over my $30 spending limit).

Who would accept such an offer? I can only imagine, but it would not be a very sophisticated user of credit. This is among the worst examples of predatory tactics I have ever seen. Needless to say, reputable lenders do not engage in these practices.

late fee for a trivial amount owing can be exasperating for a good customer. And small balances owed are quite common, given that customers do not always calculate the right allowance for a returned item, or are unwilling to send in a check for $1.65 for a small finance charge owed on a previous balance. Yes, most customers can get the late charge removed with a phone call, but many find it annoying to have to call (remember, your good customers can easily get another card). As a result, some of the big credit card issuers such as Citigroup, Discover, and MBNA have begun to move toward a flexible fee policy, for example charging $15 for balances up to $100, $25 for balances $100.01 to $1,000, and $35 for larger balances. A sliding scale of late charges that reflects the severity of the late balance owed makes good sense.

Know Where the Money Comes From

Finally, in order to understand where your revenue and your profits really come from, remember the old saying: "Keep your eye upon the doughnut and not upon the hole." For example, in the credit card business, with its four main sources of income, most income still derives from finance charges (although the interchange and miscellaneous sources of income have been increasing rapidly). The following shows the trend for the sources of credit card income over the past five years.

	1997	1998	1999	2000	2001
Finance charges	79%	75%	71%	70%	69%
Interchange/merchant fees	10	11	14	14	15
Miscellaneous fees (late charges, etc.)	9	12	13	13	13
Annual fees	2	2	2	3	3

If you don't understand "where the money is," you will not be able to plan and price a profitable product.

2. FEATURES

Next, some decisions must be made in designing a revolving credit product which, while less obvious to the customer, could still significantly affect its acceptance (and profitability). These include the selection of a grace period and minimum monthly repayment terms.

- *Grace Period. Lenders typically charge revolvers (those who do not pay off their balance in full every month) interest from the time a credit card charge is made, while allowing about a 22-day, interest-free grace period for those who pay the balance in full each month (this is down from a 25-day average earlier in the 1990s). Some aggressive card issuers charge interest from the date of purchase even when no previous balance is outstanding.*

- *Minimum Monthly Payment. The minimum monthly payment requirement can be a powerful marketing tool for some lenders. Typically, debtors are required to pay only a minimum percentage (usually 2–5%) of the outstanding balance per month in order to keep the account current. While only a relatively small percentage of people (12–15%) make just the minimum monthly payment, this method does provide a convenient way for people to meet their obligations during hard times. For instance, an offer might be made to people who are in financial difficulty along the following lines: "Transfer your balances to us and your monthly payments will decline dramatically." The offer looks like this:*

EXHIBIT 2-5
Minimum Monthly Payment

	Balance	Min. Monthly Payment
■ Before Consolidation		
– bankcards	$3,500	$105
– department stores	2,500	250
– other cards	700	28
Total	$6,700	$383
■ After Consolidation		
Credit card X	$6,700	$134

For someone tired of getting collection calls, or experiencing a period of financial distress (loss of job, divorce, heavy medical expenses, etc.), such an offer can be manna from heaven.

There are two decisions to make in establishing a minimum monthly payment policy: the percentage of the balance due that is to be paid, and the method of computing the repayment.

SELECTING THE PERCENTAGE

As noted, the minimum monthly payment can vary from 2–5% of the balance owing. To illustrate the impact on repaying the balance at these different rates, consider the amount left over for principal repayment at each one (for this example, we have assumed a constant interest rate of 18%, or 1.5% per month):

Minimum Monthly Payment

% of Balance Due	2%	3%	4%	5%
Payment on $1,000 balance	$20	$30	$40	$50
Interest paid	$15	$15	$15	$15
Principal paid off	$ 5	$15	$25	$35

Each lender must decide if the very slow rate of amortization at the 2% or 3% minimum payment level is appropriate for its portfolio (it can take eight years to pay back a fixed balance with a 2% payment, versus two years with a 5% payment).

One further key point: there are two methods of calculating the minimum monthly payment.

HIGHEST BALANCE VS. DECLINING BALANCE

With the *highest balance* method of calculating the minimum monthly payment, the lender sets a percentage due each month (e.g., 3%) of the *highest balance* owing until the account is paid off, or until a new high balance is achieved. Thus if the customer has a balance owing of $2,000 he pays $60 monthly (3% x $2,000) until the entire original charge amount is paid off. If new charges are made, the minimum payment is re-computed at the higher balance.

The second way, the *declining balance* method, calculates the percentage rate (e.g., the same 3%) but only on the current balance owing. As the principal owing gets smaller, the minimum monthly payment declines (e.g., $60, $59, $58, etc). The declining balance method means smaller minimum payments and thus extends the length of time the customer pays.

The highest balance method is a conservative method of computing: it's lower reward/lower risk for the lender because the customer pays off the amount more quickly with higher payments. For instance, assuming no new charges, repaying the total balance will require slightly more than eight years (at a 2% monthly minimum payment).

However, using the *declining balance* method, repayment can take up to *thirty-two years* to pay off a balance at the same low minimum monthly repayment rate (2%). Take a trip to Hawaii and you can celebrate paying off your card debt after thirty-two years by reviewing the yellowing pictures in your photo album!

Which is the right minimum repayment schedule? There is no one answer. Using the declining balance method there is a greater chance that something will go wrong (the customer may lose his job, get a divorce, become ill); however, you are earning the interest over a long time. The highest balance method of repayment shortens the repayment period and thus the risk. Longer terms are appropriate for a house or a car, but for convenience shopping, including typical credit card charges for items such as movies, grocery shopping, and liquor sales, the more disciplined, shorter terms may be more appropriate. Each lender must make its own decision whether the reward justifies the risk.

One note of caution: there should always be a minimum dollar amount of repayment for low-balance accounts; $20 per month is typically the minimum allowable figure.

3. ENHANCEMENTS

The most popular way to get a product accepted is to enhance it, at an affordable cost, with features attractive to the target market. Your marketing department will be delighted to assist in the process of making the product appealing to the intended market.

Following are some typical enhancements available on credit cards:

- ***Airline frequent flyer or other product usage programs.*** *People who charge on a particular credit card can receive bonus mileage or other product awards for every dollar charged. Examples include Citicorp/American Airlines, BankOne/United, US Bank/Northwest, Chase/Continental, etc. They are among the most popular enhancements, particularly with business travelers.*

- ***Affinity programs.*** *A vast number of joint ventures link card issuers and affinity groups such as college alumni, sporting associations, environmentalists, the military, etc. In return for a share of the revenue, an affinity group will allow its members to be solicited and the card branded with the group name. MBNA is the prime issuer of affinity cards today.*

- ***Credit card registration.*** *This feature covers lost or stolen cards. By calling one telephone number, a member can cancel all credit cards and automatically begin the process of obtaining new cards.*

- ***Discount offers.*** *This type of enhancement offers, for example, car rentals, hotels, airlines, shopping services, or long-distance phone calls at discount prices.*

- ***Free or low-cost insurance coverage.*** *Such coverage might include accident, disability, or life insurance (for airline trips), fraudulent credit card usage, collision damage waiver for auto rentals, and lost luggage insurance.*

- ***Warranty extensions.*** *This enhancement increases the time period of the initial warranty for new product purchases charged on the card.*

- ***VIP services.*** *This service can provide special twenty-four-hour emergency help for travelers. Assistance might include finding medical assistance or legal advice and can be offered for both overseas and domestic travel.*

- ***Travel services.*** *Such enhancements might provide auto rental, hotel or airline reservations, trip-planning assistance, and other concierge services. American Express and other premium card issuers offer excellent concierge and other travel assistance around the world.*

- *Special financial services. Several issuers provide quarterly or annual statements detailing purchases by major category of expense (e.g., airlines, rental cars, meals, hotels, etc.). These can be a real boon to small business owners who need detailed records of travel and entertainment expenses for tax purposes.*

Some enhancements may be too expensive to offer. For instance, Ford and Citicorp broke up their alliance when (it was rumored) the automobile rebate program became too costly. Other enhancements, such as special financial statements (at least once the systems are set up) may cost pennies. Some enhancements, such as special shopping services, may present an opportunity to make additional money.

As the many options clearly indicate, price cutting and relaxing the terms of repayment are not the only alternatives to product differentiation.

CREATING A BRAND

Competition often prevents an institution from designing the perfect product. It is highly unlikely that you can deliver a product with the lowest price, the best service, *and* the best features and enhancements. Compromises must be made. Is there an alternative to offering a commodity product? Aren't all credit cards, lines of credit, auto loans, mortgages, just like gold—a commodity?

One solution: create a brand. Nike, Mobil, Coca-Cola, Toyota, Ford, and AOL are all worldwide brand names. McDonald's was just another hamburger stand in the 1950s when it first came out. How did these companies get to be the international giants they are today? By creating a brand and a brand image. You know what a McDonald's hamburger and fries are going to taste like whether you're in Topeka, Kansas, Tokyo, Japan, or Melbourne, Australia.

American Express, Capital One, Citigroup, and Discover are the card issuers who have best managed to differentiate themselves from the market, with Citigroup even challenging Visa in the late 1990s in an attempt to strengthen its own name identification vis-à-vis the association's brand name. Advertising, enhancements, and point-of-sale promotions have obviously helped these two strengthen their brands, but their emphasis on expanding their card usage worldwide has obviously helped. Going into a Citigroup branch in Beijing, Kraków, or Cape Town usually means good service and an ability to take advantage of all the worldwide automated services the bank offers. This can't help but build their brand image.

The Fit between Your Product and Your Target Market

Once you have designed a product and have agreed upon a target market, yet another question needs to be answered. Have you designed the correct product for that target market? The following chart shows the possibilities for the credit card business. You will see that there are different types of customers:

EXHIBIT 2-6
Target Market—Credit Cards

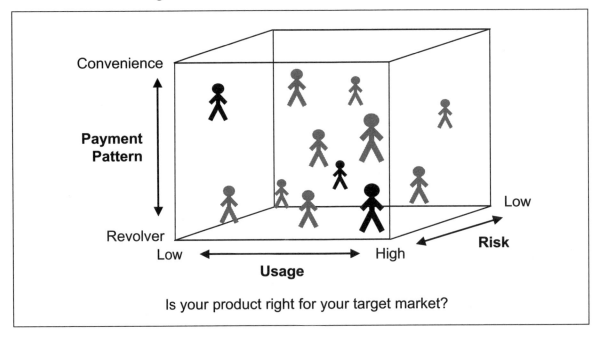

Is your product right for your target market?

The behaviors of the target market can be divided into three components:

1. Those who revolve, that is, they do not pay off their balance every month

2. Those who pay off every month and use the card as a convenience

3. High users and low users of credit cards (both of these appear in both of the above groups).

The net result, shown in the third dimension of this chart, is the degree of risk (and, ultimately, the amount of profit each category generates). The point is to make sure your product attracts the ones you intend to reach—the right customers—and, conversely, avoids attracting the wrong ones.

Let's look at three lenders who went after three different areas of the market—one marginally successful, one very successful, and one a complete failure:

Lender A

In the early 1990s, Lender A very successfully offered a credit card with no annual fee *ever* at a time when many issuers were still charging an annual fee. The response was overwhelming. Senior management spent weekends and evenings alongside regular staff replying to the millions of applications being returned. The result: a rousing short-term marketing triumph; long term, however, they attracted the low-risk, low-usage customers (upper-lefthand corner).

Because these consumers tend to pay promptly and to be low users of credit, making a profit on their accounts is a real challenge. One lender estimates that for a no-fee, convenience card account to be profitable, it takes about $75/year in interchange fees. This could require more than $500/month ($6,000/year) in charges, a figure that many business travelers achieve easily but that non-business customers may not reach with any consistency. Too many of Lender A's customers put the card in the back of their wallet as a reserve, and the challenge facing the company was to increase the customer's use of the card.

Lender B

Lender B had a very clear vision of its target market, going after the high-usage, high-risk customers, down in the lower-righthand front portion of the chart. These customers are easy to attract: they need credit. Lender B carefully mined credit bureau and demographic data to find credit card customers with a pattern of carrying high balances at several banks and retail institutions. Typically, these may have had some recent mild delinquency and may be making only the minimum monthly payments. An offer was made to these people along the following lines: "Transfer your balances to us and your monthly payments will decline dramatically." Lender B did this, of course, by lowering the minimum monthly payment required (from 4% or 5% to 2% of the outstanding balance). The fact that the interest rate charged was very high was irrelevant; the target market was attracted by the small monthly minimum payment. As we have already pointed out, however, it could take *more than thirty years* to repay the transferred credit card balance under these terms. While only 12–15% of cardholders typically pay only the minimum balance, this minimum-monthly-payment offer can be appealing to one target market. This lender knows his market and is successful, because of very tight screening, high pricing, and careful marketing. Many other C&D (subprime) lenders took too many risks with this market in the late 1990s, and many went bankrupt. We will cover subprime lending later in the secured product portion of this book.

Lender C

In the 1990s, this lender discovered the consequences of designing a product that attracted the wrong customers. The unfortunate product was a mailed credit card offer with a high initial rate of interest, and an offer that, over time, these interest payments would be rebated. The card would be "FREE." The fact that it took twenty years and a specified minimum usage to "earn" these rebates was overlooked by the less sophisticated applicants. The more sophisticated credit users saw the immediate high price, could not see how they would ever earn it back, and went elsewhere. The result was a classic case of adverse selection: the "bads" liked the offer and the "goods"did not buy it. Without the "goods" on the books, the portfolio ended up with an extraordinarily high rate of writeoffs (>20%). The product was a disaster and was withdrawn from the market.

As we have already covered, going after the "lower-front, right-hand customers" in Exhibit 2-6 can be appropriate as long as the pricing, screening, and usage by good customers offsets the added risk.

Forecast the Results (Including Profitability)

Part of the planning process should be a forecast for the first few years the product will be offered. What results are expected? How many applicants will apply each year, or what response rates are expected? What will usage be—what will be the average lines and/or average amount of the loan? What fees will be paid? What is the projected writeoff rate, in both numbers of accounts and balances?

If the product doesn't work on paper, it can't work in the real world. An example of a portfolio forecast noting some of the key items to be covered is as follows:

EXHIBIT 2-7
Portfolio Analysis Forecast

Product / Program: Bankcard / Vacation Discount Mailer

	Months Open						
	1	2	3	...	13	14	15
Number Open Accts	25,000	24,825	24,500		22,000	21,600	21,200
Total O/S ($000)	$7,500	$22,343	$27,563		$23,100	$22,680	$22,260
Avg Balance per active	$1,000	$1,500	$1,500		$1,500	$1,500	$1,500
% Open accts Active	30.0%	60.0%	75.0%		70.0%	70.0%	70.0%
% Open accts Revolving	0.7%	30.0%	50.0%		50.0%	50.0%	50.0%
% Accts Delinq 60+	0.0%	0.0%	0.0%		1.0%	1.0%	1.0%
% Accts C/O (Annualized)	0.0%	0.0%	0.0%		2.0%	2.0%	2.0%
% O/S Delinq 60+	0.0%	0.0%	0.0%		2.0%	2.0%	2.0%
% O/S C/O (Annualized)	0.0%	0.0%	0.0%		4.0%	4.0%	4.0%
Avg Bal per C/O	$0	$0	$0		$2,100	$2,100	$2,100
Gross Rev Per Active	$0.83	$21.25	$21.25		$21.25	$21.25	$21.25
Profit per Active	($7.71)	$8.44	$8.44		$3.44	$3.44	$3.44
Return on Assets	-9.3%	6.8%	6.8%		2.8%	2.8%	2.8%

Note that this forecast includes only one mention of profitability (at the line "profit per active" account). This very brief, summary number might alert management if the product is not meeting its profit objectives. Our opinion of the importance of profitability is such that we have devoted a whole chapter to it. Suffice to say, you cannot design a product without making assumptions as to its profitability: Does the product meet your corporate target? Is it profitable immediately or only over time? These subjects are addressed later in Chapter 11, Profit Analysis.

THE CRAFT OF FORECASTING

Forecasting is not an exact science. The following forecasts published by *Newsweek* in 1997 are some of my favorites.

"Stocks have reached what looks like a permanently high plateau."
IRVING FISHER, *Professor of Economics, Yale University,*
October 17, 1929

"Who the hell wants to hear actors talk?"
HARRY WARNER, *Warner Brothers Studio,* 1927

"Television won't be able to hold on to any market after the first six months. People will soon get tired of staring at a plywood box every night."
DARRYL ZANUCK, *Head of 20th Century Fox,* 1946

"Computers in the future may, perhaps, only weigh 1.5 tons."
Popular Mechanics Magazine, 1949

"We don't like their sound. Groups of guitars are on the way out."
Decca Records, rejecting the Beatles, 1962

"For the majority of people the use of tobacco has a beneficial effect."
DR. IAN MCDONALD, *Los Angeles Surgeon,* 1963

"Everything that can be invented, has been invented."
CHARLES DUELL, *U.S. Commissioner of Patents,* 1899

"There is no reason for any individual to have a computer in their home."
KENNETH OLSEN, *President of Digital Equipment Corporation,* 1977

I hope you are able to forecast more accurately than some of these geniuses of the past.

FINAL STEPS

Once the product has been designed, the lender must decide whether or not it is possible to test the product in the marketplace. If management is sufficiently patient to wait eighteen months or more, the assumptions of the product planners can be tested and the product can be amended, if necessary. The resulting delay in a full-scale introduction for the product, however, can be too costly for many institutions to accept.[2]

---

2. Despite some concerns about the ethics of such a practice, many businesses bypass the test process by "borrowing" product knowledge from competitors. This can be done by hiring employees with experience in developing or managing a similar product(s). In addition, a great deal of industry information is available by reading trade publications such as *Credit Card Management* and by attending seminars run by such institutions as Fair, Isaac, and our own, Solomon-Lawrence's *Managing Risk & Reward,* which we have run for more than fifteen years.

Testing a new or revised product can reap the following benefits:

- *No major commitment of resources is needed before gauging the results. If the product is overly successful and the lending institution will be unable to meet its customer service goals, it won't suffer the embarrassment of facing thousands of unhappy customers; conversely, if the product is a flop, it will have few public relations problems.*
- *The test period can be used to fine-tune and modify the product to meet the customers' requirements in a way that is consistent with the lender's own profit objectives.*
- *Finally, several tests can be conducted simultaneously to help resolve internal disputes over which product features will work best.*

The first rule with a test is to be sure the results can be determined clearly. The second is to be sure that someone knowledgeable is reading the results and feeding them back to management. When a carefully developed series of tests is not systematically tracked, the whole process can be a waste of time and money.

It is difficult to devote time and resources to an extensive test period; the temptation is to just plunge in with a new product. If management cannot wait, the risks of moving ahead without a test can at least be mitigated by taking the following steps:

- *Rigorously studying what the competition has done under similar circumstances and modifying these results to meet the institution's own circumstances*
- *Hiring experienced people and listening to them*
- *Watching the very early results of the product introduction closely. If justified, the key terms can be changed quickly to avoid continuing a potential disaster.*

We cover some early warning MIS in later chapters.

Approval

The last step in product design—for either a new product or a major change in an existing product—is to prepare a formal proposal documenting the decisions reached at each stage of the planning process. This document should enumerate all the remaining steps in the credit cycle to be considered before a product is introduced, including the screening process, how the accounts will be billed and serviced, collections requirements, writeoff policy, management information and, of course, a forecast that includes profitability over time.

Every product should receive a formal sign-off by several members of senior management. These signatures should represent the *individual* approval of people who have been formally delegated the authority to approve such programs. The point is individual responsibility rather than the consensus of a faceless committee. The wisdom underlying the saying "A camel is a horse designed by committee" also applies to the consumer business.

Each person signing the document should be able to add value either by asking the right questions or contributing to the product's development (i.e., he should really know the business). Approval from a senior manager(s) with no knowledge of the business is worthless. Indeed, such approval may corrupt a perfectly good proposal if it is contingent on unnecessary (or stupid) changes.

Implementation and Feedback

Formal approval is not the end of the process. In addition to the monthly (or weekly) updates on the initial forecast (see Exhibit 2-7), there should be a formal review of every existing product at least once a year. The following are the sorts of questions that should be asked:

- *Are any modifications required in the target market or terms and conditions?*

- *What has the competitive reaction been? (Remember, imitation is the sincerest form of flattery.)*

- *Were there any operating problems?*

- *What have we learned for any future products? What can we do better?*

- *Is the product profitable, and what changes, if any, should be made to increase profitability?*

- *What is our share of the market? Is this increasing or declining?*

- *Is the risk-adjusted pricing appropriate?*

- *Is our collection strategy effective, and are we staffed to meet these goals?*

Delivering on the Offer

Finally, successful product acceptance requires a business to deliver to consumers the advertised products with well-trained customer service employees. Many corporations that used to excel at answering the phone promptly and providing quick access to trained customer service representatives have begun to resort more and more to automated response systems. "If you want your balance, press one . . . If you want us to know how bad we are, press 13 . . . . Please wait for the next available representative. . . . Your call is important to us . . ." and so forth. Devoting more resources to customer service could represent a big opportunity for a company to gain a competitive advantage in today's automated world.

CAN THE PAST PREDICT THE FUTURE?

Planning (and implementation) strategies can go only so far. Real discontinuities occur in the economy, in the legal or regulatory structure, or in consumer spending habits, to upset the best-laid plans of "mice and men," as poet Robert Burns expressed it.

Who can foretell where new technologies—such as the explosive Internet—will lead? There might be changes coming in the way consumer privacy is protected, with regulations capping the amount of data available to lenders from the credit bureaus. A recession might lead to a regional or worldwide depression for the first time since the 1930s. The expected changes in bankruptcy laws, whereby more debtors with identifiable assets will be directed to pay back at least a portion of their debts, may help to curb some abuses in bankruptcy filings. Any of these factors can dramatically impact the way you do business, and no amount of planning can take every event into account.

Adapting to these changes requires great management flexibility, a lack of bureaucracy, and the ability to gather sufficient information on a timely basis to adapt to the changing world.

SUMMARY

Good planning is critical to the success of a consumer lending business. Good planning means:

- *Controlling the business by product (and subproduct)*
- *Planning the details*
- *Matching the product to the target market*
- *Knowing the competition (some are bad)*
- *Being aware of change (economic, legal, cultural)*
- *Knowing the elements of your profitability.*

If you understand the need for all of these elements and have them in place, you are off to a good start. Next we cover the steps required to execute your plans, beginning with a discussion of the powerful tool used throughout the consumer lending business: scoring.

Credit Scoring

B EFORE CONTINUING WITH further coverage of the credit cycle itself, it is first necessary to discuss the industry's most important management tool, credit scoring.

Scoring is a method for analyzing data on applicants (potential customers) and existing customers to try and predict their future performance. If used correctly, scoring systems can provide managers with an enormous amount of statistical information which they can use to control their portfolios with a high degree of predictability. We will cover the alternative method of making decisions, namely, the use of human review and judgment, in the next chapter, Acquiring Accounts.

This chapter covers the development, implementation, and monitoring of credit scoring systems, then examines how scoring is used in day-to-day operations. The level of detail should give the reader an understanding of scoring concepts, but we do not attempt to explain the technical mathematical principles necessary to develop and validate the systems. This chapter is for managers who must understand scoring without necessarily having a technical background.

THE SCORING CONCEPT

Credit scoring uses statistical techniques to identify and rank-order the *desirability* of potential customers or the activity of current customers. Desirability is defined beforehand by the user and can be, for example, profitability, risk, probability of response, willingness to renew, willingness to repay if delinquent, and so forth. Some systems identify customers with a high potential for bankruptcy, or identify accounts in collection for either no action or for special followup; some identify customers for line increases, others select customers for line reductions or early cancellation. In short, scoring can be the single most helpful tool in the arsenal of a consumer lending business manager.

THE EARLY DAYS OF SCORING

According to Gerry De Kerchove, an executive at the California-based scoring development company Fair, Isaac & Company, Inc., the first attempts at credit scoring in the loan decision process were made in the 1940s by Household Finance and Spiegel, the Chicago mail order house. The efforts by both companies were aborted, however. Much later, in the late 1950s, the American Investment Company (AIC) of Illinois asked two mathematicians, Bill Fair and Earl Isaac, to examine a small sample of loans (some of which had paid well and some of which had not) to see if they could detect any patterns that would help the company make future lending decisions.

Using discriminant analysis, Fair and Isaac calculated that AIC could have avoided making nearly 20% of the loans they wrote off. This concept was revolutionary, but the scoring system was never fully implemented because a few of the lending officers thought they could do better. Still, Fair and Isaac thought they had the germ of a good idea. They continued to improve the mathematical techniques and began converting the skeptics; the concept slowly took hold.

Such high-volume lenders as Ford Credit, Montgomery Ward, and Sears Roebuck were early converts and believers in scoring. In fact, Ford Motor Credit *had* to use credit scoring to assess auto loan applicants right from the beginning because the company, started in the early 1960s (forty years after General Motors Acceptance Corp.), had few trained lenders. GMAC, on the other hand, did not use scoring until the mid-1980s because of its pride in its experienced underwriters and because its product offering was stable.

Scoring is used in many businesses other than consumer credit. It is used by insurance companies to rank-order candidates for longevity, good or ill health, or for risk of automobile accidents. Mail order houses use scoring to develop response models. Although not highly publicized, scoring systems are also used by the Internal Revenue Service to select likely candidates for audit.

Scoring systems consider many variables simultaneously to array *groups* of applicants or accounts (not *individual* applicants or accounts) according to their level of desirability. The concept is that all members within one group have the same odds of performing in a certain way.

As we have said, scoring is used in the consumer lending field both to screen applicants for loans (regardless of how they are sourced) and to manage accounts already booked. The term *application scoring*, or *credit scoring*, is generally used to describe scoring systems that screen applicants; *behavior scoring*, or *performance scoring*, is generally applied to scores used to manage accounts already booked.

Both application and behavior scoring systems work especially well for high-volume products with lower outstanding balances (i.e., up to $15,000), including the typical Visa, MasterCard, Discover cards, the travel & entertainment cards issued by American Express and Diner's, retailers' charge cards, personal installment loans, auto loans, and so forth. Scoring provides a consistent and accurate review process at the lowest possible cost appropriate for smaller loan balance products and a way to control their loss rates.

Large lines of unsecured credit, home mortgages, and other high-value loans may require a more intensive individual review and analysis in addition to scoring, because of the larger dollar exposure and the need to evaluate the collateral in the case of secured products. In fact, the companies that dominate the home mortgage secondary financing business (Freddie Mac and Fannie Mae, see Chapter 10) *require* that each applicant be scored as part of the elaborate application process needed to buy or refinance a home.

Finally, there are two different types of scores: custom scores and generic scores. Custom scores are developed from your own data; generic scores are developed from large pools of data, typically from the major credit bureaus. If your own portfolio data are limited, or you are expanding with new products or into new geographic areas, then a generic score may be the only way to score these applicants or accounts.

Benefits of Scoring

Each type of scoring system offers different benefits. For an application system, the benefits include:

- **Objective risk evaluation.** *A scoring system eliminates personal biases in the decision process and allows for consistent decisions.*
- **Cost-efficient processing.** *Unqualified applicants can be eliminated quickly, and highly qualified applicants can be speedily approved, leaving time for the "gray area" accounts to be analyzed in detail.*
- **Statistical control of the portfolios.** *The risk of each account accepted can be described in detail with great statistical precision. The actual results over time can be charted against the predicted results to ensure that the scoring system continues to function as developed.*
- **Controlled experimentation.** *With the ability to array the portfolio, experiments can be run to accept more higher-risk accounts, to offer larger lines, to place fewer restrictions on new accounts, and so forth, so that a business can be more profitable in the long run.*

Behavior scoring systems offer the following benefits:

- **Control over account usage.** *With the risk in each account identified on an ongoing basis, the more desirable accounts (possibly low-risk, possibly more profitable accounts) can be encouraged to expand and lengthen their relationship with the institution; the high-risk accounts can be controlled or eliminated.*
- **Better authorization decisions.** *Score systems allow more consistent and speedier decisions on routine authorizations, and more flexibility*

with the difficult decisions such as allowing on-the-spot, over-limit changes. This increases customer satisfaction, can save on costs, and of course can result in greater profit.

- **More experimentation.** Champion/challenger strategies can be devised in order to constantly improve collection, line change, or authorization decisions. Under this concept, existing strategies, the so-called champions, are challenged by alternate strategies, the challengers. The winning strategies are implemented; the losers are discarded over time.

- **Improved collection performance.** A good collection model can identify high-, low-, and medium-risk accounts, allowing improved collector targeting at a lower cost. Collectors can spend their time on the most cost-effective accounts, those where they have a good chance of influencing a delinquent customer to pay. At the same time, the model will identify the lower-risk accounts that need not be contacted (and annoyed) because the odds are high that they will pay anyway.

- **Early identification of problem accounts.** A score system can use credit bureau information to identify people who are building up their level of borrowing or becoming delinquent at other institutions.

Limitations of Scoring

Scoring also has its limitations, and management must understand these before entering any project. The major limitations are:

- **Time-intensive development process.** Scoring systems take time to develop and install. A behavior scoring system, in particular, requires a well-developed internal reporting system to enable testing and implementation of different strategies. In addition, the data must be read and acted on. If management support is halfhearted, the project may not be implemented effectively.

- **Limited predictability.** A scoring system cannot identify individual good or bad accounts; it can only identify the odds that an account will be good or bad. If the odds are 500 to 1 that an account is going to be good, the decision is easy; however, if the odds are only 8 to 1, or 5 to 1, decisions are more difficult.

- **System deterioration over time.** All systems deteriorate over time as the population and the economy change. Since scoring relies on the interpretation of past performance, systems must constantly be monitored and validated to determine how well they are performing.

The benefits outweigh the limitations, but no one should embark on the development of a scoring system thinking it will be easy.

DEVELOPING A SCORING SYSTEM

Credit and behavior scoring systems obviously have very different applications, but the same general principles of development apply to both. As an example, let us examine the four steps in developing an application scoring system: 1) planning, 2) developing, 3) implementing, and 4) validating/monitoring.

Planning Scoring Systems

Because scoring systems are complicated and take time to develop, it is extremely important to assign the task of project direction, through to completion, to a qualified, in-house, management team. Planning subtasks include determining the score objectives, selecting the developer, defining good and bad accounts, and selecting the sample.

> ***Determine the Score Objectives:*** The first and most important planning step is to decide where score systems can be most useful in managing your business: To which products and what part of the credit cycle should scoring be applied? Most lending businesses today use scoring in a variety of ways, but there are always opportunities for improvement. Do some of your existing custom scores need updating? Should you develop a new score to help manage your collections organization? Are new generic scores available in the marketplace that could be used to better predict bankruptcy? Can your mortgage approval process be speeded up and improved with scoring? You must choose the objective of your scoring system before development can begin; identification of the data to be analyzed is determined by your scoring system's objective.
>
> There is no "book" solution to the number and types of scores that a well-run business needs. Since scoring has multiple uses, large-volume lenders usually need many systems.
>
> Keep in mind a few common-sense, basic rules. First, the more carefully defined the product and/or target market, the better the system will discriminate, at least until the population gets too small, at which point the score becomes statistically unreliable. Thus, one application model for each branch or store in the southeast region may do a superb job of ranking risk, but can the business afford to develop and administer the large number of models this geographically narrow definition implies? Are customers so different in each branch that multiple models are needed? On the other hand, developing one scorecard for new automobile buyers and one for used car buyers is probably mandatory, because people who buy new cars tend to be very different from people who buy used cars (particularly used cars six or seven years old).
>
> Also, there are many different populations to consider. Separate scorecards may be appropriate for "first-time credit seekers," people with

"thin files," or the true subprime market—those who have a bad credit history but may now be ready for a second chance. If you wish to target this type of customer in the future, it may be possible to screen them using generic scoring systems that incorporate appropriate discriminants for that target market. Remember, few of these applicants own their own home or have a reliable record at the credit bureau, so how would they ever get credit if you have a system that relies heavily on characteristics that do not apply to them? Few first-time or subprime borrowers would ever be accepted by a scoring system developed for the general population.

Adapting existing systems to new products can be effective if the business takes the time to validate whether the systems discriminate as intended for the new population—as long as you truly test if the system fits statistically (we cover that later). However, if a business's sole objective is to save money by applying an old personal loan system to a new auto loan product, a new line of credit, or a home equity loan product, it should watch out. An invalid score system will cause more harm than good because it typically does not discriminate well between goods and bads—letting in more bads than intended, and, more important, also keeping out potentially good accounts.

Select a Developer: Developing an application scoring system typically costs $50,000 or more and can take several months to develop, depending on the availability of data. Behavioral systems may take even more time and resources to develop, depending on the number and purpose of systems to be developed and, again, the availability of data. The first question is: Should the system(s) be developed in-house or should you use a professional score-development company?

There are several excellent, highly experienced developers of scoring systems. The largest and best known is Fair, Isaac & Company, Inc. (FICO) of San Rafael, California. In business since 1948, Fair, Isaac develops models for many of the larger banks and financial institutions. In addition, its generic risk, bankruptcy, revenue, fraud, attrition, and collection models are typically available at each of the three major credit bureaus (Equifax, TransUnion, Experían). Fair, Isaac also develops models around the world. It is hard to go wrong using Fair, Isaac, but there are alternatives.

For instance, HNC of San Diego, California, and Portfolio Management Associates (PMA) in New York City are in the top level of score developers. HNC originally pioneered the development of artificial intelligence or neural "net" score systems, systems which update themselves constantly to determine new patterns of behavior, but they also develop conventional score models. PMA is not committed to a particular mathematical technique; its approach is to work closely with clients, to train them and make sure they understand the process of development and implementation, to leave behind management information to track the scores, and thus to leave behind an organization that thoroughly understands scoring and its applications.

Using an outside developer has the following advantages:

- *Access to some of the best industry talent*
- *Unbiased opinions: no turf to protect or jobs to save, as there could be with an in-house scoring department interested in maintaining or expanding its empire*
- *One-time costs rather than continuing fixed costs to maintain the scoring department*
- *Possibly lower costs due to the competitive bidding process.*

The disadvantages of outside development sometimes include the following:

- *A "black box" approach, which means no one within the organization is allowed to, or can, understand the underlying mathematics of the system.*
- *The developer leaves the client after creating the system; the end user may be reluctant to buy the consulting expertise required to use the system at its maximum capability.*

There is no one answer. One solution may be to establish a balance—to rely on outside developers who are guided and advised by a small staff of internal experts who act as liaison with the individual business units. Some larger lenders use a combination of internal and external development to take advantage of both.

Define Good and Bad Accounts: Once a developer has been chosen, the end user must define a "good" account, a "bad" account, and an "indeterminate" account (an account that is difficult to describe as being either good or bad) from the performance of existing accounts. For a risk system, a bad account, one that would be better not to have on the books, can be defined as bad because it is persistently delinquent, or it is an actual writeoff or a bankruptcy. For an attrition prediction system, a bad account may be a profitable account which is going to leave you. The definition ideally should be set by analyzing profitability. What is the profitability of accounts that have been severely delinquent three out of the past six months, or that have been carrying only a small balance recently? Can the lender afford to keep *them on the books? This* type of analysis requires extremely sophisticated data and not all lenders may be able to do it.

There will always be a few indeterminate accounts. For a profitability-based model, accounts around the breakeven level would fit this definition. In a risk system, indeterminate accounts may have been mildly delinquent at some time but not so frequently or so severely as to warrant their being classified as bad (or good). These accounts should be relatively few in number. Indeterminate accounts are not used in the development of the system; however, they are set aside for validation purposes.

Select the Sample. The next step in developing an application system is to select a sample of accounts for analysis. The keys to obtaining an appropriate sample include the following:

1) *First and foremost, the sample must be representative of the population that the finished scorecard will evaluate.*[1] *For example, a model that ranks automobile loan applicants must be based on a population that purchased similar types of cars at similar dealerships in the past. A buyer of a new Cadillac is different from a buyer of a used Kia; the characteristics examined are different, the behaviors are different. It would be difficult to predict what a good buyer of the Kia should look like if you used the characteristics and behaviors of the new Cadillac buyer as a guide.*

2) *The sample must have the same characteristics (e.g., the same geographic and demographic profile) as the population to be scored. For example, a score used for offering a credit card to students should be developed on a sample of students, and a score for home equity lines of credit for homeowners in the Northeast should be developed on a sample of those homeowners.*

3) *Certain populations should be excluded from the development sample. For example, if, as is typical, the lender will always exclude minors in the future, it makes no sense to include them in the model-building process.*

4) *There must be at least enough good and bad accounts to provide a solid statistical basis for the system. Developers want to achieve a confidence level of 95%, meaning there is no more than a 5% chance that the model's results could come about purely by chance. Your developer can tell you how many good and bad accounts it takes to achieve this level of confidence and what sampling techniques he will use (such as stratified random sam-*

---

1. A scorecard is the end product of a scoring system. It includes all the characteristics, such as *time on job, type of housing,* etc., used in the system and the weights given to each classification used (*rents:* 0 points; *owns:* 38 points; *lives with parents:* 15 points, etc.).

pling), but a key figure to remember is that score developers usually require around a minimum of 1,000 bads to reach their goal.

5) Data must be available for the time period being analyzed. For an application scoring system, data typically come from applications and credit bureau reports from people who applied for credit one to two years ago, thus allowing sufficient time for accounts to develop a record of performance (good or bad).

6) Finally, the development sample should include previously rejected accounts, some of whom may have been good. Since, by definition, you have no record of performance on these rejected accounts, it must be inferred by obtaining credit bureau records or using sophisticated statistical techniques.

Now that you have determined your objectives, selected the developer, defined your goods and bads, and have a fully representative and accurate sample, you can develop the system.

Developing Scoring Systems

Select the Characteristics. The first step the developer takes is to examine the characteristics of all the accounts in the sample, based on whatever data are available (the data typically come from the application, credit bureau records, and possibly a demographic profile). Typical information examined can be found in Exhibit 3-1.

The objective of this analysis is to discern any patterns that can help discriminate between the good and bad applicants. In Exhibit 3-2, the score developer has analyzed the historical performance of the development sample against one characteristic derived from credit bureau information, in this case, "time on file," i.e., how long the applicant has had a credit bureau file. The breaks in time categories could have occurred anywhere (e.g., 12–15 mos., 20–30 mos., etc); however, in this example, the developer looked at accounts on file at the credit bureau in six categories, ranging from "Less than 12 months" to "Over 60 months."

Examining the data, the developer found a correlation between the amount of time the applicant had a file at the credit bureau and the performance of the account once it was on the bank's books. The data demonstrate that a far greater percentage of accounts with short credit histories at the time of application ultimately were bad than those that had a file at the credit bureau for longer periods of time. Thus, this characteristic provides a distinction between good and bad accounts.

For instance, as shown in Exhibit 3-2, people with a short credit bureau history (<12 months) had a bad rate of 25%. Conversely, applicants with long credit histories had lower bad rates and those with >60 months on file had a bad rate of only 5%. Such a straight line of performance does not always exist; often, the relationship between performance and any given characteristic is a curving or irregular graph.

EXHIBIT 3-1

Credit Scoring : Examples of Variables Examined

Sample data available from application

- Age
- Residence (own, rent)
- Years at residence
- Occupation
- Telephone
- Income
- Years on job
- Prior job
- Years on prior job
- Marital status
- Number of dependents
- Credit references (bankcards, etc.)

- Banking references
- Checking/savings account
- Collateral/equity requirement
- Credit outstanding
- Debt/burden
- Purpose of loan
- Type of loan
- Co-signer
- Same information on co-signer
- Co-applicant
- Same information on co-applicant

Sample data available from credit bureau

- Time in file
- Number of satisfactory payments
- Number and balance of various delinquencies (e.g., 30-day, 60-day)
- Length of time since last delinquency

  } for various types of loans, e. g., revolving/installment (last X months, last X years)

- Number and balance of charged-off accounts
- Number and balances of various types of loans, e.g., bankcards, retailers' cards, finance company accounts
- Number of inquiries (in last X months)
- Length of time since last inquiry
- Age of oldest/youngest trade
- Highest/lowest/total credit limits on revolving accounts
- Highest/lowest/total utilization on revolving accounts
- Total balance owing as percent of highest outstanding for various types of loans (e.g., revolving, installment)
- Number and types of trades recently opened

Other data

- Demographic clusters
- Census tract median income

EXHIBIT 3-2
Individual Characteristic Analysis

Time on File	Total	Good	Bad	% Bad	% Total
<12 Mos.	1,000	753	247	25	4.2
12–18	1,334	1,067	267	20	5.6
19–24	2,000	1,700	300	15	8.3
25–36	3,000	2,700	300	10	12.5
37–60	3,334	3,067	267	8	13.9
>60	13,333	12,713	620	5	55.5
Total	24,000	22,000	2,000	8	100.0

Conversely, analysis may show *no* distinction between a good and bad account for one specific characteristic, in which case that characteristic would not be used in the scorecard.

The score developer tests hundreds of characteristics in this manner to see if there is a difference between goods and bads. The developer searches for the stronger discriminants and tries to select those with the most power to separate good accounts from bad ones. Because so many characteristics overlap (e.g., home-owners tend to be older than renters), the next step is to statistically estimate the degree of correlation between potential predictive characteristics and remove its effect. There are well-defined legal restrictions on the types of characteristics that can be used; in the U.S., laws forbid a lender from denying credit on the basis of race, sex, religion, national origin, marital status, or source of income. In addition, the developer and the end user must agree on the desirability of using each of the characteristics found to discriminate; some are just too illogical to explain to a rejected applicant if they must be disclosed in a rejection letter.

For instance, because automobile buying is seasonal, the *month* in which a vehicle is purchased may be a statistically useful discriminant; for example, a person who buys a car in August may appear to be riskier (i.e., gets fewer points) than a November car buyer. This may be statistically valid because a person buying a new model car, typically in November, accepts the higher price for the new model versus the bargain shopper of August. Can this be explained persuasively to the customer? Imagine writing a rejection letter that says, "You have been denied credit because you prefer buying a car in August." Other, more logical discriminants must be found. The system may be less powerful, but much more defensible. The end user must work carefully with the developer to ensure that a reasonable scorecard is developed.

Select and Weight the Discriminants. From the accepted sample, the developer identifies the most powerful discriminants, considers the correlation between them and actual performance, and mathematically assigns *points* or *weights* to each one selected (get your score developer to explain the techniques used). The end result is a scoring system that contains characteristics that could look like the one shown in Exhibit 3-3.

The number of categories from the application may be greater or fewer; there may be more items from the credit bureaus or fewer. There could also be more or fewer breakpoints within each category selected. The final result allows the end user to score each applicant by adding up the points awarded, characteristic by characteristic (e.g., with this scorecard, if the applicant lives with her parents, she gets 15 points; if she is 23 years of age, she gets another 4 points, etc.). The total point count or score is translated into an "odds" quote that predicts how the applicant's account will perform over an estimated time period.

Set the Cutoff Score. A cutoff score establishes the total number of points above which theoretically all accounts are accepted and below which all are declined. Lenders may choose to override these decisions within allowable limits (overriding the cutoff score is covered later in this chapter). The most helpful tool when deciding whether to accept/decline an account is the projected approval and bad rate at each score level, as determined by the developer. See Exhibit 3-4 for a sample of this powerful tool.

There are many methods of setting a cutoff score, depending on the lender's business goals. For instance, an application score cutoff could be chosen to:

1. *Maintain a given rate of approval*
2. *Maintain a given bad/charge-off rate*
3. *Maintain any combination of approval/bad rate that is acceptable to management based on prior experience*
4. *Select the most profitable level.*

EXHIBIT 3-3
Sample Credit Scoring Table

Characteristics	Classifications	Assigned Points
Type of housing	Rents	0
	Lives with parents	15
	Owns	38
Age of applicant	18–20 years	0
	21–24 years	4
	25–55 years	27
	56 years or older	53
Household income	Unknown	22
	Less than $15M	0
	$15M–$25M	7
	>$25M–$35M	31
	>$35M–$50M	43
	Above $50M	61
Number of recent inquiries	0	66
	1–3	48
	4 or more	0
Number of satisfactory ratings	0	0
	1–2	14
	3–5	26
	6 or more	33
Number of 90-day ratings + derogatory items	0	129
	1	34
	2	13
	3 or more	0
Number of past due balances	0	38
	1	7
	2 or more	0
Number of bankcards	0	0
	1–3	40
	4 or more	53
Bankcard balances reported in last 12 months	$0 to $250	40
	>$250 to $1000	37
	>$1000 to $3000	17
	>$3000 or more	0

Minimum possible score = 0   Maximum possible score = 511

EXHIBIT 3-4

Selecting the Cutoff Score

Score	Total Percent	Goods Percent	Bads Percent	Charge-offs Marginal	Charge-offs Cumulative
500	17	19	2	1.4	1.4
450	25	29	3	2.2	1.7
400	32	37	5	3.9	2.2
350	46	52	9	4.2	2.8
300	**62**	**69**	**17**	**7.2**	**3.9**
250	65	72	21	18.0	4.6
200	73	79	34	23.4	6.6
150	85	89	59	29.1	9.8
100	100	100	100	38.0	14.1

If you are a manager who lacks good profit data, any of the first three alternatives is acceptable (and they can be adopted immediately), but you may not be getting the best performance from your portfolio. For instance, using the above chart, a manager would be able to predict the approval (62%) and writeoff rates (3.9%) at a cutoff score of 300; however, is a 3.9% charge-off rate appropriate? It depends on the product and the profitability of that product. A 3.9% writeoff rate on a credit card product is low by current standards but very high for an automobile loan, and it would be off the wall for a home mortgage product. In the final analysis, we strongly recommend that senior management select the cutoff score based on the profitability of the account. The key information required is the cost of a bad account (in higher collections costs and writeoffs) compared with the profit from a good account over the assumed lifetime of the product. The cutoff score could be set at the breakeven point for any given account, or it could be set by estimating the total portfolio profitability. We will cover profitability analysis in greater detail in Chapter 11, Profit Analysis for Consumer Products.

Other predictive models (attrition models, revenue models, collection models, bankruptcy models, etc.) require different strategies to determine what actions to take by score range. These models have no "cutoff" score. For instance, a collections model requires one strategy for lower-risk accounts, one for medium-risk, and one for higher-risk. Profitability remains the key objective, so in a collections score you would need to balance the costs of collecting vs. the dollars collected with each strategy.

It is particularly difficult to establish a firm policy by score range using a bankruptcy predictive model because a potential bankrupt looks (and often acts) very much like your best customer. The point to remember is that any scoring system merely rank-orders your accounts. Finally, you are responsible for what action to take at each score range. An interesting point about bankruptcy models, as we cover later in the chapter on collections, is that the most powerful ones today appear to be the generic bureau models that rely on data from many creditors. Your own data may not be powerful enough to be predictive.

THE DEBELLIS CURVE

One phenomenon seen on all revolving portfolios is that the profitability by score range will look like this:

EXHIBIT 3-5
Profitability by Score Range

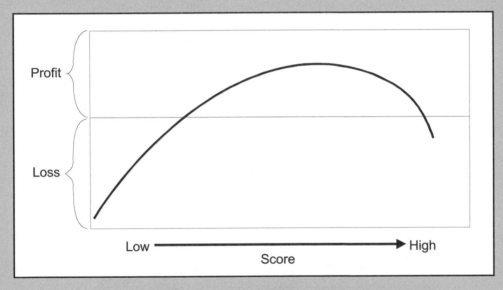

The highest *and* the lowest risk accounts are far less profitable—and possibly actually unprofitable—than the mid-score ranges. The high-risk accounts incur too many collection costs and writeoffs to be profitable; the lowest-risk accounts typically include too many people who use the card merely as a convenience (i.e., they habitually pay on time) or don't use it at all. If the card has no annual fee, a convenience customer must be very active to be profitable.

I call this the "DeBellis Curve," in honor of Joe DeBellis, founder of Portfolio Management Associates. Joe pioneered many developments in the scoring industry, including the first profitability-based mail-solicitation model for Citicorp in the mid-1970s.

Implementing the System

Steps in implementation include training your people how to use the system, determining your tolerance for overrides, watching out for scoring errors, preparing decline letters, and documenting the process.

Training. Are the people who will be using the system ready for it? The answer often depends on whether it is a replacement system or a first-time system. A replacement system may require only a few managerial changes, assuming that the prior system was running well (i.e., it was accepted by the credit organization and had good security, good monitoring, and effective performance). In other words, the old system worked but may have been deteriorating and a new system is being installed to improve the degree of discrimination. Training in this instance would merely require explaining why the new scorecard is needed and how it will improve the loan decision process.

If application scoring is new to the organization, the system must be introduced carefully. The keys to a successful launch are: 1) senior management commitment (and understanding), and 2) thorough training for all end users. If the organization perceives that management is truly behind the project, the credit underwriters are more likely to actually use the system and not try to subvert it. The more decentralized the organization, the harder it tends to be to implement a system, particularly in a branch organization where senior officers are accustomed to making individual credit decisions. Installing the system in an organization with a centralized loan processing shop is much simpler, if only because of the ease of communication and ability to control the process from the beginning.

To convert a branch organization to scoring requires a thorough, ongoing training process to ensure that the credit approvers know what scoring is and how it works: how the system was developed, why it works, the need for system integrity, and why it is superior to making individual credit decisions through the use of human judgment. For example, the underwriter (or the broker) must be taught the importance of not "fudging" the applicant's information, (e.g., "You do have a savings account, Mrs. Brown, don't you?"). The application should be complete, but not fabricated. Further, the credit approvers must know that they will see the results of scoring to prove that the system works. The results must be fed back regularly, and in a simple enough format to make the point that scoring systems indeed array accounts well and perform as predicted. One more point: it is important to show the performance of all overrides.

Overrides. Virtually all loan applications are eventually reviewed by an individual for whom the score is just one part of the decision process. Although we have discouraged individual loan reviewers from spending much time on the smaller lines of credit, any application system should allow for controlled overrides because there will always be some instances where the recommended score decision should be reversed. Usually this results from the reviewer's having additional information with which he can "second-guess" the score system.

There are two types of overrides:

- **High-side overrides:** *The score system says the account should be approved, but the reviewer sees a reason to reject.*
- **Low-side overrides:** *The system indicates the account should be rejected, but the reviewer accepts it.*

To illustrate: no system is designed to review the chairman of the board's son or daughter's application for a credit card. Although they may be just departing for college, with no credit history, these worthy individuals are going to get a card—system or no system. Similarly, some people who pass the score should be declined, possibly because of information known to the credit approver that does not enter into any statistical system (e.g., a record of constant and frivolous litigation).

Overrides and allowances will be made in such situations. But overrides should be tightly controlled, with, say, no more than 3–5% of the total accepted population on the low side and the same number for the high side, depending on the product. (The figures could be higher on larger lines and lower on smaller lines.) The most important aspect of allowing overrides is to monitor their performance.

For low-side overrides, monitoring performance is easy. Prepare a monthly report to track the accounts accepted. It will soon become evident if the overrides are justified. If their delinquency or writeoff rate is unacceptably high, cut the allowable level of overrides. In a study published by Fair, Isaac, one lender found that the only acceptable reason for a forced approval was for the sake of good customer relations (e.g., the customer or one of his close relatives maintained several good accounts or a large CD at the bank). These accounts had a delinquency rate *below* the rate at cutoff (which was set presumably at the maximum acceptable risk).

Allowing low-side overrides is very important in the indirect automobile business because it is necessary to accept some bad accounts to get a fair share of the good ones from selected dealers. Even if the bads have a very high writeoff rate, the overall profit from the business may be acceptable.

The performance of high-side overrides is another matter. Unless special steps are taken, the performance of high-side override applications cannot be tracked since the accounts have not been booked. One solution is to accept a *sample* of the accounts that would have been rejected and to track them separately (for example, by assigning these accounts to a central, identifiable, department number). If these accounts perform well over time, as the score system predicted they would, the lender would have the evidence to adjust the rate of high-side overrides allowed. Another way to track these accounts if they are not booked by your institution is to obtain the performance of the unbooked accounts by examining their credit bureau records at some later time period, say, after eighteen months. If too many of these have a good record with other lenders, you should take steps to reduce your high-side overrides; if not, keep up the override level or adjust your system's cutoff score. It is important to let the data prove the validity of your override decisions.

The system is now statistically sound, the scorecard logical, the reporting systems in place, and the whole system is technically ready to be implemented. There are a few more details to worry about.

Scoring Errors. With the automation of many scoring systems, the need to audit for errors has been reduced. Managers, however, should be aware that errors can still penetrate a system. There are two kinds of errors: 1) *critical errors*, where the scorer enters sufficiently incorrect data to allow an account that would normally be rejected to be accepted, or vice versa, and 2) *normal errors,* where the error has no real impact on the final decision. Obviously, the first type is more important, but normal errors can still impact the validity of the system.

Errors most typically occur when applications are misread manually (e.g., a 90-day delinquency is read as a 60-day). It is difficult enough to score accurately with all the time in the world, but the normal processing pressures can exacerbate the difficulties. In addition, systems that include information requiring considerable interpretation (e.g., difficult or complex occupation codes) are more vulnerable to error. Further, some applications contain conflicting data. Suppose an applicant checks off the box that says "Lives with parents" as well as the one that says "Homeowner"? Which one is right? Maybe both are. Is it worth sending the application back for clarification? Remember that any delay of this sort will sharply reduce the completed application rate. As when interpreting Florida ballots in a presidential election, the user must develop rules for reading misleading data on applications (e.g., accept the first box ticked?). An experienced developer will have rules to deal with these exceptions based on prior systems usage.

The audit department should have a procedure to sample and report errors—especially critical errors.

Letter of Decline. In the United States, the lender is required to notify the applicant when he is denied credit. The letter can give the specific reason the applicant failed the credit system and may identify the individual factors where his score deviated most from either the highest possible score or the expected average score (e.g., insufficient time at the address, no bank account). Another option is for the letter simply to advise the applicant of his right to obtain an explanation from the creditor. Management must decide, in advance, whether the principal reasons for decline will be communicated to the customer immediately or only upon request.

Documentation. It is important to have complete documentation for any installed system. One reason is the need to keep formal, internal control over the system in the event of management changes. A second is that an audit trail may be required for legal purposes. Although validated score systems are legally acceptable, in the event of a group action against the lender, there may be a need to defend the complete impartiality of a system.

Validating and Monitoring the System

Validation and monitoring steps include initial and ongoing statistical validation, the development of early warning reports, and reporting actual results over time.

Statistical Validation. A scoring system must be constantly validated and monitored during its lifetime to ensure that it is working as the developers intended, that the cutoff scores are appropriate, and that the system is in legal compliance. Using a scoring system without monitoring is like using a clock without hands (it may be working, but how would you know?).

The first step is to validate before implementation. To do this, developers typically use a holdout sample: they hold out a random sample of the accounts used to develop the system for use in verifying that the score works the same for the holdout sample as it did for the development sample. If the system has taken a long time to develop, it may be necessary to use a sample of more recent applications to verify the score. Once the system is in place and working, a lender should use several standard reports to verify and monitor the system on an ongoing basis to be sure it continues to work as intended.

- *To be sure the score is statistically powerful, use K-S or Divergence Measures.*
- *To be sure the score is likely to work in the future, use Population Stability Reports.*
- *To be sure the cutoff is appropriate, use Historical Performance Tables.*

There are two methods of evaluating performance: one is called the K-S score, the other is the divergence method. The K-S score (named after two mathematicians, Kolmogorov and Smirnoff) calculates the difference between the cumulative distribution of the good and bad accounts. Because of its shape, it is sometimes called the "football" chart as shown below

EXHIBIT 3-6
Validation

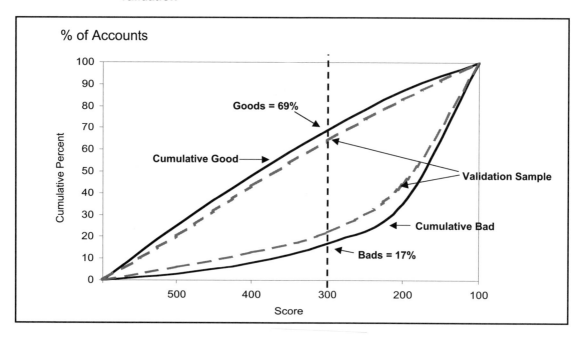

The larger the separation between the cumulative goods and bads, the more powerful the system is. A separation of more than 30 points is considered acceptable for an application score. This increases to 45 for a behavior score where, because it is based on your own data, the score should discriminate better. In the above example, the separation of 52 points (69 minus 17) is very good. The above chart also shows that the holdout sample (the inner line) validates the development sample as the two lines are very close. The K-S should be computed regularly, say, semiannually at the least.

The divergence method also can be used to determine the validity of a score system. Here, the developer calculates how often a good could be mistaken for a bad (or vice versa), or how much overlap there is between the two, as in the following example:

EXHIBIT 3-7

Divergence Method of Analysis, Score Distribution

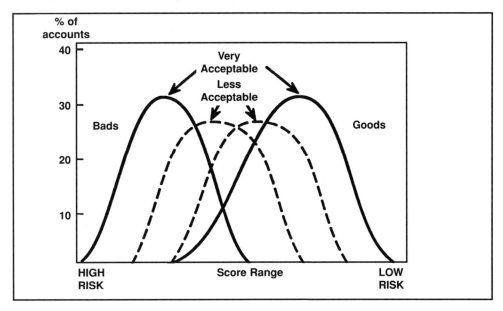

In general, the farther apart the two lines, the better the results. Your score developer can tell you how to calculate an acceptable level of divergence.

Early Warning Reports. Once the score system has been installed, you must monitor it regularly; is it performing as expected? Two important early warning reports are the Population Stability Analysis and the Characteristic Stability Analysis. The Population Stability report compares the distribution of the actual applicants by score range, either month by month or quarter by quarter, to the predicted distribution. A sample of this report is as follows:

EXHIBIT 3-8

Through-the-Door Population

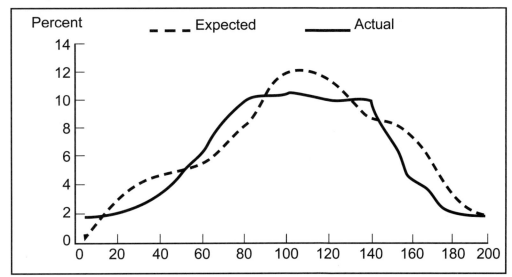

Population Stability is a good early indicator of potential problems because it tells you if the same type of people that the system was built on are still applying for credit. The assumption is that the distribution by score range will begin to skew from the development sample if the population of applicants begins to change. For example, if a lender starts a new marketing campaign targeted at applicants younger than normal, the number of younger, and possibly riskier, applicants presumably would increase. Typically, this would result in a greater number of applications below cutoff, which would result in a lower approval rate.

If the lender does experience a shift, the next step is to review the distribution of the actual score characteristics. The Characteristic Analysis Report looks like this:

EXHIBIT 3-9
Characteristic Stability

	Development Sample	Actual		
		Q3	Q2	Q1
Unknown	5%	14%	5%	8%
Less than $15M	3	3	2	4
$15M - 25M	15	14	14	15
$25M - 35M	55	54	57	55
$35M - 50M	17	14	18	16
Above $50M	5	1	4	2

The distribution of each characteristic used in the scorecard should be compared over time with that of the development sample. In the above example, does the sharp increase in the number of "Unknown" income in the third quarter—people whose income is not known or reported on the application—indicate a problem? Is it a real shift in the business or just an aberration, due to some other cause?

These reports only raise questions—they don't resolve them. Understanding the cause of the change comes only with a detailed analysis of the lender's processes and operations.

The Final Report Card. The final results, the "truth, the whole truth," for a scorecard comes when you finally get the numbers to show the actual results versus what you predicted. In the case of a scorecard predicting risk, this comes finally with the report showing actual delinquency or charge-offs by score range. Does the system work? This report card will tell you. Of course, one disadvantage is that these reports are not available until several months after the accounts are booked. In the following chart, we have tracked the actual writeoffs by score range. If the system works, the line will drop consistently as the score increases (as it does below):

EXHIBIT 3-10
Charge-Offs by Score

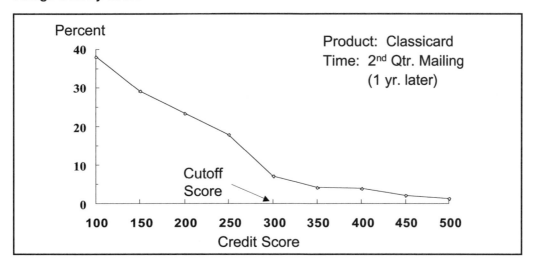

This report should be prepared for a book of business acquired during a given time period (typically three months), or for all accounts acquired as a result of a particular mailing or marketing program. A book of business acquired in the same time period and with the same screens/target market is usually referred to as a *vintage* of business (just the way winemakers identify one year's bottling); some refer to it as a *cohort* of business. Either way, it is the building block for all analyses of performance. If certain relationships between the score and the actual results look unusual, it is time for a manager to begin digging in to discover what has gone wrong.

Monitoring score-system performance with these reports gives the lender the hands to be able to read the clock. Managers would have difficulty performing their jobs without reading the reports regularly.

CENSUS BUREAU AND GENERIC SCORING MODELS

In addition to customized (in-house) scoring models, there are also *generic* models based on data available at credit bureaus for use by those who elect not to develop their own models due to insufficient resources/insufficient data, possibly because they are just entering the market with a new product. These generic models can be used independently or to supplement an in-house model.

As mentioned earlier, Fair, Isaac has been the major developer of generic models, using the actual performance of millions of accounts from many lenders on file at the credit bureaus. These include the following score models, typically adapted for use with each of the three major credit bureaus:

- *Risk models—e.g., BEACON and EMPERICA*
- *Industry-specific models for autos, bankcards, installment lending, and personal finance*

- *Bankruptcy model*
- *Revenue models*
- *Application fraud model*
- *Attrition model*
- *Collection model*

Additional models are available from other developers on both a national and a regional geographic basis. Specific products covered include:

- *Bank revolving credit lines*
- *Bank installment credit loans*
- *Automobile loans or leases*
- *Credit union products*
- *Retailer charge cards.*

Typically, the better defined the product, the better the model will fit the lender's needs. A national or very broad model may suffice, but the lender is advised to validate the scorecard with its own proposed products and target population to be confident of the final results.

Although it is always more desirable to build a custom application or solicitation score model (one lender reported that, with very complete records, it could develop its own model that would be 10–20% more powerful than a generic pre-score model), generic models are obviously effective for those whose portfolios are too small to build a system or who are too new in a business. An additional advantage to using generic scores is that most are updated every six months. When the economic environment is changing, some in-house scorecards may deteriorate faster than expected; the generic cards may be more powerful and up-to-date than an older, in-house model.

If cost-justified, both a custom model and a generic one can be used to screen new applicants or review existing accounts. Using two models can increase the discriminatory power with a large percentage of the accounts, but it also causes problem areas where information is uncertain. In Exhibit 3-11, a credit bureau score and a custom application score are overlayed: in this exhibit, 28% of the applicants would have failed both scores, and 46% would have passed both. Thus, the systems agreed on nearly three quarters of the accounts scored (which is typical of the results that Fair, Isaac reports). This result gives the lender a solid statistical basis to accept or deny credit to a large percentage of applicants.

For the remaining one quarter, one system says "go" and the other says "no go." This problem may not be as bad as it sounds; rather, it is an opportunity to improve the decision process in the gray areas.

By overlaying the two systems, it is possible to develop the combined odds and draw the cutoff line wherever the odds or "bad rate" is acceptable—regardless of the original single-system cutoff scores. A projection of the combined bad rate in each area of the combined scores is shown in Exhibit 3-12.

EXHIBIT 3-11

Using Two Scores

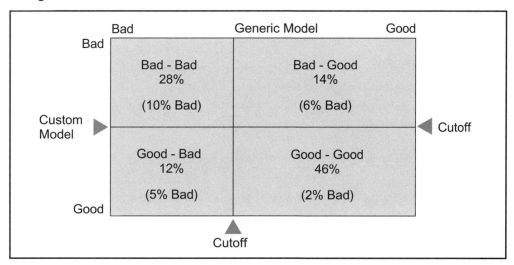

EXHIBIT 3-12

Using Two Scores (cont'd)

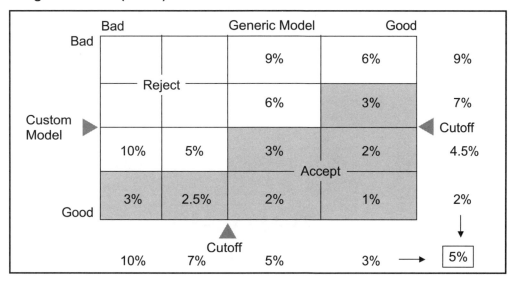

In this case, the developer accepted accounts in the shaded areas, even though one system or the other rejected the accounts. It is typical to accept more good accounts using two models. Fair, Isaac research indicates that on some models it is possible to improve the acceptance rate by 2–3% *with no increase in the bad rate.* Although this increase may not sound like much, for someone approving 10,000 loans a month, the added 200 to 300 loans could really improve the bottom line, without changing the risk.

If a lender is worried about approving too many loans that one system or the other says to reject, it could modify the approval strategy on the gray-area accounts (above) by:

- *Requiring a more intensive human review of the data (e.g., obtaining further verification or getting a second bureau report)*

- *Assigning lower initial credit lines, higher interest rates, shorter loan life, or obtaining higher down payments.*

Is it worth the added cost to use both systems? Only the business can provide the answer, but the cost of the generic models can be quite small (20 to 30 cents per application screened). Using more than one model should definitely be considered whenever it is economically feasible. Test to see if it is worthwhile.

USING TWO SYSTEMS—A WARNING

One potential pitfall is using two score systems in sequence rather than overlaying them, as some lenders have learned, to their chagrin. The score systems must be integrated and used together to guide your decision process.

One lender used the following scenario: Risk management had developed a risk-predictive model, while marketing had developed a revenue-predictive model. Marketing took the names that passed the risk model and sent offers only to those that passed the revenue model, the "higher potential revenue" customers. The end result was disaster.

EXHIBIT 3-13
Using Two Scores (cont'd)

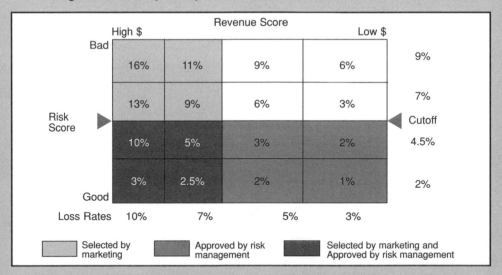

There were two reasons for this: 1) none of the potentially low-risk customers in the lower *right-hand* quadrant received an offer (remember, they were potentially low-revenue customers) and 2) those in the lower *left* portion of the quadrant (the highest risk) responded heavily to the offer. They had been screened through the revenue model as "big spenders." The end result was not enough goods from the lower right-hand side to offset the bads on the left. The lender experienced a severe case of adverse selection as a result of this targeting strategy with unacceptably high writeoff rates.

While marketing could say that all their target market had passed the risk screen, they had to learn the hard way that not all 640s (or whatever the risk cutoff score was) performed alike. Using two models sequentially can be a recipe for disaster. Get your developer to explain how the models should be integrated.

SUMMARY

Developing, installing, and making a scoring system work demands far more effort than the brief bursts of calculations required to actually develop the scorecards. A few holdouts are not completely convinced that scoring can be a very effective tool, perhaps because many lenders still do not use it to full advantage. They have scoring, but don't use what it can do to make the best decisions.

Weaving scoring into an existing organization requires strong support and real understanding from senior management. One way to reinforce the role of scoring is to include the scoring results as a key part of the language that managers use to communicate how their business is doing. For example, effective reports might say:

- *"The high-risk test group (score <180) in Alabama from the October mailing is performing better than expected; we are expanding the test to the other three states and may consider lowering the cutoff if these early results can be confirmed."*

- *"Bruce Oldsmobile contracts have the lowest average score of any dealer we service in Minnesota (292 versus 336 average) with 13% overrides; their repossession rate is twice the average rate. We are investigating to determine if this dealer's business is profitable."*

- *"The response rate in the 400–500 PBS score group was higher than expected. We are watching the early activation and usage patterns of these accounts because they are in the higher-risk range."*

This type of reporting language reflects how credit scoring is used as the way to communicate changes and performance of every phase of the credit cycle.

NEURAL NETWORKS

Professional managers constantly worry about staying abreast of the most advanced techniques for controlling and understanding their portfolios. For instance, neural networks (or neural nets) were once hailed as having the potential to revolutionize the credit-scoring industry. Are they the answer to all the limitations of scoring? Let's see.

Neural networks, which have been around for forty years, came from the world of academic research but were first employed in a significant way by the Defense Department. In comparison with conventional scoring systems, which are developed and revised only when proven to be out of date, neural nets are constantly analyzing the data they process and revising the decision systems accordingly. For instance, a fraud detection neural net would constantly be searching for new patterns of fraud. These systems are supposed to mimic the reasoning process of the human brain in that they are constantly learning from processing new data. An increasing number of non-military applications is being found every year. Some uses include analysis of huge bodies of information in highly technical, repetitive jobs, such as comparing fingerprints, interpreting medical laboratory samples (e.g., looking for cancer cells), and recognizing handwriting.

Financial institutions first began using neural networks to detect patterns of credit card fraud from their hundreds of thousands of daily transactions. Neural nets are now used to recommend collection actions, authorize purchases, and help card-processing operations, among other activities. Some users claim they recognize subtle changes in the patterns of behavior earlier than any other statistical method.

One supporter, Allen Jost of HNC, a San Diego–based firm specializing in developing, counseling, and training of neural-network-based products, believes that neural networks offer advantages over conventional credit scoring techniques. The primary advantage, in his opinion, is that they allow the rapid development of consistent and more subtle rank-ordering systems. Neural networks "converge automatically on the optimal solution," he asserts. In addition, he says, "Because of the 'automated' nature of the model-building process, neural network systems can be integrated quickly into data-processing systems."

In a recent article in *Collections & Credit Risk* magazine ("What Happened to Neural Nets?"), Mellon Bank reported that "neural nets have dramatically reduced the time needed to identify fraudulent transactions. . . . The neural network is built right into our debit card authorization system, so we know generally within ten minutes after a transaction has occurred that fraud has occurred. With our old 'rules-based' score system it took at least a day before we got any results."

Critics cite the following problems with neural networks:

- *They are initially more expensive than a single score system, although this can be viewed as the cost of buying many systems.*
- *They lack the ability to explain the reasoning behind their predictions.*
- *There is a risk of "over-fitting" the data . . . putting too much emphasis on "blips" or small departures in the data from what is usually observed (e.g., in a risk application, three accounts with prior bankruptcies perform well; bankruptcy now becomes a positive factor in a score system).*

Lenders need to make sure that the results do not become nonsensical. As with all score systems, some human intervention is necessary to ensure that the system does not go haywire and contravene established credit policies.

Buying a neural network system may be like buying a Porsche when all you do is drive to and from work on the Long Island Expressway or the Los Angeles Freeway, where the top speed is four miles per hour during rush hour. For larger, highly sophisticated lenders, the idea of using neural networks should be under constant test and review. For the less advanced, particularly those just beginning to use scoring well or for those just entering the arena, buying a neural network may be too much to take on, at first. Because not every lender gets full value from its existing scoring systems and the technology is so well developed, there may be enough left to accomplish with today's scoring systems before investing heavily in neural nets.

One solution: possibly the two methodologies should be combined. In the same 1999 article in *Collections & Credit Risk* magazine, Fair, Isaac's fraud manager described how they created a software tool to improve fraud detection by combining data from rules-based models with specific purchase information collected by neural networks. He goes on to say, "When all of these tools are properly applied, they cut down on fraud and allow credit managers to focus their resources on the most suspicious cases."

New methods of analyzing data and building scores should always be under review, but no analytic technique is ever a substitute for good data. If forced to choose, an organization is generally better off expending scarce resources on improving data rather than buying the latest analytic technique. Remember, you can't build good models with bad data, no matter how advanced the modeling technique. In summary, I recommend following the development of neural networks carefully in the future.

Acquiring Accounts

F IRST AND FOREMOST, the key to a good acquisition process (and ultimately a profitable business) is to entice desirable prospects to apply as a result of a good product offering. This means the product must be compelling and the prospect must see its benefits. After you have decided what products to offer, and where to offer them, the next step in the development of the business is to acquire the accounts. The business can be built up either by deepening relationships with current customers or by offering new/existing products to a broader base of customers. The expansion can be local, regional, national, or even international.

This chapter covers the key steps in developing new business. It discusses methods to deliver additional products to existing customers as well as techniques for acquiring new accounts. The objectives of the acquiring phase are to:

- *Entice good prospects to respond/apply*
- *Understand the risk/reward trade-offs of targeted accounts*
- *Establish a speedy, cost-effective approval process*
- *Assign initial lines appropriately*
- *Minimize fraud.*

The goal of the acquisition phase is not to catch all of the potential bad applicants; that you can never do. Rather, the goal is to have an acceptable ratio of good and bad accounts.[1] Increasing the number of goods that apply for your product or respond to your offer will lower your ultimate bad rate more effectively than working to decrease your number of bads.

The important point to remember is this: *The bad rate is a ratio—the number of bad accounts divided by the total number of accounts (or the dollar value of the bad accounts divided by the total dollar value of the portfolio).* Exhibit 4-1 demonstrates this idea.

---

1. To prevent misunderstanding, we will again define good and bad accounts. A good account, as we have defined it, is one that is profitable, or has the potential to be profitable, over time. A bad account is one that you would prefer not to have on the books, typically one with low revenue and/or high risk (with lots of delinquency, written off, etc.). As part of the planning process, each business should define what are good/bad accounts.

EXHIBIT 4-1
Impact of Negative Selection

The Universe: 1 million prospects
965,000 goods; 35,000 bads

	Product A	Product B
Offers	1 million	1 million
Accounts booked	14,325 (1.4%)	35,000 (3.5%)
Goods booked	12,750 (1.3%)	33,250 (3.4%)
Bads booked	1,575 (4.5%)	1,750 (5%)
Bad rate	11%	5%

Product B was a more compelling offer; the number of accounts booked for this product was higher than for product A. Even though more bads were booked for product B, the overall bad *rate* for the product was materially lower than for Product A. The small number of goods attracted by Product A may have resulted from a weak product, a poor offer, or bad targeting.

FINDING POTENTIAL CUSTOMERS

Traditionally, banks and other financial institutions have used their own branch distribution systems to attract new customers and expand their relationship with existing customers. To attract customers, banks built imposing downtown edifices and surrounded metropolitan areas with efficient-looking branches. Finance companies placed their branches in shopping centers or in older, working-class, urban locations. Customers were greeted by name, and the opening of an account depended mostly on goodwill and good connections.

Geographic expansion, especially the vast growth of the credit card industry and new financial services companies, many of which have no branch offices at all (e.g., the monoline card issuers and the Internet banks), has changed this personal approach to banking. Today, consumer lenders use a variety of methods to acquire new accounts and build their customer base, including the following:

- *Branch walk-ins/advertising*
- *Take-ones (brochure/applications)*
- *Direct mail/affinity group marketing*
- *Advertising*
- *Internet*
- *Cross-selling existing customers*
- *Purchase of existing portfolio(s)*
- *Indirect lending—i.e., sourcing accounts through a third party (real estate brokers, retailers, auto dealers, etc.).*

Each of these methods is covered in more detail in the following sections (the indirect business is covered separately in Chapter 9).

Branch walk-ins.

With an existing branch system, a bank or finance company has the physical presence to attract new customers, particularly first-time borrowers who may not have yet been targeted for direct mail offers. Further, a bank can take advantage of a branch's merchant and business relationships to solicit companies' employees for new accounts. Branches can be an attractive and convenient source of good business, although all applicants must be thoroughly screened, as with any other method of attracting prospects.

Take-ones.

These are brochures containing applications for credit products that are made available to potential customers at convenient retail establishments and branch outlets (information on the application is verified after submission). Take-ones allow a lender to reach customers outside its existing acquisition channels. Locations for take-one applications should be chosen carefully; although tight screening might make it possible for an institution to place take-ones indiscriminately,[2] the expense of reviewing many "no-hope" applications can be considerable. Because of their low approval rate (10–20%), lenders should not rely on take-ones to grow their business rapidly (you might pick up some marginal customers), but I have seen them used as part of special "new account solicitation" promotions, say, at a shopping mall.

Direct mail.

Direct mail means sending invitations through the mail to prospects to accept a lending institution's products and services. Almost every large issuer of credit cards has used direct mail heavily to solicit new credit card customers. The method has also been used to attract mortgage and home-equity customers and sometimes for other products. Direct mail is a *relatively* inexpensive method for reaching large numbers of people, and techniques have grown increasingly sophisticated as response rates to credit card solicitations in the U.S. have fallen below

---

2. A lender should also consider the legal ramifications of take-one placement; you could be accused of redlining if take-ones are placed only in higher-income areas. Check with your legal office.

the 1 percent range in recent years. Because of the complexity of the subject, direct-mail list selection and screening processes are discussed separately in the next chapter. A subset of direct mail is affinity group marketing.

Affinity Group Marketing.

Affinity groups consist of people who have joined or are part of an organization because of a common interest or past activity (e.g., airline frequent fliers, auto club members, environmentalists, alumni groups, museum members, etc.). The lists of members can be used as a source of direct-mail solicitations. MBNA, in particular, has successfully used affinity-group marketing to grow its card business. (It was once said that the only affinity group not solicited by them was the "Heart Transplant Survivors Association." Maybe there weren't enough members to make it worthwhile.)

Advertising.

Advertising is still widely used to gain new business. Advertising ranges from the extensive use of television by the credit card associations (Visa/MasterCard) to the daily inserts of automobile and home mortgage ads in local and regional newspapers. It remains an excellent way to gain attention and market share if done well.

Internet.

The worldwide Internet is one of the fastest growing (and potentially cheapest) ways of acquiring new customers. New specialty financial institutions have entered the market, offering potential customers a full range of banking products (loan applications, bill payment, stock trades, etc.); existing lenders are offering their customers similar services. Current low approval rates for Internet applications may improve over time.

Cross-selling.

This is an inexpensive way to expand upon an existing customer base by selling additional products to existing customers. Well-managed financial institutions exploit the fact that they are in frequent contact with their customers by mail or telephone, or with customers who walk into their branches. If customers are treated well (e.g., with good products, excellent customer service, good ATMs, short lines, and polite tellers), customers may be open to new product offers. Because the lending institution has an existing record of performance on its customer, the quality of business obtained in this manner can be carefully controlled.

Portfolio purchase.

A financial institution sometimes buys an entire portfolio, or part of a portfolio, of existing accounts from another institution. The purchase of portfolios allows the institution to expand its geographic coverage and to acquire large numbers of customers at one time. In addition, the performance of the portfolio is known. In the late

1990s, the credit card business in particular consolidated enormously. While the cost of acquiring the portfolios may have seemed high ($100 per account or more), it may not have been that much more expensive than the cost of acquiring an account by mail. As we pointed out earlier, the top ten issuers now control 78% of the business, vs. 50% or less a decade earlier. The highly competitive nature of the credit card business and the need to install sophisticated marketing and control techniques has allowed the expansionist organizations to grow at the expense of those who have been unwilling to devote the resources to learn or understand the market.

Indirect.

The term *indirect* refers to business acquired through a third party (e.g., automobile, boat, and mobile home dealers; department store retailers; mortgage brokers). The dealer or retailer sells the product, and the indirect lender finances the purchase. In effect the financial institution uses another party's distribution system to acquire customers and, typically, it is a way to grow a business rapidly. The financier pays some form of commission for the privilege, and must review the applicants carefully (remember, the dealer/broker has much to gain by getting the sale and always faces the temptation to "adjust" a customer's application).

THE INTERNET—WHO WILL WIN?

The explosive growth of the Internet has stimulated the growth of virtual bankers. Given the advantage of lower operating costs and the immense potential of the Internet as a distribution channel, it would seem that Internet-only banks would acquire credit card and other loan customers quickly. Further, with no costly branch systems and limited overhead, they can pay their depositors a higher rate of interest and attract the funds needed to build a profitable business.

While this is a compelling strategy in theory, such start-up banks as Wingspan and NextCard, Inc. have had major problems. So far, most Internet start-ups have been hampered by exorbitant acquisition costs due in part to the need to establish a brand name. For instance, Wingspan spent a reported $150 million on marketing to build its brand name, which worked out to about $1,363 per acquired account, according to Paul Jamison, a senior banking analyst for Gomez Financial advisers. That's rather more than the $60 to $75 per acquired account spent by conventional lenders using direct-mail campaigns.

In addition, the Internet customer initially was indeed a different customer (younger, more mobile, etc.), so that significant numbers of potentially high-risk applicants had to be carefully screened out. For instance, approval rates on Internet applications ran in the range of 10–15% in the first years, a rate well below other channels. Presumably this will change as the Internet customer becomes more mainstream, and the big bricks-and-mortar banks move to take advantage of that fact.

Traditional financial institutions are racing to enter the business, using all their marketing and process skills to build a long-run profitable business. American Express, Citigroup, Capital One, MBNA, Wells Fargo, and Bank of America are among the most successful in using their brand names to build their cyberspace businesses. As the use of the Internet grows, institutions that can offer customers a full range of brokerage, depository, lending, and bill paying relationships will probably dominate the market. My guess is that the old bricks-and-mortar financial institutions will be the most successful users of the Internet in the long run.

The Student Market

As new credit card accounts have become more difficult to acquire through the normal methods of mail solicitation, in-branch applications, take-ones, and so on, several lenders have turned to the student market as a new source. Citigroup, Discover Card, and American Express, in particular, have been pursuing this market, which has become a major source of new accounts for these lenders. It is estimated that 70% of the approximately 4 million full-time undergraduates at four-year colleges currently have at least one major credit card, a huge market; high school students are also being pursued.

Are students a good source of business, or should they be avoided like the plague? The benefits are obvious because many people feel loyalty to the first institution that extends them credit. Hook the student early and you have a potentially good customer for life (or at least a well-educated one). And the students need the cards to charge books, to travel home for vacations, to keep a car running, and so on. But there are always the horror stories—the $17,000 bar and hotel bill run up by a group of students; the trip around the world charged on American Express and never paid for.

One way lenders limit their liability is by offering first-time student cards with small lines ($500 or possibly $1,000 at the most) and then increasing the exposure as experience dictates. Some lenders require parent guarantees; some will deal only with students at major four-year colleges; others experiment with the lesser-known colleges and other accredited institutions. Most lenders enter the market knowing that for many of these students, limited or no information is available, with the possible exception of the existence of a checking or savings account of a few dollars. Lenders are tight-lipped about the loss rates on these cards, but indications are that students pay their bills about as well or better than their parents.

The risks are obvious, but the rewards can be very high in a world where new accounts are increasingly difficult and expensive to obtain.

Up to this point we have summarized the main ways that lenders obtain new accounts (as noted, we will cover the direct-mail process separately in Chapter 5 because of its importance in the marketplace today). In conclusion to this introduction regarding the acquisition of new accounts, remember that the *source* of a customer will closely define the quality of his business. A customer found through an existing good customer, or by a carefully targeted direct-mail campaign, has a much better chance of being a desirable customer than one generated by a take-one brochure picked up in a bar or restaurant.

SCREENING ACCOUNTS

Once the source of the new business has been identified, the next step is to set up a good screening process. The single most critical step in the management of risk in the consumer business is to put in place a carefully thought-out process that screens all new extensions of credit. The basic principles used in screening new customers is described below. The unique steps taken to screen direct-mail accounts, assess collateral (on secured products), and review accounts sourced through a third party (indirect) will be covered in later chapters.

Gathering Information—The Application

The account application process begins when a prospective borrower is asked to fill out a form to provide the lender with sufficient information to make an informed credit decision. This form can be long or short (it will vary by product), and completing it is one of the most visible steps for the customer in the whole application process.

On the whole, a lender will require a great deal more information on larger loans, including a complete financial statement from the applicant. For instance, for a home mortgage, the application should go into enough detail to determine the applicant's total annual housing expenses, property taxes, insurance, common fees on condominiums, and the like. These expenses can be significant but are of interest only on a mortgage application. You would not ask for this information for a small line of credit or for a credit card.

An application, depending on the product, could request the following information on the applicant and co-applicant's current situation and history (brief):

- *Personal background (e.g., name, address, home ownership)*
- *Employment and income*
- *Credit references plus sufficient data (e.g., Social Security number) to be able to check the credit bureau files*
- *Financial statements (typically required only for products with larger lines of credit, such as mortgages or major unsecured credit)*
- *Information on collateral for collateralized loans.*

Let's return to one of the primary goals of the acquisition process: to encourage the right people to apply. In designing the application, the trick is to balance the amount of information requested (from the perspective of a prospect completing the form) with the legitimate needs of the lending institution to make a good credit decision and service the account. If an applicant with a good credit history has the choice of filling out your competitor's short application, as opposed to a lengthy one required by your organization, which do you think he will choose? Good credit risks have options and usually do not enjoy filling out detailed forms, whereas a marginal applicant will usually complete a form of any length. Thus, an unnecessarily complex application can cost a lender its best potential customers.

Each of the functional areas involved in attracting the customer, providing service, and collecting the account (if needed) requires certain information from the application in order to do its job and therefore should be involved in the application's design.

Marketing.

The primary goal of marketing is to encourage the right people to apply for the product. The application should be easy to complete and user-friendly. Such headings as "Please tell us about yourself" can introduce the customer to questions about his job, income, and other personal details in a friendly manner.

Risk Management.

The goal of this department is to acquire as complete information as needed on the applicant to allow it to make a good credit decision. For instance, there must be enough data to fully identify the applicant. Since people move frequently, get divorced, remarry, use different professional and personal names, and so forth, this task is not always simple. In the U.S., a Social Security number should be requested to help ensure that the correct credit bureau history is obtained.

Collections.

This department requires sufficient information to find the customer in the event the account needs to be collected.

Operations.

This department needs responses that can be read easily since staff must enter the information into its records. The application must have sufficient room for people to enter the requested information.

Legal.

This department ensures that your organization meets regulatory and legal requirements (including disclosure and anti-discriminatory rules). A review of the application by your legal department is a key step in the application design process.

OTHER TIPS

- *An application should reflect the uniqueness of the target market, e.g., ask different questions of college students and working adults. There is little point asking whether a student owns a house, although data regarding summer or temporary employment, extracurricular activities, and the like could be significant.*

- *Specificity is better than ambiguity. The application should be specific in asking for personal data (e.g., date of birth, not age). When asking for income, are you interested in household or personal income? Salary or all income? Monthly or annual income? While check boxes are often used to obtain the range of income (e.g., check a box if your income is between $25,000 and $40,000), it may be preferable to ask for specific information (e.g., What is your total monthly household income $ _____).*

- *Asking for too much information, such as the account number of every credit card, bank loan, or money market account, is counterproductive. Filling in these numbers is tedious and guaranteed to discourage a good applicant. The information may also be unnecessary: in the U.S., the credit bureau record typically will contain a listing of all existing lines.*

- *Finally, a lender should always be testing new criteria that might indicate creditworthiness in the future, since today's criteria may not continue to be useful in the future. Future discriminants might include: Do you own a second home? How many cars do you own? Do you have an IRA or a 401(k) account? Are you on the Internet? It is important to select items today that might help legally discriminate between good and bad customers in the future. Only by testing some seemingly far-out questions today to see if in fact they do discriminate between good and bad applicants, can a lender stay ahead of the crowd.*

Standard Screening Steps

The next step in acquiring accounts is to review the new account applications. The process can be streamlined (see below), but there should be a standard review process. The typical process a consumer lending business uses includes the following steps:

- *Review the application for accuracy and completeness; reject those not meeting minimum requirements (e.g., under minimum age).*
- *Obtain a credit bureau report.*
- *Score those applicants passing the preliminary screen.*
- *Evaluate the results and determine if additional information is required.*
- *Compute a debt-burden ratio (this step may not be taken for all products).*
- *Review for fraud.*
- *Verify the customer information and/or collateral; adjust the deal (e.g., on autos) if necessary.*
- *Make the final decision and notify the customer of the decision; accept a limited sample of rejected accounts for test purposes.*

The underwriting/screening process looks like this:

EXHIBIT 4-2
Underwriting Process

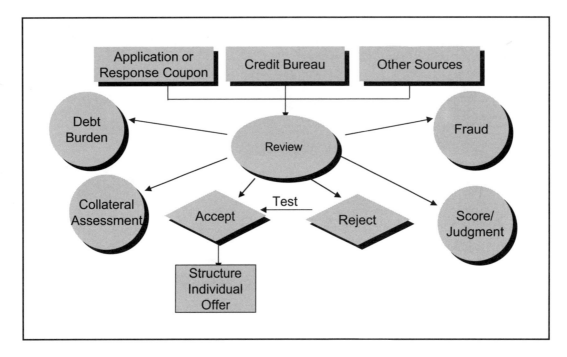

Initial Screens

The new account process, even for a home mortgage application, must be streamlined and automated to the extent possible. Under this process, applications that fail to meet minimum standards are rejected with only a quick review; the most promising applications are selected for speedy processing, and the rest are given a more intensive review. This approach can save money and improve the quality of the decisions because the lender can devote more time to the truly difficult determinations.

Quick Kill.

Some circumstances that would qualify an application for a quick kill would include:

- *Failing to meet a minimum age or minimum income requirement*
- *Failing to meet a minimum score (custom or generic)*
- *Prior bankruptcy or an obviously fraudulent application.*

An incomplete application may or may not be subject to a quick kill. One so obviously deficient in information as to be unreviewable may be rejected, but others, where only minimal information is omitted, should be followed up for more detail.

Speedy Approval/Automated Underwriting.

With carefully written rules, most applicants can be put through a rapid, highly automated approval process. Such an approach is absolutely necessary for the indirect-sourced automobile business, where dealers scatter applications like confetti at a wedding. Typically, the first to reply (with a competitive rate) has the best chance of getting the contract. Even home mortgage applications now can be speedily approved, as we discuss later. And, remember, not all the applications you approve will be booked; many of the good applicants will be accepted by another lender, so the cost per account *actually* booked is the important figure to watch. One caveat: the initial approval can be conditional, subject to customer and collateral verification including further checks if anything misleading turns up.

A smart lender will examine its rules to see if it is processing the most applications for the least cost, while still maintaining control of the decision process. For instance, if a lender is offering a new product to an *existing* customer, it may be able to derive all the information internally, and score it, without bothering the customer.

The depth of a credit evaluation depends on the amount of risk involved, which varies by product. As we have said, screening prospects costs money; if the dollars at risk and the associated profit are small, an institution can't afford to spend much money screening the customer. On a large credit line, it must probably spend more to make a sound decision. Screening costs can vary from less than $10 to $20 per new account to thousands of dollars for an intricate examination of a home mortgage application. The point is to keep the investigation cost in line with the product, represented as follows:

EXHIBIT 4-3
Credit Investigation

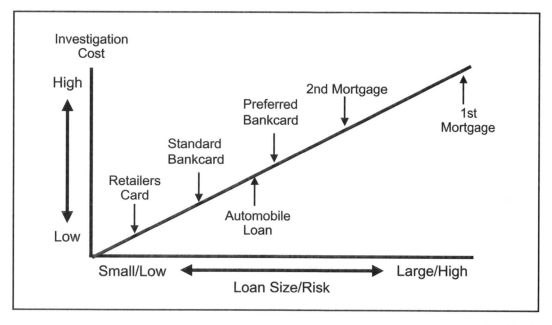

By way of example, an evaluation for retailers' cards, which carry small balances, may include scoring the completed application, period (hopefully with a good generic score for first-time credit users, since many people start their credit life with a department store account). For upscale credit cards with higher potential liability and greater potential for fraud, a more thorough investigation is required; if conflicting data are found, a second credit or merged bureau report can be ordered.

First mortgages and the larger home-equity loans (> $25,000) require more investigation of both customer and collateral. Some form of property appraisal is essential if a home is being purchased or refinanced. Credit investigations for smaller second mortgages (< $25,000) and other products fall somewhere between the above categories. A small second mortgage/home equity applicant should be reviewed to determine if she is qualified for an unsecured loan; if she passes this screen, a lien can be registered on the property to provide additional security, and the appraisal process can be less rigorous for these loans.

Account Screening: Judgmental vs. Credit Scoring

Typically, after an initial screening, each application for a loan in the U.S. will be entered into the lender's existing loan origination system, where a credit bureau report will be obtained/scored. As noted in the last chapter, credit scoring is the most desirable method for screening your potential customers. Occasionally, the portfolio is too small or unique to be able to use a proprietary or even a generic score and the only alternative is using human judgment. Aside from this situation, a validated, professionally developed scoring system should be used as a key step in screening prospective customers.

JUDGMENTAL SCREENING

Most experienced lenders have a series of rules they swear by: Older people are more reliable than young ones, a homeowner is a better bet than a renter, a white-collar worker is a lower risk than a blue-collar worker (but beware of lawyers, they are litigious), and the list goes on. It is a body of knowledge built up over time, and every decision that the expert makes uses this knowledge. Historically, judgmental experts made their decisions considering the three Cs: character, capacity, and collateral. Character equates to the client's willingness to meet his obligations in the past and, today in the United States, is based primarily on credit bureau information. Capacity is the client's ability to meet current and future obligations out of current income (debt burden), and collateral refers to the value of the item being financed. These rules are defined by experience developed over time, and are often called expert systems.

EXPERT SYSTEMS

Expert systems are designed to clone the expertise of the bank's most knowledgeable people—to condense their experience and wisdom into a set of rules for less experienced people to follow. The expertise to be cloned could be loan underwriting, collection experience, authorizations, or some other aspect of the business. If an institution is relying on judgmental screening, it must, at a minimum, document its procedures to help achieve consistency. For instance, the written policy must establish the minimum criteria for approval, such as:

- *Legal age to contract*
- *Income*
- *Time at job*
- *Time at residence*
- *Loan-to-value ratio on secured loans*
- *Credit bureau experience*
- *Debt-burden standard*

On the basis of these criteria, the lender might develop the following rules which underwriters would then follow:

Reject applicant if:

- *Income is less than $25,000.*
- *Time with employer is less than one year.*
- *Time on credit bureau file is less than one year.*
- *Any delinquency is found on file.*
- *More than three inquiries have been made in last six months.*

Or:

- *Accept if applicant has only one exception (e.g., time with employer is less than one year) and income is >$40,000.*

One place where expert systems are helpful is in guiding the entire front-end application process—to set up rules such as when to require more information from an applicant, when to get a second credit score or credit bureau report, when overrides are appropriate, how much debt burden to perform, how much information to verify. And they are particularly useful in pre-qualifying applicants for home mortgages. Historically, applying for a mortgage can be a time-consuming, tedious process. Now, however, the automated underwriting systems—expert systems in effect—developed by the two major, government-sponsored mortgage lenders, Fannie Mae and Freddie Mac, can speed up the process significantly. With the aid of these automated systems, branch personnel are able to guide a potential customer quickly and professionally through the maze of applying for a mortgage, and they can suggest ways of meeting problems that may arise. We will cover this later in describing the mortgage underwriting process in Chapter 10.

Problems with Judgmental Screens

Some basic limitations are inherent in all judgmental systems.

Inconsistency. Despite written rules, achieving consistency is difficult. Underwriters bring their own biases to the process, and even the same underwriter might make a different decision on the same application on different days (or even before or after lunch, particularly if a martini or two is imbibed with the meal). This is just human nature.

Lack of Feedback. Few lenders actually analyze the results of their judgmental system. For instance, how good is a decision to exclude all people who have "Income less than $25,000"? What happens if a lender accepts such candidates? The institution should be able to prove statistically that its decisions are the best possible; unfortunately, few lenders conduct such examinations by accepting a sample of applicants who do not meet their judgmental criteria and tracking the performance of this sample portfolio over time.

Inflexibility of System. It is difficult to modify and/or control a judgmental system in light of changes in the economy, the product offering, portfolio experience, target market, competition, or legal and regulatory changes. A change in any of the above requires reexamining individual criteria to determine which should be modified and how they should be modified. For example, should a slowing economy require a higher minimum income or a longer time at a residence or on a job? And if changes are made to a judgmental system to increase the quality of the portfolio, the lender must retrain all the people involved in making the credit decisions.

Lack of Reporting. There is no statistical way to describe a portfolio after it has been acquired judgmentally. If a lender makes 2,000 loans in one month with a judgmental system, theoretically they must *all* be good or they would not have been approved. However, some loans will be bad, but the lender cannot array the portfolio and describe it statistically as can be done with a score system. With a score system, for instance, you can describe the risks of a drive to gain more profitable business from a new target audience and track the results over time. We gave some examples of the type of information that can be gleaned from scoring systems at the end of the last chapter.

Imprecision. Judgmental rules are "go/no go," with no in-between positions. For example, an applicant's having some minor delinquency may cause automatic rejection. A scoring system, on the other hand, assigns weights to various characteristics (after a careful analysis of their impact over time), and no single one may be cause for rejecting an application. With scoring, a minor delinquency, for example, can be offset if all or most of the other characteristics analyzed score high.

For all these reasons, a judgmental screening system is recommended only as a supplement for a high-volume business. Such a system could be used, for instance, to determine if new information can affect the decision . . . information that does not enter into the score system (e.g., the applicant has a major business account at the branch, she's the Chairman of the Board's daughter, or the credit bureau finds three records on the same person at different addresses). Here, judgmental screening may add value to a score system, but the decisions should be tracked like all overrides.

HUMAN UNDERWRITING VS. THE COMPUTER

For those who still believe in the infallibility of humans, it is sad to report there is ample evidence that scoring systems do a better job (higher approval rates, lower losses) than most human reviewers or underwriters in processing and approving consumer loan applications. In addition to the loan-processing cost savings realized with a computerized scoring system, these systems have proven, time and again, to be more consistent, reliable, and predictive than human reviewers.

A carefully developed, validated, and implemented scoring system will virtually always beat the record of the human underwriters. In the more than two hundred times we have run an application approval exercise in our *Managing Risk & Reward* seminar, in only a few instances have human underwriters even equaled the scoring system in reviewing ten applications (no one has ever beaten it). One major gain in scoring versus judgmental screening typically comes from a higher approval rate. Human reviewers tend to be conservative, particularly when management has a tendency to fire underwriters who make too many bad loans (as defined by management, usually without regard for the overall profitability of a product). Thus, scoring equals more accounts on the books, more predictability, and more consistency, all of which mean improved profits.

Credit Bureau Reports

We have already talked about getting credit bureau reports and scoring them. By way of background information, credit bureaus are simply "libraries" where creditors regularly report on the performance of people doing business with them. In the U.S., subscribers include banks/finance companies, retailer card issuers, doctors/medical facilities, local/federal governments, and utilities, among others. Access to this vast data bank traditionally has been restricted to existing and prospective creditors; however, individuals can obtain a free copy of their own credit file if turned down for credit, and they can usually obtain a copy of their report, at a nominal cost or free of charge, from the bureaus at any time. You can even access your own credit file on the Internet.

EXHIBIT 4-4   Sample Credit Bureau Report

Here's an ACROFILE PLUS report enhanced with these options: Equifax Risk Score '98, SAFESCAN, On-Line GEO Code and On-Line Directory.

OPTIONAL FEATURE: Equifax Risk Score '98 returning credit scores from 1-999 – and up to four reason statements explaining that score's most significant elements. Reasons can be given to applicants not meeting your criteria. The higher the score, the lower the serious delinquency potential.

```
 EFX RISK ASSESSMENT SCORE: 389
 REASON CODES: 00003 00036 00001 00007
 NARRATIVES:
 LENGTH OF TIME ACCOUNTS HAVE BEEN ESTABLISHED
 NUMBER OF BANK REVOLVING ACCOUNTS WITH REPORTED LATE PAYMENTS
 NUMBER OF CONSUMER INITIATED INQUIRIES IN THE PAST 6 MONTHS
 TOTAL AMOUNT OF AVAILABLE CREDIT ON ALL OPEN ACCOUNTS
 **********************************************************************
    SAFESCAN WARNING:
    INQUIRY ADDRESS HAS BEEN ASSOCIATED WITH MORE THAN ONE NAME
    OR SOCIAL SECURITY NUMBER. THOROUGH VERIFICATION SUGGESTED.
 **********************************************************************
    SSN ISSUED -65                                     STATE ISSUED- GA
 *GEO CODE: MSA 0520 STATE 13 COUNTY 121 CENSUS TRACT 0065.00 BLOCK GROUP 1
 9412,MAIN STREET,ATLANTA,GA,30302
 INQ CURRENT ADDRESS (STANDARDIZED)  FOUND ON GEO CODE DATABASE

 * 001 EQUIFAX CREDIT INFORMATION SERVICES    -      P O BOX 740241
       1150 LAKE HEARN DRIVE STE 460 ATLANTA GA 30374-0241 800/685-1111

 *CONSUMER,JOHN,Q,JR,    SINCE 03/10/73  FAD 06/22/98        FN-238
 9412,MAIN STREET,ATLANTA,GA,30302,TAPE RPTD 07/93
       TELEPHONE NUMBER  (404)555-1212 CRT 07/93
 410,ORANGE GROVE,DR,SAN JOSE,CA,95119,CRT RPTD 06/91
 46,KENNEDY,DR,DETROIT,MI,DAT RPTD 01/86
      ****ALSO KNOWN AS-CCONSUMER,ROBERT****
 BDS-03/03/49,SSS-900-00-0000 SSN VER: Y
 01 ES-ENGINEER,ACME MFG,ATLANTA,GA,EMP 06/93,VER 03/96
 02 EF-ENGINEER,CENTRAL POWER,SAN JOSE,CA,,,,LEFT 05/93
 03 E2-ENGINEER,MAJOR MOTORS,DETROIT,MI,,,,LEFT 05/91

 *SUM-04/73-01/98,PR/OI-YES,COLL-YES,FB-NO, ACCTS:8,HC$450-87595, 4-ONES,
    1-TWO, 1-THREE,1-FIVE, 1-OTHER.
 INQUIRY ALERT - SUBJECT SHOWS 4 INQUIRIES SINCE 05/98

 ***** PUBLIC RECORDS OR OTHER INFORMATION *****
 04 07/95 BKRPT 111VF116, 95-453657,LIAB$25600,ASSET$10500, EXEMPT$100,
          INDIVID, PERSONAL,DISMSD CH-7
 05 05/97 ST JD,111VC51, $500,DEF-S,88776,VISA,SATISFIED,08/97
 ***********************************************************

 ***** COLLECTION ITEMS *****
 LIST   RPTD  AMT/BAL   DLA/ECOA  AGENCY/CLIENT          STATUS/SERIAL
 04/97  11/97  $532     11/97     111YC363 ACB COLLECTIONS UNPAID
               $300      I        DR JONES                202012
 ****************************************
```

ⓑ OPTIONAL FEATURE: SAFESCAN, Equifax's nationwide fraud prevention system, automatically alerting you through one of 17 warning messages to known or potentially fraudulent information—providing a clear message when credit, employment or other application information should be examined more closely before granting approval, cross-selling or making management decisions.

ⓒ OPTIONAL FEATURE: Equifax's On-Line GEO-CODE service providing valuable geographic address information:

Metropolitan Statistical Area (MSA; state; county; census tract; block group (street block or area within census tract); geo-coded inquiry address plus nine-digit zip code; and one of these messages: found, not found or full zip code not found.

ⓓ Comprehensive consumer ID information — including complete name, ID and address information, with current and

former addresses and telephone numbers (when available) identified by reporting method (when available) — for verifying key information.

ⓔ When available, employment history including last reported and up to two former employers plus position titles, company names, locations and employment dates.

ⓕ File summary showing critical public record,

account status and other information for fast evaluation.

ⓖ An "Inquiry Alert" section showing an unusually high number of inquiries have occurred within the past 90 days. (Inquiry listing at end of report.)

ⓗ Public records/other information and collection items sections listing complete dates, amounts, collections agencies, court records and outstanding balances.

ACROFILE PLUS

A trade section providing up to a seven-year history of an applicant's account activity that clearly identifies creditors, debt payment performance, current account status and more — in plain language for easy evaluation.

24 months' inquiry history.

OPTIONAL FEATURE: Equifax's On-Line Directory™ service automatically identifying names and telephone numbers for all inquiries plus names and numbers of all tradeline and collection item creditors — and, upon request, addresses for all tradeline, inquiry and collection item creditors.

OPTIONAL FEATURE: Confirmation that applicant-provided information has been "SAFESCANNED" — monitored by SAFESCAN, a fraud prevention system option.

```
PAGE 2 OF REPORT
FIRM / ID     CODE       CS RPTD LIMIT  HICR BAL $   DLA MR (30-60-90+)MAX/DEL
ECOA/ACCOUNT NUMBER         OPND P/DUE  TERM         24 MONTH HISTORY
---------------------------------------------------------------------------
ATL FIN VS   *111FS26     R5 06/98 3000 ---- 2832    02/98 75      (01-01-01)
I/4453                       03/92 700  140          432**********/***********
            ACCOUNT CLOSED BY CREDIT GRANTOR

WACH IL      *111BB771     R1 06/98 5000 ---  4500    05/98 71
I/432704567                  07/92 ---  100

LORD & TAY   *111DC151     R3 06/98 ---  478  356     04/98 57 (04-02-00) 06/94-R3
J/175                        09/93 50   25           2**********2/*232********

SEARS        *111DC29      R1 06/98 1000 ---  110     05/98 99 (01-01-00) 07/93-R3
J/5540                       04/73 ---  10

      REVOLVING TOTALS            9000 478  7798
                                  750  275
---------------------------------------------------------------------------
AMEXTRVLSV   *1110N259     01 06/98 ---  450  123     06/98 41
J/86934                      01/95      123

      OPEN TOTALS                 ...  450  123
                                  ---  123
---------------------------------------------------------------------------
HFC  *111FP439             I1 05/98 ---  4200 933     11/97 28
C/12566843                   01/96 ---  18M

PAINE/WEBB   *111FM1117 I2 05/98 --- 87595 37345     04/98 65 (01-00-00)
I/7785632                    12/92 750  750          ***********/*2**********
      HOME LOAN
      INSTALLMENT TOTALS          --- 91795 38278
                                  750  750
---------------------------------------------------------------------------
      GRAND TOTALS                9000 92723 46199
                                  1500 1148
---------------------------------------------------------------------------
WACH IL      111BB771         08/96 ---  ---  ---     08/93
  4567                        07/92
      LOST OR STOLEN CARD
*INQS-BURDINES    111DC304    06/22/98  HECHT CO    111DC2872    05/15/98
   FRIEDMAN'S     111JA105    05/12/98  SUNTRUST    111FM6875    05/11/98

CONSUMER STATEMENT      RPTD  12/97  PURGE 12/99
I HAD FAMILY PROBLEMS AND COULD NOT PAY MY VISA BILL.  I TRIED TO PAY IT BUT MY
ACCOUNT WAS CLOSED BEFORE I COULD WORK IT OUT.

* MEMBER #    COMP. NAME   TELEPHONE   * MEMBER #    COMP. NAME    TELEPHONE
 111YC363  ACB COLL    111-1111111     111FS26    ATL FIN VS  111-1111111
 123 MAIN ST                           813 FULTON ST
 OAKFORD            GA 30000-0001       ATLANTA            GA 30300-0001

 111BB771   WACH IL    111-1111111     111DC151   LORD & TAY  111-1111111
 717 SEVENTH                           965 HOWELL
 CHICAGO            IL 60000-0001       DALLAS             TX 75000-0001

 111DC29    SEARS       MAIL ONLY      1110N250    AMEXTRVLSV    MAIL ONLY
 CALL 1-800-801-2055                   P.O. BOX 100
                                       MIAMI              FL 33000-0001

 111FP439   HFC        111-1111111     111FM117   PAINE/WEBB    MAIL ONLY
 818 EIGHTH AV                         P.O. BOX 990
 NEW ORLEANS        LA 71000-0001      NEW YORK           NY 10000-0001

 111DC3D4   BURDINES   111-1111111     111DC2872  HECHT CO    111-1111111
 475 AMERICA ST                        908 FIRST
 ANYTOWN            NY 10000-0001       BALTIMORE          MD 20000-0001

 111JA105   FRIEDMAN'S 111-1111111     111FM6875  SUNTRUST    111-1111111
 865 SECOND AV                         234 THIRD ST
 CLEVELAND          OH 40000-000        CHARLOTTE          NC 30000-001

&
END OF REPORT EQUIFAX AND AFFILIATES - 07/31/98          SAFESCANNED
```

A sample credit bureau report is shown on the preceding pages.

Three major credit bureaus—Experían, Equifax, and TransUnion—dominate the U.S. industry, having bought many of the independent agencies over the years (although some smaller, independent agencies still exist). Along with this centralization of databases, the quality and thoroughness of the information has improved substantially over time. Obtaining a credit bureau report and a score on every new applicant is a critical step in any new account process. As we already covered in the Scoring chapter, there are risk prediction scores, bankruptcy scores, generic revenue scores etc., all based on credit bureau data. The information gleaned from bureau reports can be the most significant part of the application process.

The bureaus may differ in some of the following ways:

- *Completeness of records (merchant and customer)*
- *Timeliness of updating*
- *Geographic coverage*
- *Accuracy of information*
- *Ease of ability to read data (matching algorithms)*
- *Products offered (generic scores)*
- *Fragmented file[3] suppression*
- *Pricing.*

On the basis of these factors, creditors generally select a primary and a secondary vendor for each geographic area in which they are doing business and tend to use these vendors until a change is justified. Each vendor is constantly trying to upgrade its services, so it is important not to get tied to one or two bureaus without a continuing competitive analysis. Just because a lender has selected one bureau as the primary bureau one year does not mean it will be the best the following year.

Credit bureau reports can be difficult and time-consuming to read and analyze. A good application processing and scoring system scores and interprets these reports automatically.

If a lender has any doubts about the information contained on one credit report (e.g., if the information is too limited or suspect for any reason), a second report should be ordered from another agency. The second report might contain information from an earlier address or a variation of the name that could change a lender's decision. Remember, reports are relatively cheap, and the potential for loss so high for some products, that it is shortsighted to try to save some money on a second report if there is any reason to doubt the data. Further, it is possible to order a merged report from an independent agency which specializes in such reporting. Credco, a California-based company that merges credit files for mortgage lenders, once did a study showing that no report from any single bureau had more than 72% of all month-

---

3. A file is fragmented when a consumer has more than one file, each with incomplete information. Fragmentation might occur due to a misspelled name, a different version of a name (John Jones vs. John R. Jones), or a recent move to a new address.

An acquaintance recently requested a summary of his credit bureau records from Privacy Guard, a credit search firm. At his request, Privacy Guard contacted the three bureaus with his correct name, address, and Social Security number, and received the following summary of his files as of June 1999:

EXHIBIT 4-5
Merged Credit Report Summaries

	SSN: 000-00-0000 7 MAIN STREET WESTHAMPTON BEACH, NY 11978	SSN: 000-00-0000 7 MAIN STREET WESTHAMPTON BEACH, NY 11978	SSN: 000-00-0000 7 MAIN STREET WESTHAMPTON BEACH, NY 11978

MERGED CREDIT REPORT SUMMARIES

	TRANS UNION	TRW/EXPERIAN	EQUIFAX
TRADES			
TOTAL	21	21	17
REVOLVING	14	16	10
INSTALLMENT	3	5	7
MORTGAGE	4	0	0
OTHER	0	0	0
ACTIVITY: # OF			
CURRENT ACCTS	21	19	16
DELINQUENT ACCTS	0	2	1
INQUIRIES 12 MTHS	5	1	1
PUBLIC RECORDS	0	0	0
COLLECTION ITEMS	0	0	0
BALANCES			
TOTAL	601,380	303,539	9,346
REVOLVING	5,000	1,588	798
INSTALLMENT	8,132	0	8,548
MORTGAGE	588,248	301,951	0
OTHER	0	0	0

As shown, one bureau reported his total debt at $601,380, the second at $303,539, and the third at $9,346. All three were wrong: my friend reports that his total debt is in the $400,000 range, primarily a mortgage on his home. Further, there was no consistency as to the amount of installment, revolving, or mortgage loans. My friend says he has been borrowing and repaying home mortgage and automobile loans for many years, and he is a constant user (and re-payer) of credit card debt. He has lived at the same address for more than twenty years, is married to the same wife, and has had a stable career with two major corporations. In other words, he is no fly-by-night borrower. But, boy, were the bureau reports inconsistent! The world is not yet perfect.

"First, let me pull up your file."

ly payments, more than 64% of all trade lines, or better than 36% of all inquiries. The cost of a second report should be compared to the value of the information added.

Despite recent improvements, credit bureau data are still problematic, and the industry is incurring wide publicity for inaccurate reports and failure to cure inaccuracies. Currently, there are some 450 million reports on 120 million adults, which is why it is so important to get a correct, complete report on an applicant, and why items such as birth date and Social Security number are so important. It is worth noting, however, that Social Security numbers are estimated to be available on only about two thirds of all files.

Debt-Burden Analysis

Debt-burden analysis on a consumer account is equivalent to the cash-flow analysis performed by commercial lending officers on corporate accounts. This is a traditional task of the commercial lending officer, who has accurate tools to work with, including certified financial statements, established sales records, and the like. The concept of debt-burden analysis has often carried over to consumer lending, but it is difficult to get good financial data on the average individual. Self-employed consumers, in particular, are even more difficult to judge. Their tax returns are sometimes masterpieces of creativity with the sole objective of reducing their tax liability. A cursory review would eliminate all but the largest and/or least creative, who cannot control (i.e., minimize) their taxable earnings.

For these reasons, and particularly because reliable data are very difficult to obtain, most lenders should spend as little time and effort as possible reviewing a consumer's ability to pay on the smaller loans. A more detailed process to measure income and verify assets is appropriate only on large credit lines if cost-justified (or is required on home mortgages; see below).

DEBT BURDEN—REVIEW METHODS

There are several methods of looking at the customer's debt-burden levels and comparing these with established ratios:

- *Minimum income requirement establishes a minimum dollar income level to qualify for the credit product— say, $40,000 for a gold credit card.*

- *Debt-to-income ratio compares an applicant's monthly debt, less housing, as a percentage of total gross monthly income—say, 15–22%.*

- *Disposable monthly income involves an elaborate calculation to determine an allowable minimum monthly margin after deducting total debt-service expense from gross income—say, $600 to $1,000/month.*

- *New monthly debt to monthly income ratio compares the monthly payment for the requested credit as a percentage of monthly income—say, 16–18% for an auto loan.*

- *Total housing debt to income includes all housing costs (e.g., mortgage, real estate taxes, house insurance, and association dues) as a percentage of gross monthly income—say, 28–33%.*

- *Total debt plus housing compares all debt (e.g., monthly car payments, other monthly payments, child support, alimony payments, and all housing expenses) as a percentage of gross income—say, 36–42%.*

Note: I have deliberately avoided recommending a precise allowable ratio for each method of calculation because of the difficulty in setting and proving that these ratios are correct in most instances. The numbers cited are merely guidelines, and any lender should be prepared to develop its own simple (I hope) guidelines. Any debt-to-burden ratio is fraught with many problems. For example,

1) *While an automobile costs (almost) the same in every state, living costs vary significantly. For instance, housing, transportation, and living costs in general are very different in New York City, San Francisco, Charlotte (North Carolina), and Oshkosh (Wisconsin). A 16% ratio could be overstated in one location and way understated in another. An automobile might be a necessity in Jacksonville but a luxury in Chicago, where public transportation is excellent. How do you take these factors into account with just one formula?*

2) *Lenders try to "guesstimate" how consumers will handle their obligations in the future. The life-cycle status of consumers constantly changes, however: they get married, divorced, lose jobs, gain or lose*

overtime, etc. Lifestyles differ as well: some save every penny possible for a rainy day; others spend everything by the tenth of the month and live on borrowed funds for the remainder. Some consumers work "off the books," and their incomes and assets are hard to quantify. In short, consumers are diverse, and some can be volatile.

Is debt-burden analysis worthwhile? Does a high debt ratio correlate with poor performance? Obviously, common sense requires that a lender not approve an obviously inappropriate loan for an individual with a low income, but that could be established with very simple rules, such as excluding people with incomes less than $15,000/year.

The usefulness of debt-burden guidelines should be tested from time to time to see if they really add value (and can you prove they add value?). In other words, a statistical sample of accounts that failed the debt-burden hurdle should be accepted and tracked to see what would happen if only the simplest or even no calculations were done. Do the test accounts perform as well as standard accounts? If so, you may be able to minimize or eliminate the debt-burden calculation. One more point: allow for regional variations. Each lender should be able to adjust these debt-burden guidelines to reflect such variations or they may lose good business to a competitor.

One final point: the housing market has rules on debt-burden ratios (set by the quasi-governmental agencies, Fannie Mae and Freddie Mac), particularly when a lender decides to sell or securitize its loans on the secondary market. Here the appropriate D/I (debt/income) ratios are critical because buyers for these loan packages require certain standards from lenders. We cover these ratios in Chapter 10, The Home Mortgage Business.

Customer Verification

Up to this point, if the screening process says go, the final step is to verify the information on the application. Here again, the trick is to balance the cost of verification with the potential gain of ferreting out those few minor fraudulent or misleading applications. At best, a lender can hope only to pick up the casual offender, someone who might recently have lost a job, overstated his income, or uses one name where there is good information while concealing another name with an older, poor record. A determined fraud may not be caught by anything other than a highly professional criminal investigation process.

It is always important to know the identity of the person to whom credit is being extended. Automated processes can verify the validity and consistency of the applicant's Social Security number, zip code, and telephone area code. If this information checks out, no further verification is needed on smaller lines of credit (< $5,000). If further checks are required, the applicant's credit bureau record (e.g., employment, major lines outstanding, marital condition, and the like) can be verified against the customer's application; major differences or unexplained items should be examined further, but again do not spend money here unless you can justify it by testing.

STANDARD VERIFICATION

As noted earlier, the depth of investigation (i.e., time and money spent) should be in direct proportion to the risk and profit inherent in the product. A lender should not spend more money acquiring an account than can be profitably recovered over time.

The following major items can and should *always* be verified:

- *Identity. Is the customer who she says she is? Is the right person actually applying, or has the identifying information (e.g., name, Social Security number, etc.) been stolen?*

- *Fraud detection. The standard credit bureau fraud detection screens absolutely should be used as a regular part of any consumer credit screen. These models contain a constantly changing list of names, addresses, post office boxes, and other factors where fraud has been detected. They also check Social Security numbers to screen out people using, for instance, a deceased person's record.*

The following major items should be verified when the risk warrants it:

- *Employment. Where does the applicant work and is he still employed?*
- *Income. Can the applicant's income be verified?*
- *Address. Does the applicant live at the address stated?*

TWO TYPES OF FRAUD

Identify Theft

Identity theft has become a growing problem. For example, an office manager applying for a $175,000 first mortgage on a home she hopes to buy is shocked by her immediate rejection because of a poor credit record. She learns that she is reported as owing $22,000 on a Volvo and has three new, severely delinquent accounts for American Express, MasterCard, and Visa. This report baffles her because she has only one or two retail-store cards (all current), pays most of her bills in cash, and drives a paid-up (and beat-up) 1995 Chevrolet.

The office manager is a victim of identity theft—people steal good credit histories and then use the information to charge as much merchandise for themselves as they can, at least until the lines are cancelled. They obviously have no intention of repaying. One method used by identity thieves is to obtain computer access codes for the credit bureaus from a legitimate merchant and then search the files for someone with a similar name and good credit. It is even possible to buy medium- or top-quality credit names depending on price!

"Credit Repair"

For a fee, so-called "credit repair" agencies work to destroy valid but, needless to say, unfavorable credit bureau information on existing customers. They flood bureaus with challenges to existing information. If the bureau does not respond by verifying that the information is correct within a certain period of time, legally the record must be deleted. As a result, the customer gets a clean report and can start applying for credit all over again!

Credit bureaus and financial institutions are constantly working together to try and stop these scams, but fraud is difficult to eradicate entirely.

COMPLEX VERIFICATION

Larger lines of credit require more checking; this can involve calling the place of employment, attempting to verify the actual job, and, wherever possible, getting some idea of income. For a mortgage application, it may be necessary to get income information from a signed tax return, the applicant's current pay stub, or a W-2 form. These last two items should be accepted only from well-known employers because they are easy to fake. If there is any doubt about the business, contact the Better Business Bureau or some other local business organization to verify the company's credibility, time in business, and other factors.

For self-employed consumers, any or all of the following items should be obtained:

- *Copy of a current financial statement (audited, if possible)*
- *Signed tax return(s)*
- *Business checking records*
- *A partner's statement.*

In sum, the verification process should be carefully designed to reflect the best balance between cost and the need for sufficient information to make an informed decision. The verification process to prove the existence and value on collateral products is discussed in later chapters.

Completing the verification process marks the end of the standard customer screening process in which the customer completes an application and the lender follows a constant decision-tree process to winnow out the very good and the very bad. This process allows the lender to devote most of its resources to the mass middle market, which involves the hardest decisions. The final step is to make the decision whether to accept, reject, or modify the loan terms and to notify the customer.

NOTIFICATION OF REJECTED ACCOUNTS

Letters of decline are required in the United States when an applicant is denied credit. Two acts—the Fair Credit Reporting Act (FCRA) and the Equal Credit Opportunity Act (ECOA), which have slightly different applications—require that the lender notify the consumer with details of the reasons he has been denied credit.

When an applicant has been denied credit on the basis of human judgment, the reason can easily be determined and conveyed to the customer ("insufficient income," "too much delinquency," and so forth). After all, the decision to deny credit typically has been made by an underwriter trained in the bank's procedures and there is at least a basis for denial ("I'm sorry, madam, you failed to meet our qualifications").

When, however, an applicant is denied credit wholly or in part because of scoring, lenders have a problem. Basically, the applicant is being rejected because she "failed to get enough points." Government regulators find this unsatisfactory and conclude that people should be given reasons for being denied credit (presumably so they can try and correct these deficiencies and obtain credit in the future). As mentioned in Chapter 3, Credit Scoring, the letter can list the specific individual factors where the applicant's score deviated most from either the highest possible score or the expected average score. These explanations usually run along the following lines:

1. *Serious delinquency, derogatory public record, or too much collection activity*
2. *Proportion of balances to credit limits too high on revolving bank accounts*
3. *Too many accounts with balances owing*
4. *Amounts owed on accounts too high.*

Another option is a letter simply advising the applicant of his rights to obtain an explanation from the creditor. Management must decide, in advance, whether the principal reasons for decline will be communicated to the customer immediately or only upon request.

If the decision to reject is based on information from a credit reporting agency, the applicant must be given the name of the agency where his record was checked and informed of his right to contact the bureau directly to obtain a free copy of the report. According to Equifax, fewer than 10 percent of all consumers ask for their files and few of these decisions are ever reversed, but the process must be followed.

LINE ASSIGNMENT

One final step remains in the process: deciding what initial credit line to assign. If the customer has requested a particular loan amount for a specific purchase, such as a home or an automobile, the loan-to-value and debt-burden ratios are examined and the loan approved, modified, or rejected. For other products, such as unsecured loans or lines of credit, credit cards, department store cards, etc., there are less-well-defined rules. The objective is to balance portfolio health, considering both the risk and the competitiveness of the offer. Historically, the typical methods used to assign lines are by:

- *Score*
- *Census tract median income*
- *Household-cluster income*[4]
- *Debt burden*
- *Any combination of the above.*

4. We will cover the concept of obtaining household cluster information in the next chapter, Direct Mail.

Today, lenders also examine, for each targeted customer, the current line size and usage data on existing, competitor products (all information available from the credit bureau). They then apply some common-sense rules to setting the line size. If a targeted account is already a very low user of credit vis-à-vis his available credit lines, does it make sense to offer another high line? Probably not. If, however, line usage is relatively high and the risk score is appropriate, a higher line offer may be justified.

Regardless of the method used, the key question is: how big should the initial lines be? Alan Schiffres, from Portfolio Management Associates, makes the following point in his lecture on the subject in our *Risk & Reward* seminar:

> "Typically, initial lines should be assigned as low as possible while still being sufficient to entice the right customers to apply and use the product. Lines can then be increased over time as performance warrants."

Alan's rationale is based on two pieces of information. First, the average credit line available to Visa and MasterCard holders is currently about $7,500 in the United States; the average balance outstanding on these accounts is about $2,400. Clearly, most people are *not* using the majority of their lines. The second piece is that when a revolving loan is written off, it is usually at or near the top of its line. Thus, good customers are not using their available lines, but the bads are.

Let's see where this takes us. Credit losses are usually expressed in value, which means both the *number* of accounts charged off and the *balances* of those charged-off accounts are taken into account. The credit loss budget is developed using the following calculation:

EXHIBIT 4-6
Computing Credit Loss

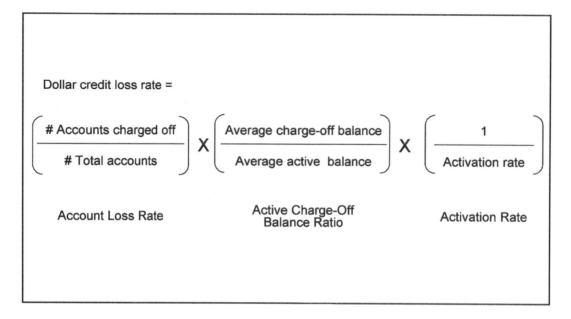

The first part of the equation deals with the number of accounts. The application score used when putting the accounts on the books usually controls the account loss rate. For example, if the projected account charge-off rate at a certain cutoff is 3.0%, that means that 3.0% of the *accounts*, not 3.0% of the *balances*, will be charged off.

The second part of the equation deals with the average balance of the accounts, both bad and for the total portfolio. We've already said that most accounts charge off at or near their credit limit, so the dollar amount ultimately charged off is heavily influenced by that account's line limit. Therefore, in order to control the dollar amounts that go bad, we must control the credit limits associated with the accounts that go bad. And since we don't know which specific accounts will go bad, that means we must control the limits associated with all accounts. To illustrate this point, the following exhibit shows how to determine what ratios must be achieved to make a specific credit loss budget.

EXHIBIT 4-7
Making Credit Loss Budget

		Charge-Off Balance Ratio					
		0.5	1.0	1.5	2.0	2.5	3.0
	1.0	0.5	1.0	1.5	2.0	2.5	(3.0)
	2.0	1.0	2.0	(3.0)	4.0	5.0	6.0
Account Charge-Off Rate	3.0	1.5	(3.0)	4.5	6.0	7.5	9.0
	4.0	2.0	4.0	6.0	8.0	10.0	12.0
	5.0	2.5	5.0	7.5	10.0	12.5	15.0
	6.0	(3.0)	6.0	9.0	12.0	15.0	18.0

In this example, we are saying we want a 3% charge-off rate, which is 3% of the *dollar* value of the total portfolio. The left side of the chart shows different *account* charge-off rates, possibly based on a score cutoff. The top shows different *dollar* charge-off rates. If we use a cutoff score that says we will have a 3% account charge-off rate, then the average dollar value of the accounts charged off must be the same as the average dollar value of the good accounts. If we alter the cutoff on the score so that the account charge-off rate is 2%, then the average dollar value of the charged-off accounts can be 1.5 times the average dollar amount of the good accounts to achieve the same 3% writeoff goal. This actually is more realistic, since, as we have already noted, a typical good account will have average balances which are much less than the available line.

In Chapter 6, Portfolio Management, we discuss how to control balances once the accounts are on your books. For now, it is important to note that as lines are increased but go unused by the good customers, the ratio of bad balances to good balances keeps getting higher. In order to maintain a specific credit loss budget as the lines get larger, you have to keep lowering the *account* charge-off rate. As the account charge-off ratio keeps getting lower, you ultimately squeeze yourself right out of the business.

Which goes back to the second part of Alan Schiffres's statement—you can always raise lines later as a pattern of usage and payment unfolds, particularly with the aid of behavior scoring.

As you can see, there is no one way of arriving at your profit goals, but line assignment is obviously a critical task. This is the final point we will cover in the account acquisition process. In the next chapter, acquiring accounts by direct mail will be discussed in more detail.

Direct Mail Account Solicitation

AS EVERYONE KNOWS—everyone, that is, with a stable mail address or who stays at one address for more than a few weeks—direct mail is the way many financial institutions build their businesses, in particular, their credit card businesses. While the Internet is becoming increasingly important and branch networks remain a good source of new business, particularly abroad, direct mail remains the medium of growth in credit cards for the more aggressive financial institutions. Direct mail campaigns have also been used to promote almost every consumer asset and liability product available in the marketplace, including savings accounts, money market accounts, checking accounts, automobile financing, unsecured lines of credit, and a variety of mortgage products, but credit card offers remain the leading direct mail product. If you have not been sent four or five offers for a credit card in the past month, you might want to check to see what's wrong.

The underlying objective of using direct mail to acquire accounts is to get the largest number of good customers for the least cost. The direct mail process begins with the financial institution selecting the target market and the type of lists it wants its customers to come from, then selecting the screens necessary to whittle down the list to the most likely targets, and then mailing the surviving names. The advantage of direct mail is that the lender is being proactive in selecting the type of customer it wants to solicit, rather than waiting for applicants to come into the office or apply over the Internet. If you can reach your targeted customers with a well-conceived, attractive offer of credit and a short application form (these offers are virtually all pre-screened), you can make it easy for the potential customers to accept.

The disadvantage of direct mail solicitations today is that everyone uses them and response rates are way down. Currently, between three and four *billion* offers for credit cards are mailed each year in the United States, and as the response rates have fallen to less than 1% (0.6% in 2001), financial institutions have had to devise increasingly sophisticated (and sometimes costly) techniques to target and screen their customers. The phrase *data mining* is often used to describe the process by which the most sophisticated financial institutions, such as Citigroup, Capital One, and First USA, gather information about individuals to precisely target them. Considering the high cost of acquiring good accounts by other techniques (portfolio purchase, brokers, branch sales, etc.), direct mail still remains a valid way of getting new business at an acceptable cost . . . but only if done correctly.

As with other ways to expand a business, direct mail works best when the product being marketed is somehow differentiated. In the past, AT&T's "no annual fee, *ever*" campaign caught the market by surprise and was an extraordinary success. Similarly, the Monoline companies' early "no annual fee gold card" gained market share for organizations such as Advanta, First USA, and Capital One. Some lenders have gained market share with high loan-to-value second mortgages offered to homeowners. But most consumers receive far more mail than they can absorb, so most offers end up in the trash unless they stand out quickly in some way. Credit card balance-transfer programs with a low, introductory rate ("Platinum card—2.99%") are still popular with many issuers,

EXHIBIT 5-1
Direct Mail Solicitation Process

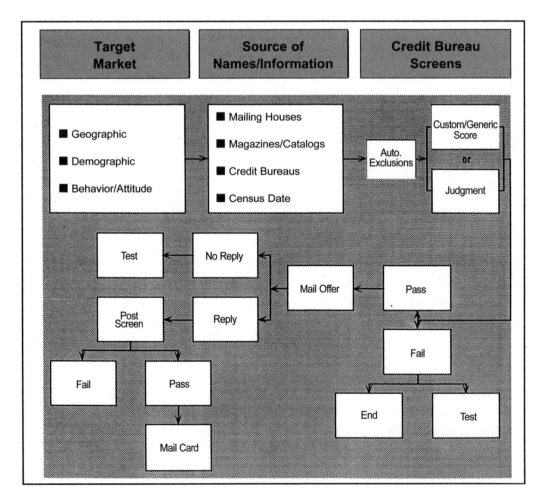

but these must be carefully tracked to ensure long-term profitability. No, a lender cannot make a profit with an interest rate of 2.99% (or 0%); the only way to make these offers profitable is by retaining customers even as the rate increases over time.

Before detailing methods of soliciting customers by direct mail, let's look at an overview of the process as shown in Exhibit 5-1.

The first step is to prepare an overall plan that covers the following:

- *Determining the overall program objectives, including creating pro forma financials*
- *Selecting the target market—by geography, income, buying habits, etc.*
- *Selecting the source of names to be screened*
- *Designing the offering package appropriate for the target market*
- *Devising the screening process*
- *Preparing a post-screen process*
- *Administering and tracking the program, including identifying the metrics (the management information) you need to measure the results*
- *Testing alternate processes to improve the results.*

PLANNING

The first step is to design the overall program objectives. These objectives could be along the following lines:

Primary Objective: To achieve an after-tax return on assets of 1.5% by the third year on every mailing, and 2.0% from there on.

Secondary Objectives:
- *To increase the credit card portfolio by 200,000 accounts per year*
- *To expand the target market with offers in two new regions while maintaining the same rate of penetration in existing markets*
- *To test six new selection and screening processes vs. the existing processes*
- *To gain 50,000 new customers from the recent merger with South-Central Bank.*

Once the overall objectives have been selected, the target market for your mailing should be defined, including where the people live, their demographics (income, age, etc.), and an understanding of their behavior, including risk and credit usage and any lifestyle factors (e.g., golfers, etc.) that may make them desirable targets. Let's examine each of these in more detail.

Target Marget

Geographic target. How far from the home office or operating base does a lender wish to solicit its customers? Does it want to go after a rural or urban market, does it go statewide, regional, national, or overseas? It may want to restrict any mailing to its home state or nearby region (several states), or it may decide to undertake a national mailing. As a general rule, only the larger organizations have the processing, operational, customer service, and collection abilities to solicit nationally. Most, however, can handle accounts within their state or nearby geographic region, particularly if the institution has a readily recognizable name. Advertising can help differentiate the product, but there are few Citigroups, Capital Ones, or Discovers that can afford to spend enough to gain national recognition for their cards. Finally, be aware of regional economic conditions . . . regions do vary in their economic health, as we have already covered in Chapter 2, Planning Consumer Products. One further caveat: beware of the legal implications of mailings restricted by zip code. Be sure to consult your legal department on this subject.

Demographic target. What type of customer is a lender looking for? The total universe can be disaggregated in many different ways, including by income, age, sex, education level, household size, home ownership, and so forth. It is critical to define what you are looking for early in the process, as these decisions will affect your marketing programs as well as your credit criteria. Through the name-selection process we describe later, you can, for example, go after only well-educated, middle-aged people with high incomes who live in wealthy communities. Be aware that because these people are solicited often, their response rates typically will be low. There are many other target markets, such as college students, newly retired professionals, new homeowners, people with young children, people with lower incomes but who are homeowners, and so on. Those with the courage to seek a target market that has not been heavily solicited could gain an advantage . . . as long as they don't "bet the bank" on a large mailing with limited or no prior experience with that target market.

Behavior/lifestyle target. There are powerful ways to determine the behavior and lifestyle of a target market that can help a lender define the riskiness of a mailing and focus the product offering to those most likely to respond. One important first decision is: Are you looking for people who use credit heavily and revolve or those who pay their bills every month? If your product offering is based on attracting revolvers, particularly those to whom a low minimum monthly payment is critical, you can obtain information to target them from the credit bureaus. Conversely, if you are offering mileage enhancements to frequent flyers, you will want to target high users of credit, typically business travelers or wealthy retirees. If your product is designed to attract people with special lifestyles such as motorcyclists, golfers, skiers, or pilots, tools are available from your list suppliers to define those potential markets closely.

Once you have selected the target market, the next step is to obtain a source of names and addresses to use in your mailing that will give you the best return for your money.

Sourcing the Names: List Selection and Screening

You can build lists using internal information, or you can purchase lists using external information.

INTERNAL LISTS: CURRENT CUSTOMERS/ PRIOR MAILINGS

If you have been doing mailings for many years, start by reviewing your past mailings. You should have vast records of the names that you solicited in earlier mailings and you will know a lot about the performance of the accounts that you actually booked. You should also be able to learn from both previously successful and unsuccessful mailings. Further, if you are offering a new product, a good place to start is with your own current customers. As we have said before, many financial institutions overlook their own customers as a target market for new products; after all, you already know a great deal about your customers and have some idea of the value of the relationship. Another good source of names would be accounts acquired through a recent merger with another financial institution, particularly if the institution has been slow in the past to solicit its own customers. If you believe you have mined your own customers and data to the extent possible, the next step is to go outside and acquire new mailing lists.

EXTERNAL LISTS

At its simplest, a direct mail campaign can be aimed at a very broad list of names which can be purchased from the major direct mailing houses such as Donnelly, MetroMail, or Polk. These organizations compile names primarily from automobile registration lists, telephone listings, and Census Bureau data. Although it is true that you can obtain some good differentiation (e.g., a Lexus buyer may be wealthier than a buyer of a Ford Focus), these lists are relatively undefined and so you will not know much about the behavior of the names you receive. This can make it expensive to reach a highly targeted group of names (e.g., high-income golfers over 35) and could lead to a low response rate.

Another source of names would be to extract them directly from the credit bureau files—this is called a *direct extract list*. Extraction can be done by providing the bureaus with the criteria you are looking for, such as revolvers, high users of credit, mild delinquency, etc. Using these criteria they can develop a list that meets your target market. Some lenders use these lists alone, but the larger and more sophisticated mailers use much more advanced screening techniques described below to select their targeted names.

Another way to define the behavior and lifestyle of your target market better is to choose your names from the following, more focused, lists:

- *Magazines and periodicals (e.g.,* Forbes, Boating, Golf & Travel, House & Garden, Time, Newsweek, Vanity Fair, Byte, Gourmet, Architectural Digest, Popular Mechanics, Road & Track, Modern Maturity, *etc.)*
- *Catalogs (e.g., L.L. Bean, Bang and Olefsun, Lands' End, Sears)*
- *Affinity groups (e.g., doctors, accountants, college alumni, lawyers, AARP or AAA members, NFL season ticket holders, airline frequent flyers, etc.)*
- *Internet purchasers (eBay, Amazon, Priceline, etc.).*

You can obtain a profile of the demographics/behavior of the people from each issuer and determine if they meet your goals. For instance, each magazine list will have detailed demographics regarding its readership, such as: 67.4% male; 86.7% attended college—40% of whom attended graduate school; 53.6 married; 21% own weekend or vacation home, etc., etc. The source of the names will yield different response rates and different loss rates even though you may use the same credit criteria on each list. A subscriber to AARP's many services (including its magazine), which are aimed at retirees, will behave very differently from a subscriber to *Hot Rod Journal.* Savvy mailers build on their previous experience and are always testing new areas—whether to expand their universe of customers, to test response rates on existing or new products and the validity of the risk screens, or whatever.

In addition, the individual characteristics (demographics) of the potential mail lists can be further defined by obtaining lifestyle/geo-demographic information on the names from some mailing specialists such as ClusterPLUS, Claritas, PRIZM, or MicroVision. As noted earlier in this chapter, the term *data mining* is often used to describe the process by which direct mailers obtain sophisticated information about the names they wish to target. These companies each use their own statistical methods to break down the United States into small "clusters" of neighboring households with similar characteristics. For instance, ClusterPLUS analyzes over 1,600 lifestyle factors to divide the country into its cluster groupings. By cross-referencing data from many sources (including the Census Bureau), these companies can very narrowly define the composition of a neighborhood down to a target as small as ten to fifteen households. This allows a mailing to be very carefully targeted to the type of people that you want to solicit, including the names, age, income, education, household size, whether or not they are homeowners, and so forth. These additional screens can help define your target market very precisely to help offset the high costs of mailing and low response rates.

One point to remember: the use of a clustering screen or any of the behavioral lists noted above can reduce the number of names sent to the bureaus for final screening, thus holding down credit bureau costs. Is it worth the extra time and cost? Only a professional marketer can judge the cost/benefit ratio, and it is mandatory to keep the record of past mailings (the responses, activations, usage, and profitability) to determine which methods of targeting and screening are truly worthwhile. (Be aware, however, that the cost of maintaining a database of all previously mailed names can be high.) If you do not have the expertise to design a mailing, many large and small mailing houses are eager to provide their expertise to guide the list-selection process. They will advise on list selection and screening methods, and will handle or "fulfill" the mailing on behalf of any lending institution.

By the time a sophisticated mailer finishes, she can know enough (some say too much) about an individual to have a very complete profile. Some potential targets sound like the personal ads placed in local publications: "34- to 40-year-old male, recently moved, homeowner, likes to golf, travel, uses credit cards heavily, but pays on time."

TARGET MARKET/OFFERING PACKAGE

The next step is to design the appropriate product offering to attract your potential customers.

The offering package should include:

- *The customer communication (the letter, the return envelope, and any brochure or pamphlet explaining the offer)*
- *The coupon/application with sufficient information to enable identification and verification of the applicant*
- *An expiration date*
- *All required legal disclosures.*

You will have only a few seconds of attention from the average good consumer before the mailed offer ends up in the wastebasket (rest assured that bad prospects will examine the offer closely—they really want the credit!).

Savvy marketers understand this and pay close attention to the envelope design to increase response rates. Most offers print the key selling points on the envelope: for example, a low initial rate, the ongoing rate if this is particularly competitive, the credit line ("up to $20,000"), the fact that it is a gold, platinum, or titanium card. A lot of gimmicks are used today to make a mailing stand out, like adding a secondary window where an intriguing offer can peek out beside the recipient's name. Some issuers today use complex, colorful packages stuffed with photographs and stickers that customers are urged to peel off and apply to a specific place on the return letter. Only by repeated testing can an issuer find how to design an offer that attracts the right customers. Finally, it has to be easy to apply; the potential customer should have to fill in only a minimal amount of information, return the application, and she will receive at least a minimum line of credit, subject to a post-screening process.

Of course, all *details* of the terms and conditions must be spelled out (usually on the back of the offering letter), including when/if the pricing changes, the grace period (the number of days allowed to pay off new charges in full without any interest charge, usually if there is no previous balance outstanding), when/how any late or over-limit fees are to be charged, and the method of computing the balance owing. Your legal department should review this material carefully.

It is important to make the return coupon, the actual application, as brief as possible. A recent offer from a major bank looked like this:

EXHIBIT 5-2
Invitation Coupon

Note the statement of a credit line "Up to $100,000." Virtually every mailer includes some such "up to" restriction on the amount of credit actually to be granted. This gives the lender great flexibility in setting the actual line in case the post-screen process turns up a deterioration in the criteria used in the pre-screening process. Somewhere the offer should also state that once you return the application, you may be subject to a further screening process and may not be accepted if you no longer meet the screening criteria. One final point: the offer should expire at a predetermined date to minimize the possibility that further substantial changes to the credit report will take place (e.g., bankruptcy, job loss, etc.).

THE CREDIT SCREENING PROCESS

The final step is to obtain information on each name you wish to solicit to determine its creditworthiness. In the pre-approved process typically used in credit card direct mail offers, every name on the selected list, regardless of how it is derived, undergoes a series of credit screens. A first screen would be to automatically exclude the names of people whom you would never accept. Typical exclusions could include those names with:

- *A prior bankruptcy, usually up to 10 years; although some aggressive lenders solicit this market, they are the exception.*

- *Major derogatory information, such as too many 30-, 60-, or 90-day delinquencies (current or recent).*

- *High fraud potential (from a credit bureau fraud screen).*

Those names passing the initial screens are then scored using either a generic scoring system (based on generic bureau data) or a custom system (if you have sufficient data from previous mailings to develop one). Generic score models are now sophisticated enough to screen and rank first-time or new users of credit, people with thin files (i.e., few credit lines), and of course, heavier users of credit. The proliferation of different types of score models also makes it possible to use both a generic and an in-house system to identify the names passed by both systems, the ones failing both, and everyone in between. This must be subject to the warning discussed in Chapter 3, Credit Scoring, that the score systems be used simultaneously, not in sequence. Those passing all the screens are now mailed an offer of credit, subject only to the limitations written into the offer and a final post-screen.

Post Screening

For a pre-approved or pre-screened offer, you have provided the credit bureau with a request for all the names that pass your screen (length of time at bureau, number of open accounts, type of accounts, bureau score, etc.), and these names become your mailing list. A typical mailing, however, can take several weeks or months to gather the data, send out the mailing, and obtain the responses, so it is important to have a post-screen process in place to 1) check that the forms have been completed correctly, and 2) ensure that the people responding still meet the original criteria. The mailer has one last chance to severely limit the offer if the applicant does not continue to meet the same criteria employed at the time of the initial screen, or to cancel the offer entirely if there has been a *material* deterioration in the person's credit history. In the U.S., the Federal Trade Commission (FTC) requires that a minimum line of credit be offered to any name that 1) has been screened at the credit bureau and 2) meets your criteria, but it does allow a cancellation of the offer for material deterioration in creditworthiness such as a bankruptcy or severe delinquency. Today, pre-approved offers typically use such words as "Just mail back the enclosed form to apply for your account" or "This is a Personal Invitation for an offer of credit" to give lenders a legal way to exclude those who fail to pass a post-screen.

Two types of applicants will be identified for special action during the post-screen process. The first group are the outright declines (say, 5–10%) because they now materially fail to meet the original criteria. The second group are those whom you probably would prefer not to have on your books but who have not deteriorated sufficiently since the offer was made to be able to deny them credit outright. In these cases, the credit line assigned can be substantially lower than the "up to" offer in the original mail piece, sometimes as low as $500. Another alternative is to reprice the higher-risk accounts as soon as allowed under your published terms.

At a minimum, a post-screen will allow a lender to identify borrowers likely to be a future problem, even if it must accept them with a minimum line because of the wording on the mailer. These accounts should be placed on an alert system in collections for speedy action and early closing in the event of any sign of a problem in meeting the contractual obligations.

One final point: it is very important to test and learn from each mailing. For instance, you should send out offers to a sample of those who failed to pass your screens. Is there anything you can learn from these offers? Are they really that bad? While you will pick up some good accounts, are they really worth it when you consider the performance of the whole group you failed? Test, test, test, and try to learn for the next mailing.

ADMINISTERING AND TRACKING A MAILING

Every mailing should have a detailed flowchart to track and audit 1) the materials production, 2) the name selection and screening process, 3) the returned coupon review, and 4) the actual card issuance. Because these steps are often performed by outside suppliers, set up an audit process to ensure that your mailing is run as planned. Is the name selection accurate? Are the screening steps appropriate? One technique here is to use "seed" names, i.e., names you place in the list so that you will receive the mailing directly, as if you were a prospect, to determine if the material arrives promptly and accurately.

The final step in a direct mail campaign is to make sure that the key variables' results are tracked in order to improve the performance of future mailings. These include all the factors that go into a profit model, including the average balance per active account, cost per account acquired, revenue, operating expenses, delinquency, and charge-off rates. One important early warning of the success/failure of any mailing comes from tracking the response rate by score range. Early information such as the following could prove to be very useful in predicting the success/failure of a mailing and can also give an early warning about a potentially risky portfolio so that defensive action (e.g., hiring more collectors) can be taken—an appropriate action for this mailing since more lower-scoring responses than forecast, and fewer higher scoring responses, were received.

EXHIBIT 5-3
Response Rate by Score

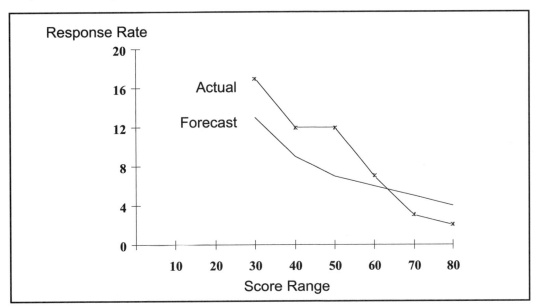

The following chart summarizes some other key variables to track versus the original forecast.

EXHIBIT 5-4
Tracking MIS

	Month 13				Month 13		
	Forecast	Actual			Forecast	Actual	Difference
Number Open Accts	22,000	14,107		Number Open Accts	22,000	14,107	(7,893)
Total O/S ($000)	$23,1000	$9,458					
Avg Balance per active	$1,500	$1,154					
% Open accts Active	70.0%	58.1%		Number Active	15,400	8.196	(7,204)
% Open accts Revolving	50.0%	40.2%		Number Revolving	11,000	5,671	(5,329)
% Accts Delinq 60+	1.0%	2.1%		Number Delinquent	220	240	20
% Accts C/O (Annualized)	2.0%	2.0%		Number Charged-Off	37	24	(13)
% O/S Delinq 60+	2.0%	3.2%		Number Active, but	15,180	7,956	(7,224)
% O/S C/O (Annualized)	4.0%	11.9%		not delinquent			
Avg Balance per C/O	$2,100	$3,979					
Gross Rev Per Active	$21.25	$16.35					
Profit per Active	$3.44	($4.92)					
Return on Assets	2.8%	-5.1%					

These results indicate a problem: the mailing is not achieving the results intended. Problems include:

- *The number of open and active accounts is way below estimate.*
- *The average balance at charge-off is almost twice the forecast, resulting in much higher than planned writeoff rates on outstandings.*
- *The accounts are unprofitable.*

It is now up to the issuer to find out what went wrong and to learn how to revise the next mailings. By continuing to track the results of a mailing over time, some results will finally become obvious, as in the following two charts.

Exhibit 5-5 shows that each succeeding mailing is getting worse. The second chart, which segments the third mailing, shows there are still many good (low-risk) accounts within this mailing; only a portion are high-risk and should not be included in subsequent mailings. Segmenting the MIS allows you to better understand where the problems are.

These simple summary reports do not give you all the answers, but they certainly lead to many questions, which helps to identify the problem(s). Now it is up to you to find those answers.

EXHIBIT 5-5a
Gross W/Os by Mailing

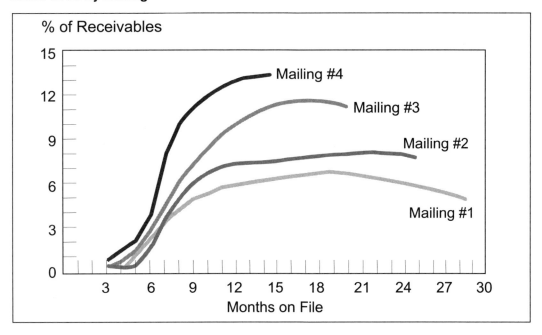

% of Receivables — Months on File

EXHIBIT 5-5b
Mailing #3 – Vintage by Score Range

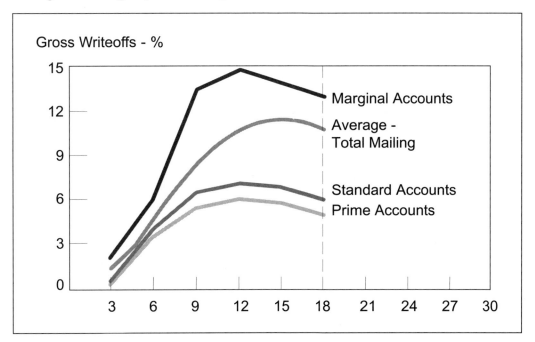

Gross Writeoffs - %

MAILING FRAUD

Mail-intercept fraud used to be a problem. Professional card thieves would be on the alert at post offices where mass mailings of cards were made. With the right contacts in the post office itself, some cards could be intercepted and used before the issuer was aware they had been stolen. The use of "dead" plastic—that is, sending cards that cannot be used until the intended recipient has called and given some identification—has helped minimize the problem significantly, but at a cost. Some issuers question whether the cost justifies the risk of fraud, which appears to be so minimal today. Alan Schiffres addresses this problem in our seminars by questioning the participants as follows:

"How many of you have fire insurance?" Virtually every hand is raised.

"How many of you think you will have a fire next year?" Not one hand is raised.

"How many of you will buy fire insurance next year?" Virtually every hand is raised.

Having made his point, Alan goes on to point out that if the card issuers do not use dead plastic, word would quickly get out, fraud losses would climb, and the costs would far outweigh the cost of administering the dead plastic program. Using dead plastic is an insurance policy.

Two final points: 1) Make sure the activation requirement is very obvious to the customer to avoid the embarrassment of a possible reject the first time the card is used, and 2) track and follow up on nonactivated cards to determine why they have not been used.

SUMMARY

In using the direct mail method to acquire new customers, a very precise process is the key to building a good quality portfolio at an acceptable cost. Once an account is on the books, a lender can do only so much to change its quality. If the right customers are not selected to start with, the portfolio can never be profitable. In the next chapter we explore what can be done to manage accounts once they are booked.

Portfolio Management

F OR A LENDER, one critical aspect of managing consumer credit is handling customers in a way that encourages the good ones to maintain and expand their relationship, while controlling and, if necessary, terminating the relationship with the bad ones. The overall objective of portfolio management[1] is to improve the portfolio's profitability by managing the following areas:

- *Handling routine transactions*
- *Meeting your customer's service needs (inquiries, complaints, etc.)*
- *Cross-selling products and services*
- *Controlling the performance of accounts on the books.*

Poor handling of a customer and his account in routine areas can cause some to move to another lender, especially the good ones who have many alternatives. We will cover these areas briefly, before moving on to more risk-related areas.

HANDLING ROUTINE TRANSACTIONS

Some routine customer service and maintenance steps must be in place to manage a portfolio effectively. I call them routine because they are repetitive, necessary transactions in running a business, but they do not require advanced statistical techniques to manage. For example, the institution must be able to:

- *Disburse funds*
- *Issue plastic/checks*
- *Issue statements*

---

1. Throughout this chapter we use the terms *portfolio management* and *account maintenance* interchangeably; both are used in the industry to describe the management of accounts that you have already booked.

- *Record transactions*
- *Process payments*
- *Handle inquiries*
- *Handle disputes*
- *Change addresses*

In this context, the word *routine* is also used only as a reminder that the customer *expects* these transactions to be routine. It does not mean they are mundane or easy to manage; on the contrary, they are as difficult to handle as any step in the credit cycle. Also, while these routine transactions do not have the potential for large profit improvement that the less routine steps do, as we have already noted, they do have a downside risk: while it is difficult to gain customers by handling these transactions well, it is assuredly possible to lose customers quickly by making too many errors. Remember, these tasks are the only contact you have with many customers; installment loan customers can easily choose to try another lender for a new auto loan or mortgage, and credit card customers may receive two to three offers a week from other lenders, so their moving on is simple.

The Cost of Maintaining Accounts

Operating expenses, which typically include the costs of maintaining and collecting accounts on the books, vary as a percentage of the average balance outstanding from 10 to 20 basis points (.10–.20%) on a typical first mortgage loan, all the way up to 3.0–5.0% or more on a credit card. The wide range is due to the differences in average balance (it costs the same to send a bill or handle routine customer service calls for a $100,000 mortgage loan customer as it does on a $1,200 average balance credit card) and the varied operating functions that need to be performed on each product. Although few lending institutions have failed because of high operating costs, these costs obviously have a significant impact on the profitability of a business.

Portfolio maintenance operations should be viewed as a very precise process with paperwork or electronic data coming into the "factory" where they are handled by a number of different people and departments who have clearly defined and measurable goals. This is a pass/fail world where transaction goals are met or not met. The departments meeting their goals should be rewarded, and those that fail should be subjected to a thorough review and analysis. If the goals are found to be wrong, they should be revised; if they are proper, then the cause of the problem must be found and changed.

A well-run operation should fully cover the more mundane questions such as:

- *How many times does the telephone ring before it is answered? What is the telephone "abandon" rate? A customer can take only so much*

Muzak or not-so-subtle sales pitches while waiting for a human being to answer. After ten or so rings, or five minutes of Muzak, many customers will hang up and may be lost forever.

- *How many days does it take to answer a written inquiry, and do these responses satisfactorily address the customers' problems?*

- *How many problems can be answered either automatically ("if you wish to learn your account balance, press 1") or by a service representative on the first telephone call?*

- *Can the authorizations representative approve an over-limit charge for a good customer while the customer is waiting in line at a grocery store? In order to do so, the approve/reject parameters must be clearly delineated within your organization.*

A lender must be able to answer these types of questions quickly. Senior managers should establish guidelines for such quality decisions at the highest level, and the guidelines should be tested regularly. I even recommend that, periodically, the president or a senior executive should call his own organization anonymously to experience firsthand how the average customer is treated. This experiment can provide a wake-up call for senior management.

An organization's effectiveness depends on its ability to anticipate, and then to process, each transaction. This requires a constant exchange of information among all departments. If a lender conducts a new mailing, signs up new dealers, or enlarges its geographic coverage, each action will have an impact on the volume of transactions throughout each department. *Anticipation* of new business, not *reaction* to it, is the key to a well-run organization. Here, again, forecasting is a powerful tool to understanding the expected impact on all aspects of the business.

In-House or External Operations

Another question to be resolved is which functions should be performed in-house and which farmed out to one of the major data-processing houses. As a general rule, it makes little sense for smaller financial institutions to try to emulate the larger companies, such as Citigroup and American Express. The major processing houses like First Data Resources, Total Systems, etc., have built-in volume efficiencies that smaller institutions can enjoy. There is no one rule on when a business has sufficient volume to be able to do its work in-house. Rather, this is a matter to be analyzed continually. Further, there is no rule saying that *all* functions should go to an outside processor or stay in-house. For example, a business may feel that customer relations is so important that it must be kept internal in order to maintain absolute quality control, but that new account processing, bill payments, and some collection activities can be outsourced.

PORTFOLIO MANAGEMENT

The introduction to this chapter briefly described the primary objectives of portfolio management: to encourage good customers to use your products and to identify and control losses on the bad customers. For the remainder of this chapter, we will cover the following areas of portfolio maintenance[2] where good management can have a significant impact on the profitability of the organization along with a discussion of behavior scoring as a tool to help you in this process.

EXHIBIT 6-1
Key Areas for Credit Management

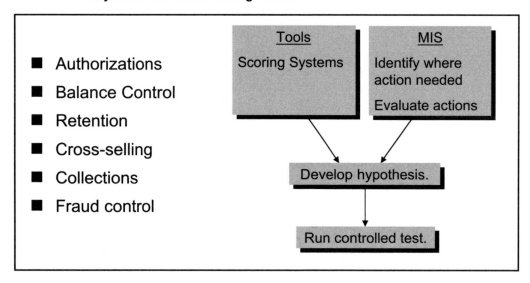

The process of managing the accounts you have booked begins with the release of money (for installment loans) or with the establishment of a revolving line of credit or the issuing of a credit card(s). Now you have an account and a customer. This funding process should be routine with an installment loan, assuming the lending institution has completed a normal review of both the applicant and any property used to secure the loan.

A revolving line raises different issues because, to a great extent, the customer controls when/how the money is to be drawn down. It is possible for people to obtain a credit card, immediately put it in their wallets, and hardly ever use it. Here, the expense to the lending institution of maintaining the account can more than offset any revenue the card might generate. Or, the customer can proceed to travel around the world, charging goods and services at a rate far exceeding the amount the lender had initially authorized. For these reasons a process must be in place to control the ongoing flow of funds and eliminate fraudulent or unauthorized charges.

To understand the key areas of account maintenance identified above (author-

---

2. With the exception of collections, which, because of the importance of the subject and the specialized operations it requires, will be covered in two later chapters, 7 and 8.

izations, balance control, etc.) as they relate to credit cards and other revolving lines of credit, you need to understand the powerful tool of behavior scoring (as opposed to application scoring), which is widely used to control portfolios today.

Behavior Scoring

The development of application scores was discussed in Chapter 3; performance or behavior scores (the names are used interchangeably) go through the same steps of planning, development, validation, implementation, and monitoring as an application score. This discussion examines the highlights of this process as they pertain specifically to behavior scores, with the understanding that much of the conceptual ground has already been covered.

When developing a behavior score, the first decision to make is: What is the objective of the scoring system (the first step for developing any score)? Typically behavior scores are developed to array accounts from most to least:

- *Profitable*
- *Creditworthy*
- *Transaction-oriented*
- *Attrition prone*
- *Collectible*
- *Bankrupt prone*
- *Likely potential for fraud.*

Both application and behavior scoring use past performance to predict future behavior. However, there are differences between the two scoring concepts:

- *Behavior scores have great predictive power because they are based on information contained in a lending institution's master file (e.g., whether a customer made or missed a payment; whether an account balance increased or declined). While these scores also can include credit bureau data (the same as application scoring), using actual results from your master file is usually more powerful than using information obtained from the potential customer's application.*

- *Behavior score models can be applied to every account for every transaction, every day, every month.*

- *A lender can constantly test and monitor different strategies to derive the maximum benefit from behavior score models, the same as with application scores.*

PLANNING AND DEVELOPMENT

One basic question is whether the lender has the necessary systems and data to develop behavior scores. You should have records of actual account performance for a minimum of 12 months (18 months would be better). There should be enough bads to ensure that the model is statistically sound (possibly fewer than the 1,000 required for the development of an application model, say 250 to 500). Profitability models should take into account all the factors that determine profitability (e.g., revenue items such as balance, payment, and usage patterns, as well as cost items, including collection expense and writeoffs). Since seasonality is so significant in historical account balance and payment performance, performance data should be randomly selected and not be unduly influenced by one season or another.

DISTRIBUTION OF PROFIT

One point about profitability: as noted in the scoring chapter, every revolving portfolio we have looked at shows a distribution of profit by incidence of risk that looks like the following:

EXHIBIT 6-2

Behavior Score—Portfolio Distribution

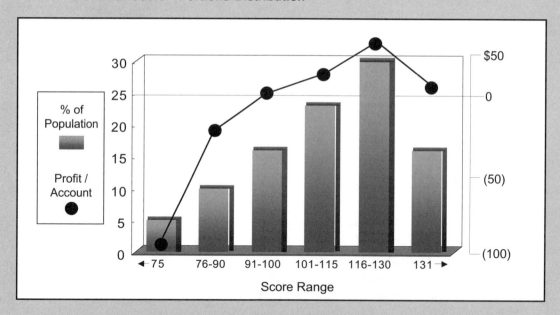

What this indicates is that the most profitable accounts are in the middle range of the score, and that the lowest and highest scored accounts are either unprofitable or only marginally profitable. The lowest-risk customers don't use revolving products much, so revenues from these customers barely (or don't at all) offset the cost of maintaining the account. The higher-risk (i.e., lower-scoring) customers tend to use revolving credit a lot; their revenues may be high, but the losses are high as well, again resulting in poor profit performance. Every institution should review its accounts to see if they follow this pattern. One of the major benefits of scoring is to obtain the MIS to thoroughly understand your portfolio.

If you have the data in readable form, the next step is to choose a developer. As with an application score, should the score be developed internally or by an outside vendor? Both courses of action have a plus and a downside. Internal people understand the portfolio better; they may pick up on some information that outside vendors might miss because they are able to research their own files better. Additionally, much is learned about the portfolio during the research phase; obviously it would be better if internal people learned this information so it can be applied in other areas. On the other hand, outside vendors are exposed to more score systems and may be able to apply what they learn to your development project. Some companies use a combination of internal and external resources to benefit from these advantages.

The score developer next selects the records for analysis and identifies the variables to be examined. As with application scoring, the lending institution provides the definition of good and bad accounts, while the developer of the system selects the sample of accounts to analyze and the variables to examine, and begins to analyze the data to determine the characteristics that best predict performance. Here are some that might be examined in developing a risk model:

EXHIBIT 6-3
Example of Variables Examined

• Payment trend	• Current delinquency status
• Purchase trend	• Current amount due
• Credit score (new accounts)	• Amount past due
• Date opened	• Amount 30 days past due
• Date of last payment	• Amount 60 days past due
• Date of last limit increase	• Amount 90 days past due
• Current status	• Amount 120+ days past due
• Current amount of purchases	• Highest balance ever
• Current balance	• Maximum delinquency ever
• Current amount of payments	• Number of times 30 days past due
• Current cash advance balance	• Number of times 60 days past due
• Current credit limit	• Number of times 90 days past due
	• Number of times 120+ days past due

The developer examines as many characteristics as possible until it can identify the most powerful discriminants. As with an application score, the final step is to validate the results with a holdback sample. Using standard statistical techniques, the developer prepares a scorecard, which might look like this:

EXHIBIT 6-4
Performance Score (Example)

Characteristics	Classification	Points
Time on books	< 6 mos.	0
	7-12 mos.	40
	13-24 mos.	242
	25+ mos.	384
High delinquency last 12 months	0 - 30	0
	31 - 60	-65
	90 or worse	-134
Ratio of current balance to credit limit	0 - 50	0
	51 - 80	-96
	81 - 100	-130
	> 100	-137
Current cash advance balance	0	89
	1 - 100	0
	101 - 250	-67
	251+	-180
Number months currently delinquent	Inactive, 0	120
	1	0
	2	-80
	3	-140
	4+	-300

GENERIC BUREAU SCORES

Up to this point, behavior scoring has been described in terms of a customer's performance on a lending institution's own accounts. A great many unexpected events may affect its customers, and some changes can cause a good account to turn high risk, such as a complicated divorce, the loss of a job, a serious health problem. Other changes can be good, such as having two incomes as the children grow older, getting a promotion, etc. Typically, customers have additional accounts with other lenders. Here is where the generic credit-bureau-based risk identification models, available from Fair, Isaac (Horizon, Empirica, ScoreNet, et al.), can be used. From these reports, the lender gains an understanding of the customer's relationship with other lenders: how many credit lines he has, how well he is meeting any obligations, and, most important, the trend of change in a customer's obligations—is he using his lines more? Is minor delinquency becoming more frequent? All of this can be statistically interpreted to help guide the lender. When and how should these models be used? Time and costs prohibit fully researching the status of every account every month with the credit bureaus; quarterly may be sufficient. Also, a bureau score can be obtained whenever a lender is faced with a decision to change the existing price, to lengthen, expand, or deepen the relationship with an account, or when some deterioration becomes evident in the customer's relationship with you.

Generic scores such as Fair, Isaac's Horizon score can be particularly useful in predicting bankruptcy. In June 1998, Fair Isaac reported[3] that Horizon identified three times as many bankrupts as did issuers' own behavior scores when focusing on the lowest-scoring 5% of the total population of accounts which were current. This makes sense, since a person does not declare bankruptcy because he is behind on just one account. Virtually all bankrupts are having trouble with multiple lenders, and if you restrict your analysis to your own accounts, the chances are very high that you will be surprised when the customer decides to take that route.

One warning—before taking any adverse action such as terminating an account before its normal termination date, reducing an existing line of credit, or changing the cost of credit partly or in whole on information contained in a credit bureau report, lenders should be aware of the legal ramifications of such an action. Do the terms of your agreement allow such actions? How will you notify the customer? Remember, the customer must be given the reasons for such "adverse actions." It is not sufficient to say "your bankruptcy score is too high." As with applicants denied credit, the customer must be given specific reasons justifying the change in terms (e.g., too many accounts showing 30/60-day late payments; too much utilization of available credit on revolving accounts, etc.), along with the name of the reporting agency.

As with solicitation scoring, outside bureau scores can be used in conjunction with an internal behavior score as a very powerful tool to assess risk. Using two scoring systems might be done monthly or quarterly for all active accounts not in collections. Or, if you have an early warning system to identify accounts with a high probability of attrition, obtaining information on what they are doing with other lenders could be helpful. The combined information value—and in particular, noting where the score systems agree or disagree—can be especially useful.

Once you have developed the score(s), you can begin applying them in authorizations, balance control, retention marketing, cross-selling, and fraud control—indeed, throughout all of portfolio management, as we will now cover.

Authorizations

It is possible today for financial institutions in the United States to review and approve/reject virtually every credit card purchase as it is being made (this may

---

3. In its publication *Bureau Scores Today*, which reports news of Fair, Isaac credit bureau scores.

take some time to become standard around the world). This is a vast improvement from the days when each merchant had a floor limit (i.e., each transaction below a certain dollar amount, the floor limit, would be approved without any review), and few transactions went all the way back to the card-issuing bank for review. Thanks to advances in technology, approximately 99% of all transactions today can be reviewed through the following process.[4]

EXHIBIT 6-5
Bankcard Authorization Process

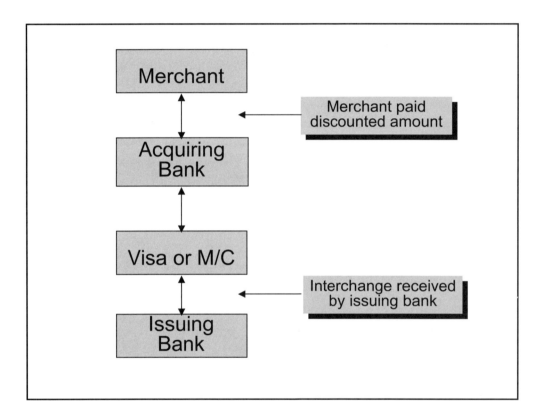

As shown in this chart, to obtain authorization for the transaction, the merchant enters the amount and date of purchase and then either swipes the customer's card at the merchant terminal or enters the card numbers via a telephone line connection. The information goes to the merchant's acquiring institution (merchant bank), which then sends the information to the appropriate card processor's network (MasterCard or Visa), and is then forwarded to the customer's issuing bank for review.

---

4. This process describes a bank-issued credit card transaction. Discover, Diner's, and American Express have both the merchant and consumer as customers, so their transactions simply go to their own authorizations network, which returns the decision to the merchant.

Once the request arrives at the issuing bank, the credit management department has several choices. It can:

- *Approve the transaction if the account is open, under limit, and not currently delinquent.*

- *Approve the transaction even if it is over the current line limit.*

- *Send back a "call me" message if fraud is suspected. This requires that the customer contact the issuer, typically by telephone immediately, in order to verify the transaction and/or his identity before the transaction can be approved.*

- *Request that the card be picked up if the account is severely delinquent or if fraud is detected.*

- *Reject all others (e.g., high risk, over-limit transactions).*

Here is the key to the process. The issuing bank has only a few seconds to review and make a decision. Most transactions fall within these categories and are speedily accepted/rejected. There are always, however, some difficult decisions. For instance, should it issue an on-the-spot line increase or reject a purchase that would take the customer over her limit? The whole authorization process—from merchant to the network, to the approving bank and back—should take less than ten to twenty seconds. How long will a customer wait at a checkout counter or the gas station for approval? How long will a sales clerk wait with a long line of customers wanting to pay for their purchases? Not very long! Each institution must have a good process in place to make these sorts of decisions. Scoring can be a powerful tool in this decision process (e.g., approve up to a 10% line increase if the score is >790; a 20% increase if the score is >820, etc.).

Once the decision is made, it must be routed back to the merchant and the customer through the same network. Interestingly, nearly 97% of all transactions going through this process are approved. Only 2.5% to 3.0% are declined, and only a very small percentage (less than 1%) are referred for a manual review (i.e., "call me"). A customer might expect a "call me" if he is making a once-in-a-lifetime purchase of a diamond engagement ring. You don't want to irritate a customer with a "call me" for purchasing $37.20 worth of groceries, unless there is a very good reason such as a suspected fraudulent transaction.

As we said, 99% of transactions go through this electronic review process; what about the other 1%? These are transactions made when the system is down for maintenance or overloaded, say, late in the afternoon or on Christmas Eve (when every male shopper finally begins his shopping), or when a regional breakdown occurs. In these cases, when the issuing bank cannot be contacted, Visa and MasterCard are authorized to use a set of rules given by each bank to accept/reject each purchase. Some banks are conservative, others go with the odds and provide a wide range of authority for Visa/MasterCard. Whatever happens, the results should be tracked and changes made to your rules if your results indicate you have been too tight or too loose.

Authorization is primarily a concern for credit cards and travel and entertainment (T&E) cards. In the case of an advance of funds for a customer writing a
check on a check-access account, the decision is relatively simple. If the line is still
available and the account is not seriously delinquent, the advance will be
approved; if not, the check will not clear.

One final issue for all credit card and revolving credit lines: When should
payment be credited, since checks can bounce (NSF, or insufficient funds). If a
payment is credited too quickly and thus increases the available line (i.e., the
"open-to-buy"), an account can quickly go over limit if additional purchases are
made (and authorized) and the payment check then bounces. Establish a realistic
time for checks to really clear!

Since virtually all credit card purchases can now be authorized/declined with
precision by the card issuer, balance control is an important part of the account
maintenance process. Tightly controlling the credit lines for customers and their
over-limit requests means increasing usage by good customers while curtailing
usage by the bads.

Balance Control

In Chapter 4, Acquiring Accounts, we discussed the importance of identifying and
achieving an appropriate target level of losses. This means controlling both the
account charge-off rate and the *amount* charged off in order to meet the credit loss
budget. A good score system(s) will help you achieve the targeted *number* of
accounts written off, but you need a process in place to control the average balances outstanding on all accounts in a portfolio in order to achieve the credit loss
budget goal.

As discussed earlier, a fundamental truism of revolving accounts is that bad
accounts tend to write off at, or slightly above, their credit lines, while good
accounts tend to maintain average balances well below their credit lines. This can
be seen in the following portfolio balance figures arrayed by delinquency:

Exhibit 6-6 shows a credit card portfolio with 30-day delinquent accounts
having balances 40% higher than accounts whose balances are current; the 60- and
90-day delinquent account ratios are even higher. If your charge-off balance ratio
goal is 1.3, this target has already been exceeded by accounts 30-days delinquent
(their ratio is 1.4) and even more by the more severely delinquent accounts. This
scenario is not unusual in the real world. As credit lines have grown larger to
attract customers (lines are frequently used as a marketing tool), the task of maintaining a reasonable target ratio has become more difficult. The problem can be
attacked on two fronts: by encouraging good customers to use more of their lines,
and by identifying potential bads early and discouraging/preventing them from
exceeding the target ratio goal.

The goal of balance control is to take action on accounts that are *current* but
have higher than normal average balances to determine whether they are getting

EXHIBIT 6-6
Typical Portfolio Usage

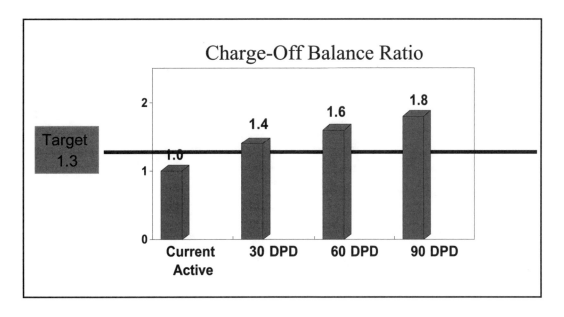

into trouble. This action should be taken as early as possible. The art of balance control management is to not irritate good customers (by premature aggressive action) while preventing risky accounts from growing. By segregating the portfolio and identifying accounts that appear to be running up higher balances, these accounts can be targeted for review as they exceed the average *current* balance, but before they go much higher.

It is critical to use a targeted behavior score to assess balance account risk and to identify the accounts for action. This includes getting information on these accounts from outside sources, including a current scored credit bureau report(s), to determine if the customer, while current with you, is getting into trouble with other lenders. If the account appears to be in difficulties as identified by a low score, this could be a signal for immediate action on your part. If justified by the size and potential profitability of the account, you might also ask the customer for updated information not available from the credit bureau (does he have a 401k account? any mutual funds?). This may not be worthwhile for a $850 balance credit card customer, but it may well be a good idea on a large line of credit or a long-term small business customer. Good balance control is critical to maintaining a profitable portfolio.

Retention Marketing

A well-run business follows its MIS on good accounts to determine if it is losing its best customers. If you see data like these, you are probably in trouble:

EXHIBIT 6-7
Account Retention

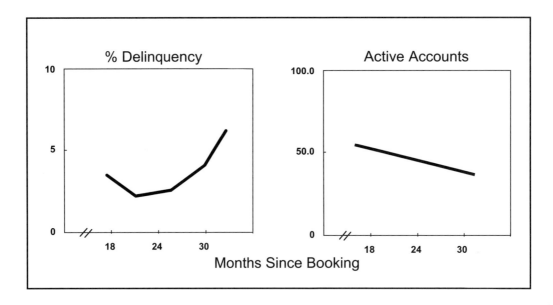

In the 1990s, balance consolidation (BalCon) programs, offering extremely low rates to encourage customers to switch their accounts to a new lender, became all the rage. Many customers who accept the mailed offer stay with the lender only while receiving the discounted promotional rate, then move on when the balance reverts to the full rate. Goods can always go to a competitor, with or without a promotional come-on; bads stay because they have no choices. In response to the sometimes alarming rate of attrition in credit card portfolios, it is vital for a business manager to identify the major reasons that the best customers are leaving and to work out programs to help slow down the loss of business. The questions to be answered include:

- *Why should the customer use your card or product, rather than a competitor's?*
- *Is your pricing so inflexible that your customers are stolen away by even a small price reduction?*
- *Are your lines of credit competitive, or have they been so carefully controlled that the competition has stolen your best customers?*
- *Is your handling of customer service complaints a problem? Can you afford to add enough resources so that a customer calling in will talk to a trained, knowledgeable person within a reasonable amount of time?*
- *Are you offering meaningful enhancements on your product, or are you annoying your customers by placing so many restrictions on the benefits that no one can take advantage of them?*

- *Are you waiting for customers to cancel their cards before trying to make them happy?*
- *Which customers should be offered additional products?*

There is rarely any one reason for a particular business to have a rate of attrition higher than normal. A detailed analysis of the reasons its customers leave must be prepared. Some lending institutions have specialized units to handle customers who cancel their accounts. In addition to offering benefits to try to keep customers, the representatives in this unit should also be detailing the reasons for cancellation so that the institution can identify and rectify the problems before annoying further customers. You should also be reviewing your products' features and enhancements regularly and emphasizing the ones that customers like the best.

ADDITIONAL STRATEGIES TO RETAIN YOUR GOOD CUSTOMERS

In addition to the strategies above, there are some other methods that can be used to retain good customers:

1) Reward customers who travel. High-spending customers who travel a lot are a good target market for special action. You should be able to identify hotel, airline, and rental car charges, both at home and away from home. If there is little or no record of such usage, your customers may be using a competitor's card to make these arrangements; they may never think of using your card because its line limits are so small, or there is little reward if they do use it. For these top-of-the-line customers, a targeted mailing, or a telephone contact, offering a special fare offer or another travel reward, may bring their business to you.

2) Grant an immediate line increase. Sometimes a customer will discover that they have reached the top of their credit line only after making a purchase which is rejected at a crowded checkout counter. With a good authorization process in place, this embarrassment can be avoided by an on-the-spot line increase. The decision should be based on a well-tested, automated review process, typically including the current score, but some human intervention may be necessary in marginal cases. Resolving casual or inadvertent over-limit charges by good customers can help you retain your better customers.

3) Change terms and conditions. Lenders have increasingly begun using a change in the terms and conditions of revolving products to reward good behavior (low risk/high usage) and to penalize poor behavior. Few customers object to having their pricing reduced, being awarded a skip-payment, or having fees waived. Surprisingly, there may also be few objections if the opposite occurs (e.g., pricing is raised, extra fees imposed, etc.) as long as those selected for such action are carefully selected and are given appropriate notification. After all, these people really need credit and some just need time to get on their feet again after a temporary dislocation in their lives. Price is not the problem for these customers; continuing availability of credit is. Pricing for risk at the time of application/solicitation is not new. Stratifying pricing and terms for existing customers—making riskier accounts pay for the risk while attempting to keep the best customers from moving to a competitor solely because of price—makes good sense today.

CROSS-SELL PROGRAMS

As noted earlier, a financial institution has an excellent opportunity to improve its profits for little extra cost if it can encourage its customers to increase, lengthen, or deepen the current relationship with existing or additional products. For instance, it makes sense to target your good customers with a new offer of credit six months or so before a boat loan, an auto loan, or a lease car program matures. This can keep a customer from migrating to the competition. Some lenders send a pre-approved check to selected customers, good for the purchase of an automobile or a boat at any authorized dealership, after making the appropriate updated credit check (including getting a current bureau score). Surprisingly few institutions actually take advantage of this type of cross-selling. The area of cross-selling is a fertile field for marketing. There is no harm in contacting customers, thanking them for the business already received, and rewarding them with an offer of further credit—provided, of course, that you have the tools to separate the good customers from the bad.

One more important item to cover in account maintenance is control of fraud.

CONTROLLING FRAUD

The war between fraud perpetrators and lenders is constant, but financial institutions have come a long way in the struggle. Both major card associations and the other card issuers (e.g., American Express, Discover Card) are very active in trying to identify and provide advice and direction to control fraud in the credit

EXHIBIT 6-8
Card Fraud (Worldwide)

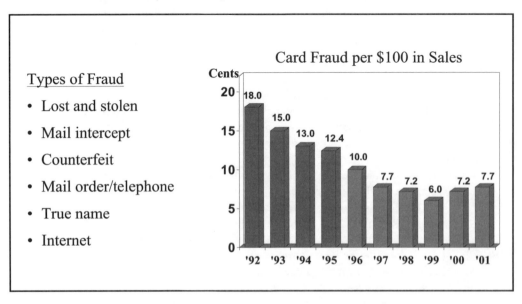

card industry. Although the line between fraud and writeoffs is not always easy to discern (e.g., is a series of new charges, just prior to bankruptcy, fraud, or should it be classified a writeoff?), fraud is typically defined as the deliberate purchase of goods or services on credit with no intention of repayment. Frequently, fraud is perpetrated by rings of criminals who steal cards, counterfeit cards, use false data to obtain loans . . . in fact, use every trick in the book to defraud lenders. While fraud losses in the credit card business are down to less than one half of the level of ten years ago, as shown in Exhibit 6-8, the total number still adds up to more than $1 billion a year in the U.S. alone.

Following are definitions for the major types of fraud:

1) **Lost and stolen:** *A valid card is lost or stolen and used by an unauthorized person.*

2) **Mail intercept:** *A new card is stolen while in transit to the authorized owner.*

3) **Counterfeit:** *Valid-appearing cards are manufactured.*

4) **Mail order/telephone:** *An account number is used by an unauthorized person.*

5) **True name:** *A card is obtained by using another person's good name, Social Security number, etc., but with a false address.*

Because most unauthorized charges made on lost, stolen, intercepted, etc., cards at retail outlets appear legitimate, the cost must be absorbed by the issuing financial institution. As long as the merchant has followed the appropriate authorization procedures, these transactions cannot be charged back to the merchant; however, fraudulent mail order charges often can be charged back, at least those where there is a customer complaint; remember, not everyone reviews their bill in detail every month, and sometimes small/infrequent fraudulent charges may not be noticed by a legitimate cardholder. After all, the goods must be shipped somewhere so the perpetrator can pick them up. If this address is different from the legitimate customer address on file, there are grounds for a charge-back. Catalog issuers recognize this as a cost of doing business, and the extent to which they check whether the address is correct depends on how hard they have been hit with fraud in the past.

In the past, control of fraud was left to specialists with backgrounds in police work. These professionals, who often had close contacts with local enforcement officials and federal agencies such as the FBI, worked to identify the pattern of violations by professional rings and then devised ways to control it. Individual fraud was usually isolated and manageable, but the major rings wreaked havoc through massive and repeated schemes. As technology improved (e.g., the electronic verification of virtually every transaction, the introduction of holograms to forestall counterfeiting, and current improvements in the use of magnetically encoded data), so did the ingenuity of the criminals. Because of the dollars involved, the war will never end, but it is hoped that losses at least will not increase to the levels of the past. The very fact that the bad guys know a strongly concerted effort is being made to control fraud helps to deter them. If it were easy to create fraudulent transactions, there would be millions more.

Because fraudulent card usage so closely resembles usage by a good customer (at least at first), control of fraud is now being assigned more and more to the risk management area. The purpose is to help line managers develop policies and procedures which avoid turning off good customers (with excessive controls) while still quickly identifying fraudulent usage.

The three keys to controlling fraud are 1) the introduction of tight controls over every phase of card issuance and transaction authorizations; 2) the ability to generate, analyze, and act on timely, worldwide transaction data; and 3) the continuing introduction of technology to help offset the professional thieves. Some lenders have found neural net score systems, with their ability to identify the pattern of a string of charges, very useful in the early identification of fraud (see Chapter 3, Scoring, for a fuller discussion of neural nets).

THE ART OF FRAUD CONTROL

A friend told me about an extremely impressive example of fraud control. American Express called to ask if she had recently made some out of town charges; she answered no. Although she still had the card—a corporate card used extensively for business travel—in her possession, the recent usage was suspect. Someone had made three purchases, all for gasoline and in a short period of time, totaling about $60. The Amex fraud detection system picked up the abnormal pattern of usage. How often do you charge three tanks of gas in one day? Not very often. The perps were probably testing the card, but very stupidly, it turned out. When my friend did not recognize the charges, Amex immediately shut down the card and re-issued another one.

One key point: the faster fraudulent usage can be identified, the faster the card can be shut down and losses controlled. Following are some of the daily steps essential to controlling fraud on existing accounts:[5]

- *Lost and Stolen: Identifying out-of-pattern spending—the number, dollar amount, and type of all new charges by merchant/location, particularly on new accounts.*

- *Counterfeit: Placing verification digits on the card's magnetic strip and the account master file . . . not on the card face itself.*

- *Mail order/Internet: Authorize only to recognizable card member address; the merchant is responsible under "card not present" rules.*

- *Establishing clear start/stop dates on each new/renewed card.*

---

5. Steps to control fraud when accounts are acquired were covered in Chapter 4, Acquiring Accounts.

Someday personal identification numbers (PINs) may be required at the point of sale to confirm the identity of the person making the charge, similar to the requirements for debit and automatic teller (ATM) cards. This would be another powerful weapon in controlling all but the most determined frauds, but will customers and merchants be able to tolerate the slower approval process? Only time will tell.

TEST AND CONTROL GROUPS

The value of any retention marketing, cross-sell, line increase, or change-in-terms decision can be improved by testing. If a financial institution develops a plan to, say, increase lines for a selected group of accounts meeting its basic criteria, how can it know if this strategy is the best one possible? Can it be improved? If *all* accounts meeting one set of criteria are treated alike, the organization will never know the answers to these questions. The basic concept of devising strategies, testing them, and then using the results to further refine processes relies on having a control group upon which no action is taken. Only then can you compare the test and control portfolios to be sure that any changes in the test group are a result of the test strategies.

Control groups look exactly like the test group, e.g., in terms of average balance, the time of analysis. Statistical tests are run to ensure that both groups are statistically alike.

When running a test, it is helpful to articulate a set of hypotheses, similar to a forecast, about what is expected. Following is a sample:

	Test Group	*Control Group*
Average Balance	$1103	$1083
Action	Increase lines by $1000	None
Hypothesis	Revenue will increase by 20%	No change
	Delinquency will increase by 18%	
	Writeoffs will increase by 22%	
	Profits will increase by 30%	

The results of this test must be reviewed in great detail. The sample analysis below shows that while the test succeeded (the average return on assets rose 36%), performance varied widely *within* the test group. To gain more information, the test group had been divided according to the percentage of line used before the increase program was instituted.

EXHIBIT 6-9
Credit Limit Increase Analysis

Credit Limit Increase Analysis
9 Months Later

				Original Balance as % of Credit Line					
				<25%		25-75%		>75%	
	Test Group	Control Group	Change	Test Group	Change	Test Group	Change	Test Group	Change
Average Balance	1431	1097	30%	275	175%	1750	35%	1950	15%
Avg Net Revenue	139	119	17%	19	90%	165	20%	207	9%
Operating Costs									
- Collections	13	10	30%	2	300%	15	30%	20	21%
- Other	75	75	0%	75	0%	75	0%	75	0%
Writeoffs	28	21	33%	4	100%	34	39%	40	21%
Total Expense	116	106	9%	81	5%	124	12%	135	8%
Profit per account	23	13	77%	-62	8%	41	52%	72	10%
ROA	2.14	1.58	36%	-30.06	-67%	3.12	15%	4.92	-4%

As shown, the customers who had some need of a higher credit line—those whose original balance was in the middle of the range (they used between 25–75% of the available credit line)—improved profits the most. This means that enough goods responded to the offer to offset the anticipated increase in collections and writeoffs. This was not the case for the original low-balance accounts; while some in the group responded to the increase offer, the increased usage by the goods could not offset the materially negative impact on profits because of the high collections and writeoffs associated with the few high-risk accounts that took full advantage of the offer. And while the heavy credit users also responded (they were already using >75% of their lines), this cohort also had a negative impact on profits. If this line increase program were to be rolled out to additional customers, based on this MIS the rollout should be limited to those using 25–75% of their current line. If more detailed MIS is available, you might be able to target the line increase program even more specifically.

The possibilities for applying test and control strategies to portfolio management decisions are almost endless. All lenders should, therefore:

- *Limit the number of strategies tested to a manageable figure.*
- *Give the strategies time to work.*
- *Really monitor the results.*
- *Be sure the control group is of sufficient size and statistically similar to the test group so that results can be read accurately to be used predictably.*

When a lender can finally demonstrate that its programs are successful, there should be no room for doubt that the test was impartial, objective, and thorough.

In the next chapter we cover how to handle accounts that start to go bad and require proactive handling. We call the subject collections.

Collection Strategies

U P TO THIS POINT we have concentrated on the process of planning a consumer lending business, acquiring accounts, and maintaining them. If you have done the job well, *most* of the active accounts will pay their bills on time, either by paying in full every month or by making a large enough payment to stay current. Some accounts, however, will become mildly delinquent (once in a while or repeatedly), some will become severely late in their payments, and some will go to bankruptcy or charge-off. Collections is a vital part of managing consumer credit and every lending institution needs a collections unit to deal with these problem accounts. This chapter will give some strategic guidelines for managing the collection process; in the next chapter we will cover the day-to-day management techniques required to execute these strategies.

Imagine, for a moment, designing a credit product with no collection department (think of the money you would save). You would quickly recognize the need to select your customers very carefully, for instance, choosing only those from the "A" and "B" score ranges . . . or possibly only the highest-scoring accounts. This would certainly reduce the size of your target market, the number of accounts you could book, and your writeoffs. But would it also reduce your profits because you are unable to get enough good and marginally good accounts to build a real business? Would you just become a small player in a big league, watching your competitors grow at your expense?

To summarize, if you remember only one thing from this chapter it is that:

An organization with a strong collection capability can gain a strategic advantage over the competition by being able to accept higher-risk customers; that is, it can go deeper into a highly competitive marketplace in search of business!

Innovative lenders, particularly those who are growing their portfolios, view collections as an opportunity to outdistance their competition. It is a fact of lending that in order to grow your portfolio, you must be prepared for growth in your delinquents, the subset of accounts that is not paying as well. This means adding collectors, training them, and planning for the technical resources needed to handle the workload *in advance* of the actual acquisition campaign. You must take the time to prepare collections for the onslaught of new business, particularly with a risky target market.

The delinquent portfolio differs from the portfolio as a whole, and has the following characteristics:

- *While human intervention is the exception in managing accounts which are current, human intervention is the rule for managing the delinquent portfolio; this can be expensive.*
- *The likelihood of obtaining payment(s) from a delinquent customer depends heavily upon the actions you take during the collection phase.*
- *Because collections is heavily people dependent, good management and leadership really matter.*

How important is the collection process? Once accounts are on the books, collection costs and writeoffs account for nearly 90% of the operating costs for a credit card portfolio. For this reason, a relatively small change in collection performance can cause a major improvement (or deterioration) in profitability. With collections having such high leverage on the profitability of your portfolio, it seems evident that collections simply *must* be a core competency of lending.

First, let's look at an overview of the collection process and define a few of the important terms used.

EXHIBIT 7-1
Collection Process

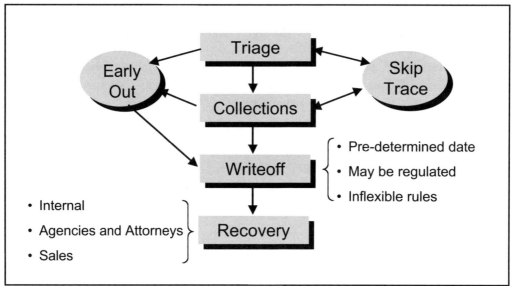

We use the medical term *triage* to describe early-stage collection activity. During natural disasters or battles, patients are triaged, divided into three categories by doctors or emergency medical workers: those who are mildly injured and will live without immediate help, those who are unlikely to survive regardless of what you do, and those who will benefit from immediate medical intervention. Good medical practice prescribes working on the last group first.

A similar concept works well in the early stages of delinquency. Because the volumes can be huge, you need to sort the high-risk from the low-risk customers. Triage can be applied, even before an account becomes delinquent,[1] by categorizing the accounts as high and low risk (more about how to identify these high- and low-risk accounts later). You need to identify 1) those who will pay with no action on your part; 2) those who have no intention of paying; and 3) those who might not pay without action but can be persuaded to pay. To the extent possible, as we cover in the following pages, collection activity should be targeted to this last group.

The collections process continues with some early-stage collection accounts moving on to the next stage, which we call *collections*; hopefully these will only be 10 percent or less of the early-stage accounts. The accounts that move on, however, are a hard-core group who have now missed two or three payments. Getting them to pay will be difficult because most of them can't (or won't) pay . . . or at least they can't pay all their creditors because they do not have the money. Consequently, many (50–60% or more) of these later-stage accounts will eventually be written off (typically after 120–180 days past due); they become *writeoffs* for accounting purposes. Each product must have a stipulated, predetermined writeoff period; in the United States, banks are regulated in terms of when they must write off an account (e.g., for credit card lenders, this point is typically no later than 180 days past due; for other products, this can range from two months to fourteen months past due, but is most often 120–150 days).

It is, nevertheless, possible to obtain small amounts of money from these written-off accounts, months and even years, after they have been written off; balances paid after they have been written off the books are called *recoveries*. Recoveries occur as a result of collection activities by your internal collections unit, by outside attorneys or collection agencies, or through the sale of written-off accounts to companies that specialize in this type of business. *Early out* means accelerating an account from one phase of collections to another because of risk, e.g., sending a very-high-risk account to a lawyer when only 45 days past due. Finally, *skip tracing* refers to the process of finding customers whom you cannot initially locate.

---

1. Some lending institutions make a customer service call, sometimes out of the collections department, to ensure that a new customer has received his bill and is aware of the contractual terms for payment.

This is merely an overview of the complete collection picture; we cover each process in detail in the following two chapters.

DEVELOPING A COLLECTION STRATEGY

Developing a collection strategy is typically the responsibility of the risk manager, while executing the strategy is the responsibility of the collection manager. Our lead instructor on collections, Don Griffin, uses the term *Aim* to describe the strategic part of the process and *Fire* for the tactical part. Prior to starting a leading collection agency, Integratec, Don served as a colonel in the U.S. Army, which may account for the terminology.

Collections entail many strategic decisions: Whom do you want to contact? When do you want to contact them? At what point do you want to make an intervention—10 days past due, 45 days past due? How will you contact them (e.g., by phone, by mail)? How will you identify low- vs. high-risk customers?

EXHIBIT 7-2
Collection Decisions

Identifying what needs to be done	Getting it done
Strategic Decisions • How are accounts ranked for collection actions? • How do accounts flow through the process? • What payment options and methods should be employed? • How is work allocated across the organization? • What is the organizational structure? • What are its broad goals?	**Tactical Responsibilities** • Maximizing right-party contacts. • Maximizing payments -- both number and dollar amounts.

As we mentioned, here we cover the steps in developing a solid collection *strategy*; in the next chapter we cover the *tactical* steps needed to manage a collections organization.

Whom to Contact, and When

The earliest stages of delinquency, when customers have missed perhaps one or two payments, always constitute the majority of the delinquent portfolio. While early-delinquent account volume is very high, the vast majority of these early accounts will typically pay with little or no effort. So the early strategy must be to:

Concentrate your collection efforts on the accounts *least* likely to pay.

Placing the collection effort on the accounts *most* likely to pay, produces several negative results:

- *You waste time and money, since most of these people will pay on their own.*
- *You irritate good customers.*
- *You dilute your collection efforts, failing to concentrate your capability on the accounts that will yield to attention.*

On the other hand, the volume of accounts that are 60 days past due or greater—that have missed three or more payments and are in the collection stage—is, happily, much smaller. Unhappily, however, the vast majority of these accounts typically will *not* pay despite your best efforts to collect. So the later-stage collection strategy must concentrate the collection effort on those accounts *most* likely to pay. And, again, failure to do this has negative consequences:

- *You waste time and money by going after those who won't pay, no matter what you do.*
- *You frustrate your collection force with impossible tasks.*
- *You dilute your collection efforts by failing to concentrate your capability on the accounts where intervention can make a financial difference.*

While concentrating your efforts on the *least* likely to pay in the early stages of delinquency and on the *most* likely to pay in the later stages makes good sense, this has not been the traditional way that collection organizations have been run. Let's see what most collection operations look like today.

Exhibit 7-3 represents typical delinquent account volumes by "bucket" or stage of delinquency. First, some definitions of the terms used in the chart. Column one is the number of accounts in *Bucket 1,* those that have missed one payment due date and are therefore 1–29 days past due/delinquent. The last column, marked *Charge-Off,* is the point at which the lender declares the loan a loss and "charges off," or "writes off," the account. The term *Collection Effort* refers to working to obtain payments before charge-off; as already noted, *Recovery* means the efforts to get payment after the account has been charged off.

EXHIBIT 7-3
Traditional Collection Operations

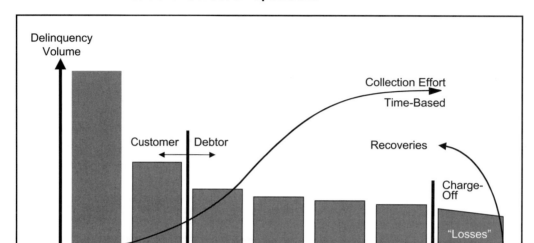

As pictured in the chart, the number of accounts in each stage of delinquency drops off quickly at first and then declines very little in the later stages of delinquency. At the late stages, the portfolio consists mainly of people who truly can't pay or are unwilling to pay. At some point, typically when an account reaches 60 days past due (by missing a third payment), lenders begin to view the account holder as a debtor rather than a customer. At this point the lender may change the collection objective from collecting the past due amount to collecting the full balance on the loan. At this stage of delinquency on a secured loan, the lending institution should begin warning the customer about the possible repossession of the automobile and the seriousness of the foreclosure process for a house.

The curve in the chart reflects the typical amount of effort by most lenders to collect their past due accounts (and what it feels like to be a customer in terms of the pressure brought to bear by the collections operation). In the earliest stage of delinquency many lenders employ their least experienced collectors and supervisors; account loads per collector may be as high as 1,000–2,000, and generally, collectors apply a light touch. Just before charge-off, however, these same lenders typically allocate their most experienced collectors and supervisors, provide them with low account loads per collector (say, in the 250–350 range), and give them more freedom to "make a deal."

On the surface, this picture seems logical enough from the lender's point of view, but let's look at it from the customer's point of view. When consumers get into financial trouble, it typically affects their ability to pay on multiple financial obligations; this usually results in collection calls from several different creditors. Someone in financial difficulty may be getting collection calls about the mortgage, car payments, utility bills, credit cards of various types, doctor bills, student loans, installment loans, and even taxes. Additionally, when a consumer with multiple obligations gets into financial difficulty, he has a certain priority of payment . . . which bills he will pay first, which last, which not at all. When does he make these *pay/neglect* decisions? Since bills typically come once a month, the consumer is forced to decide within 30 days of being short on funds. In sum, he at least mentally starts sorting bills into either the "pay pile" or the "neglect pile" very quickly. And the skill required of a collector to *change* a consumer's mind—to pay one account over another once the decision has been made—is much more difficult than influencing the initial decision. Putting these points together gives us two important principles of effective collection practices:

Collections is a very competitive business! You must distinguish yourself to become the payment of choice.

***And*, you must be the first call to influence the customer's pay/neglect decision.**

Each consumer has her own priority of payments. When we ask participants at our seminar "which bills will you pay first?" they invariably answer home mortgage payments. From there it varies somewhat, but taxes usually rate high, along with auto loans and utility bills. Doctors and dentists usually rank around the bottom, along with student loans. Credit cards are typically somewhere in the middle, but when customers have more than one card (and most do; the average number of cards per household is five or six), one card may be ranked high and the rest low. Consumers know the importance of having at least one card if they have to travel or have special needs.

While the above priority of payments is typical, there are always exceptions. For instance, people living in a major metropolis, such as New York City or San Francisco, may put an auto loan at the bottom of their list—after all, public transportation is an acceptable alternative in these cities. People in Jacksonville or Columbus, on the other hand, can't go to or from work, or get groceries or other vital services without a car (possibly two, one for the husband and one for the wife), so automobile payments rate very high in those places. Some people see that if they don't pay the mortgage, they can pay a lot of other bills. We have also found very different priorities abroad. In Colombia, taxes rated at the bottom of the list, doctors at the top. There is no one simple answer. People will always have a built-in priority about which bill to pay first and which last when they get into financial difficulty. As the lender you have to deal with this and remember that you have only a brief moment to distinguish yourself through collector skill and become the payment of choice.

Interventions can be determined either by time in the process or severity of risk. The traditional collection process is time-based, building up in intensity over the six months or more that the account is in collections. The *number* of payments past due drives what collection action to take next. Often, the traditional process brings in the strongest collection tools late in the process.

Since, however, the accounts that will go to write-off are all in Bucket 1 at some point (except maybe bankruptcies), a better alternative is a risk-based process.

Identifying Low- and High-Risk Accounts

With a risk-based process, the first step is to triage the delinquent portfolio, identifying and segregating high-risk accounts for acceleration through the process. This process of segregating early-stage accounts into those who will "pay on their own" and those who need prompting can be done judgmentally or with scoring. There are clear early indicators that an account is at high risk of becoming a loss:

1)   *A low credit or collection score (more about scoring later)*

2)   *New accounts, say those on the books for less than three to six months, missing one or more payments (particularly "first install-ment—no pay" accounts)*

3)   *Accounts at or above the credit limit*

4)   *No phone contact with the customer after seven to ten days of attempts, including at night and on weekends*

5)   *One or more broken promises to pay or no promise to pay*

6)   *Returned mail*

7)   *High cash advances, particularly with a new account.*

High-risk accounts are placed with the best collectors and even sent to outside collection agencies or for legal action when risk is clearly high—the choice is based on the outcome of the last collection action, not simply on the passage of time. For instance, if the customer becomes abusive or hostile, there is little point in your collections department continuing to make call after call when it is obvious he is not going to pay you.

In many collections operations, with one or more of these indicators present, the collection response is to continue to call routinely and to increase intensity (at least perceived intensity) only as the account proceeds through later buckets. However, you cannot afford to wait until the next bucket to increase collection activity on these high-risk accounts; the account must be accelerated to more intense treatment regardless of the number of payments past due. More attention improves the odds of changing the customer's mind and eliciting payment.

Collection Scoring

Generic or custom scores can be developed to identify the highest-risk accounts among those that just became delinquent. Typically, these scores are based on customers' past payment behavior and demographics. For accounts that have been in the collection process for a month or more, however, a customer's payment probability no longer depends only upon the customer's own attributes; now the actions of the collections operation also affect the outcome. Scoring that takes into account collection actions is much more complex and has not been readily available, so the application of collection scoring has been limited primarily to the very earliest stage of delinquency. This may be changing with some of the work being done by Portfolio Management Associates and the Colorado-based consulting group NAREX.

Existing automated collection software (i.e., the software used to run auto dialers—see Chapter 8, Collection Tactics, for details on this topic) was written to support the traditional time-based collection process and has impeded the use of collection scoring; the software makes it cumbersome to move high-risk accounts out of their time-based buckets for accelerated handling. While a number of sophisticated (and expensive) collection scoring systems are on the market, as a result of the above factors, the *application* of these scores has not, typically, been very sophisticated. The predominant use of collection scores today is to determine on which of the first thirty days of delinquency an account is to be introduced to collection calls, after which all accounts are treated the same.

Following is a highly simplified picture of how collection scoring might be used to shift collection effort by relative risk in the early stages of delinquency.

EXHIBIT 7-4
Sample Collection Strategy

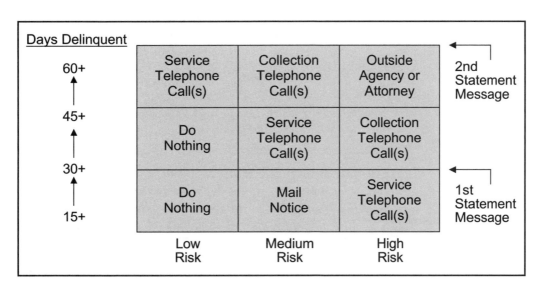

The next chapter covers what to say to customers once you have reached them by phone. There is, however, another strategic decision to be made when designing a collection operation: Where should the collectors be located geographically? (This decision impacts the organizational structure.)

Selecting Collection Sites

Large collection operations can choose the number, size, and location of their collection sites. This is a strategic decision with significant impact on both performance and costs. Some argue that local collectors, with the same regional accent as customers, will be more successful than collectors attempting to collect across the country. We believe that this advantage, if any, is small and have never seen it quantified. Most large collection operations are quite successful calling from multiple sites spread across the country, calling customers locally or in any other region.

One decision is how many sites to maintain. Obviously having a single site reduces costs by avoiding duplication of equipment and staff. A single site also makes management somewhat easier since only one location needs to be overseen. On the other hand, multiple sites have their own advantages. Among these are:

- *You have the ability to benchmark one site against another (although you can also do this within a site by having at least two groups compete on similar accounts).*
- *You have an emergency backup in case one site goes down.*
- *You avoid pressuring a local job market. In many markets, a collection site of around 300 people is about as large as can be sustained without stretching recruiting efforts . . . and is also a reasonable span of control for a site manager.*
- *You are able to put special functions, such as a bankruptcy control unit, in one site while relieving other sites of multifunction requirements.*

Other issues regarding site location include:

- *Avoiding areas with many other collection, telemarketing, or customer service operations (collectors may be available, but turnover and wage competition will be a problem).*
- *Choosing areas with military bases and colleges, which can provide a good source of talent but also, frequently, a high turnover rate.*
- *Having at least one site on the West Coast. The obvious advantage is being able to make calls to the East Coast or Midwest during the key early evening hours from a site where those are still "normal" working hours.*

Measuring Results

Another step to consider in this planning phase is measurement. How do you forecast your levels of delinquency and writeoffs? How can you evaluate the performance of the collections operation?

FORECASTING DELINQUENCY AND WRITEOFFS

The ultimate measurement of risk management is losses as a percentage of outstandings—in the past, currently, and most important, in the future. The earlier you can predict your future losses, the better chance you have to influence those results. This is particularly important if the projected losses are higher than expected. A powerful tool to forecast the performance of your portfolios and future losses is to follow the flow of delinquent accounts through each stage of delinquency, and ultimately through writeoff, and then to use this history to project the future. This reporting process is called the *net flow forecast* or, simply, the *roll rate*. The following chart illustrates how this forecasting tool works.

EXHIBIT 7-5
Sample : Net Flow

Month	Total	Current	30-59	60-89
Jan.	$720.6	$498.9	$171.1	$18.4
Feb.	742.1	515.6	34% → 169.6	9.6% → 16.4
Mar.	755.2	541.6	29% → 150.4	8.7% → 14.7
Apr.	772.1	547.5	31% → 169.3	9.8% → 14.7
May	781.3	551.5		

Receivables $'s in 000's

Roll Rate. The roll rate is the percent of account balances (or number of accounts) that "rolls" one month later to the next bucket or stage of delinquency. As shown above, the roll rate from current to 30–59 days past due has averaged about 30% for the past three months (Jan. to Feb. 34%, Feb. to Mar. 29%, and Mar. to Apr. 31%) and a bit over 9% from 30–59 days past due to 60–89 days past due. These historic roll rates can help forecast future delinquencies. For instance, we can estimate that the 30–59 day delinquencies will total about $164 million in May, based on the assumption that an estimated 30% of the current total in April will flow through or roll to May (30% x $547.5 = $164.3) and the 60—89 day delinquency will be *perhaps* 9.5% x $169.3 = $16.1. You estimate the percentage by looking at the past, factoring in current conditions (e.g., in April, people get tax refunds and may have some extra money to make payments), and using your own (or the collection manager's) experience. Used in this way, the roll rate is a reasonable predictor of *gross* writeoffs out to about six months in the future (see below for the computation of *net* writeoffs).

The roll rate has several disadvantages as a measure and predictor. Obviously, it is simply an average of past results with a bit of "guesstimating" of the future results added. It cannot anticipate and forecast fundamental economic changes, or changes in the number of consumers electing to take bankruptcy, or the fact that the marketing department changed the target market several months ago. Some of these problems can be mitigated by following "vintages" of business, that is, business put on with the same credit standards, in the same region, and at the same time. This will allow you to see that the problem is a portfolio of business acquired, for instance, through a new spring mailing campaign aimed at higher-risk customers, rather than the fall mailing to college students.

Migration Report. A more meaningful strategic *and* operational measurement is sometimes called a migration report, a delinquency matrix (DM), or "was-is" report. This report allows managers to analyze what is really happening to the delinquent portfolio by showing where the delinquent dollar balances (or number of accounts) in each bucket came from. For instance, it is possible to analyze the contents of Bucket 3 last month and where they are this month. Possible alternatives include:

a) *Made no payment—the account rolls to Bucket 4 (bad)*

b) *Made one payment—the account remains in Bucket 3 (OK)*

c) *Made multiple payments—the account moves back to an earlier bucket (best).*

This detailed type of MIS enables a manager to measure the effectiveness of the collections organization. Typically this is done by comparing similar portfolios assigned to different collectors . . . is one collections department getting a higher percentage of multiple payments? Is another recording a very high rate of "no payments"? This detailed method of analysis should be used by collection managers.

Net Writeoff. Up to this point, we have been talking about forecasting *gross* writeoffs; but standard management reporting (and accounting records) requires a *net* writeoff number because that is the figure included in your reported profits

EXHIBIT 7-6

(Kwik Kash—1999 and 2000 Total Portfolio)

		KWIK KASH					
		1999 Total Portfolio					
	Average	Writeoffs ($ 000's)				% Writeoffs	
	Receivable	Gross W/O	Bankrupt	Recovery	Net W/O	Current	Lagged*
JAN 99	$250,660	$215	$137	$64	$288	1.38%	1.40%
FEB 99	$237,618	$210	$138	$58	$290	1.46%	1.58%
MAR 99	$255,950	$222	$135	$57	$299	1.40%	1.39%
APR 99	$296,006	$203	$130	$60	$272	1.10%	1.21%
MAY 99	$319,334	$204	$178	$68	$314	1.18%	1.30%
JUN 99	$354,200	$228	$167	$73	$322	1.09%	1.86%
JUL 99	$385,194	$216	$238	$64	$391	1.22%	1.87%
AUG 99	$416,739	$218	$223	$57	$385	1.11%	1.94%
SEP 99	$459,268	$265	$227	$63	$429	1.12%	2.01%
OCT 99	$482,850	$494	$235	$70	$659	1.64%	2.67%
NOV 99	$514,065	$438	$350	$70	$719	1.68%	2.70%
DEC 99	$552,311	$595	$363	$78	$881	1.91%	2.98%
TOTAL 99	$377,016	$3,508	$2,521	$782	$5,249	1.39%	1.91%

		KWIK KASH					
		2000 Total Portfolio					
	Average	Writeoffs ($000's)				% Writeoffs	
	Receivable	Gross W/O	Bankrupt	Recovery	Net W/O	Current	Lagged*
JAN 00	$645,487	$786	$409	$77	$1,118	2.08%	3.48%
FEB 00	$623,725	$1,005	$532	$90	$1,447	2.78%	4.17%
MAR 00	$625,919	$1,242	$755	$97	$1,900	3.64%	4.96%
APR 00	$637,446	$1,936	$870	$125	$2,681	5.05%	6.66%
MAY 00	$646,776	$1,625	$986	$130	$2,482	4.60%	5.79%
JUN 00	$660,574	$1,803	$881	$126	$2,558	4.65%	5.56%
JUL 00	$664,292	$1,506	$868	$118	$2,256	4.08%	4.19%
AUG 00	$674,753	$2,053	$862	$126	$2,789	4.96%	5.37%
SEP00	$688,761	$2,395	$1,040	$124	$3,311	5.77%	6.35%
OCT 00	$678,824	$2,201	$1,391	$233	$3,359	5.94%	6.32%
NOV 00	$686,463	$2,456	$1,017	$233	$3,239	5.66%	6.01%
DEC 00	$697,415	$2,662	$1,013	$217	$3,458	5.95%	6.28%
TOTAL 00	$660,870	$21,671	$10,624	$1,696	$30,598	4.63%	5.52%

* Net W/O's as a % of receivable 6 months prior

(typically as part of the "reserve for writeoffs" calculation). Net writeoffs are determined by taking the *gross* forecast numbers and 1) adding in the estimated number of accounts/dollars that will go bankrupt over the next X months (remember, bankruptcies can occur at any stage of delinquency[2]), and 2) deducting the dollars recovered from accounts already written off. A completed forecast of net writeoffs for two years is shown in Exhibit 7-6.

LAGGED AND CURRENT REPORTING

One concept essential to forecasting and reporting on loss rates is that of *lagged* versus *current* reporting. The last two columns in Exhibit 7-6 include

---

2. There is no magic formula for estimating bankruptcies. I would base this estimate on the history of bankrupts in each state or judicial region (if possible), adjusted for the current trend.

two calculations of writeoffs each month. For example, in January 2000, the current w/o (writeoff) rate is 2.08%, the lagged is 3.48%. The underlying assumption is that a fast-growing (or rapidly declining) portfolio can distort reported loss rates. First, note the extreme differences between the lagged and current numbers for the last few months of 1999 and the first few months of 2000; note also the very rapid growth in the total receivables level: from $250 million in January 1999 to the $500–$600 million range just 12 months later. Reading just the current numbers, you would say this portfolio is performing well in 1999 (current writeoffs are in the 1–2% range); but the inherent rate of writeoffs is much higher than would be reported if you did not "lag" the results (look at the March 2000 results). Let's see how this works.

If your standard writeoff policy is to write off an account after 180 days past due, it takes six months for the account to age through the buckets (unless the account is written off early). Typically, writeoffs are calculated by annualizing the given month's writeoffs (or the year-to-date writeoffs) and dividing this figure by the total outstandings for the same month, calculated as follows:

EXHIBIT 7-7
Measuring Writeoffs

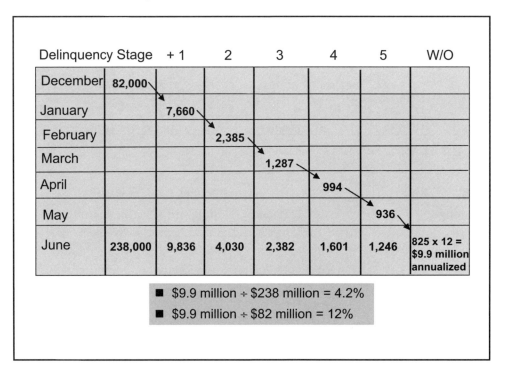

Delinquency Stage	+ 1	2	3	4	5	W/O
December	82,000					
January		7,660				
February			2,385			
March				1,287		
April					994	
May						936
June	238,000	9,836	4,030	2,382	1,601	1,246	825 x 12 = $9.9 million annualized

- $9.9 million ÷ $238 million = 4.2%
- $9.9 million ÷ $82 million = 12%

Using this method of calculation, the portfolio in Exhibit 7-7 wrote off $825,000 in June and reported an annualized writeoff rate of 4.2% (calculated as follows: $825,000 X 12 [months] = $9.9 million, divided by the total receivables for June of $238 million = 4.2%). But this is a very fast-growing portfolio. To get a clearer picture of the loss rate in such a case, one should compare the current month's losses with the outstandings six months ago (in this example, only $82 million), since today's writeoffs come from those outstandings. This is referred to as a "lagged loss rate." In a fast-growing portfolio, the result will typically be dramatically different and a much more realistic indicator of delinquency and losses.

In the above example, the lagged annual rate of writeoff is really 12% ($825,000 X 12 divided by $82 million = 12%). The sharp growth in total receivables in recent months buries the real truth. Many businesses have used the unlagged method of calculation to play games—to hide the truth for a period of time.[3] When growth ceases, all such games come to an end. Note that if you don't lag a shrinking portfolio, writeoffs are *overstated*. And lagged reporting adds nothing if the portfolio is stable.

This covers the management reporting of writeoffs. We will say more about the operational measurements of collections performance in the next chapter.

THE NEXT STRATEGIC BREAKTHROUGH?

Collections is a tough, demanding business. The weak of heart are in search of a black box solution that will suddenly improve collection results. Several years ago a black box solution seemed to be the predictive dialer, which keeps the collector supplied with a constant stream of calls and account information (see Chapter 8, Collection Tactics, for details). Dialers were a competitive advantage to those who had them until nearly all large collections operations obtained them. A similar result can be seen with the advent of collection scores—an initial competitive advantage, followed by a return to a level playing field in a very competitive business. And so it goes with hopes raised by Internet collections, home-based collectors, time-to-call software, and other approaches for converting collections into an easy endeavor.

Alas, no long-term black box solution will solve a task so heavily dependent upon individual collector skill. No investment in collection software, dialers, scoring, facilities, and so forth will distinguish your collection results if the collector lacks skill when the customer says "Hello." The winning strategy is to keep up with technological advances that work (not all of them do) while distinguishing your collection efforts from the competition with exemplary collector sales skill. In the following chapter, we address the tactical part of collections—the management of the people who carry out the actual work of collections.

---

3. Wall Street analysts, however, follow the lagged numbers closely.

SUMMARY PRINCIPLES FOR
THE RISK MANAGER

In conclusion, I would like to stress again the importance of using a risk/action-based collection strategy, that is, to focus your collection effort on accounts where good collection work will bring incrementally better results. Scoring can be a big help to target these accounts. Don't use a long, drawn-out, time-based collections process. With the right strategy in place, you can be the one to make the "first call" . . . important to becoming the payment of choice. As we have seen, the consumer makes pay/neglect decisions early; talking to the customer before that decision is firm and before your competition does provides a definite performance edge. Design your collection strategy to take advantage of these concepts.

Collection Tactics

F YOU HAVE FOLLOWED the concepts outlined in the previous chapter, you will have a clear idea of your strategic collection goals. You will have defined which accounts are to be contacted and when they should be called; you will have established good forecasting procedures; and you will have set up and staffed your collection sites. Now the goal is to get back the most money possible from your delinquent customers, cost effectively and, obviously, without violating any laws. Let's first address the steps necessary to manage your in-house collectors and then we will cover some of the steps in the management of outside collection resources.

In simplest terms, a collections operation starts by buying time from collectors. Labor is the major cost of the collections operation. Once collector hours are paid for, the rest of the collection job has two main components: *production* and *conversion.*

Production refers to the raw material of collections—namely, a phone contact with a delinquent customer. The objective is for collectors to be in contact with as many customers as reasonably possible during every paid collector hour. Obviously, increasing the number of contacts increases the probability of payment. Contact production is influenced by staffing levels, time and day of the week of calling, use of systems (including dialers), and workforce discipline. This is a production management function, not unlike an automobile assembly line. The senior management at the collection site usually exercises control of these aspects of the collection job.

The second dimension of the collection job, *conversion,* means turning customer contacts into payments. Conversion is skill-based, depending directly upon the call skills of the collectors. In turn, collector call skills depend directly upon the skills of first-line supervisors. Specifically, they depend upon first-line supervisors' being able to diagnose collector performance problems and to coach collectors in developing call skills. The tactical execution of the collection strategy by collectors is essentially telemarketing. It is relationship selling by phone with the objective of collecting money and returning delinquent customers to the profitable fold of the lending portfolio. Collections operations have many components—how to staff, what technology to use, how to organize workflow, how to manage compensation, etc.—but it is helpful to boil the job down to these two simple dimensions and to stay focused on what really matters in collections operations.

First, production and conversion are helpful divisions of management labor. Senior managers can focus on driving contact production such as dialer campaign design. At the same time, first-line supervisors can focus on improving and maintaining collector skills to produce as much money as possible from every customer contact—the main responsibility for first-line supervisors.

Obviously, achieving the best collection results requires competence and coordination in both areas of the task. Providing a low number of contacts to very skilled collectors will waste their skills and reduce the cost-effectiveness of the operation; on the other hand, a great contact production rate followed by poorly skilled collectors means that you will be very effective at sending bad messages to many customers!

Roger Willis, a well-regarded consultant to the collections industry, developed the concept of illustrating the key steps in getting from paid hours to payments as a pyramid, and Don Griffin has added his own details of the steps for this pyramid as follows:

EXHIBIT 8-1
The Roadmap to Payments

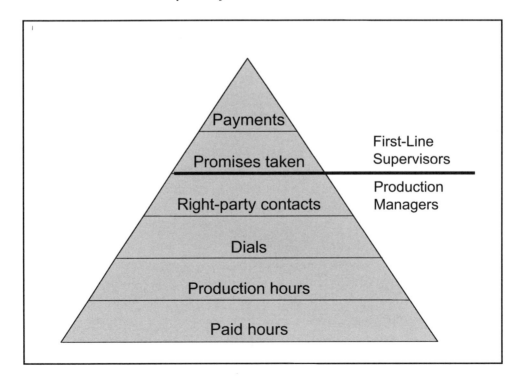

What to measure is always an issue in collection operations, because so many things can be measured (e.g., the number of collectors employed, their average monthly cost, number of calls made, etc.) that staying focused can be difficult. Simple MIS giving at-a-glance diagnostics are the most useful. As suggested at the start of this chapter, the heart of the collections operation is converting paid collector hours into customer payments. So, this "Roadmap to Payments" chart (Exhibit 8-1) is a good, first "instrument." For example, say one collection site produces $500 in customer payments for every paid collector hour and a second site working on similar accounts produces only $400; that is significant management information. The "Roadmap" allows management to peel the onion and see which components contribute to the difference. For example, is the difference between the two sites due to better production capability (the number of paid hours, production hours, dialers, and right-party contacts) or due to conversion capability, the sales skills as reflected by the number of promises taken and the number and amounts of payments received? This MIS can be a very powerful start to improving performance.

Assigning goals to each level of the pyramid in the above chart is a good start for a collections operation MIS. Further, these goals and measurements can be calculated at various levels: individual collector, a team of collectors, or the total collection site. For example, the following might be good weekly goals for lower-risk and higher-risk collection groups using predictive dialers:

	Low-Risk	High-Risk
Production Hours as % of Paid Hours	85%	85%
Contacts per Production Hour	10	5
Promises Taken as % of Contacts	85%	75%
Promises Kept as % of Promises Taken	65%	50%
Average Payment Size	$140	$100
Expected Value of a Paid Hour	$657	$159

(Sample calculation: 85% Paid Hours x 10 contacts/hr. x 85% promises x 65% promises kept x $140 average payment = $657)

The pyramid as diagnostic tool can also identify specific opportunities that can drive better results. For example, if a collector has a low average payment size, perhaps she needs help in negotiation skills. If another collector has a low percent of promises taken, perhaps he is easily brushed off by the customer's initial objections. With this information, the supervisor can work with the collector to try and improve the specific skill deficiency.

Let us now turn to collection operations tools and practices.

COLLECTION SYSTEMS AND DIALERS

Collections operations of any appreciable size operate on mainframes or PC networks using collection software, which may be a module of the loan system or stand-alone software. In either format, it typically provides:

- *Interface to the loan system*
- *Basic delinquent account information*
- *Allowance for collector notes*
- *Management reports such as roll rates and inputs to collection MIS.*

Large operations almost universally use predictive dialers, sometimes called auto-dialers. The dialer receives a download of delinquent accounts, sequences the accounts for calling based upon user-defined rules, and then uses a software algorithm to optimize calling. The algorithm attempts to predict the phone-dialing rate that will keep all collectors busy while also avoiding timing problems that cause customers to hold or hang up.

What the collector hears is a *beep* in his ear, immediately followed by a computerized collection screen on the customer who has just said "Hello." The collector wastes no time listening to the phone ringing, busy signals, or even answering machines, if this recognition feature is programmed. As soon as the collector finishes the call and releases the account, another customer is ready to be talked to. Experience indicates that concerns about collector burnout on a dialer are unfounded. When the dialer is properly run, collectors are kept busy doing what they are paid for, and their day goes by quickly, without boredom.

Following are some advantages of a predictive dialer. The overwhelming numerical superiority of the first two illustrate why large collections units must use a dialer.

- *Allows account loads of 1,000–2,000 accounts per dialer collector vs. a maximum of 300–350 with a manual system*
- *Makes over 100 attempted calls for every collector hour vs. a maximum of 120 attempts a day with a manual system*
- *Provides management with multiple ways to prioritize accounts*
- *Provides valuable performance reporting inputs*
- *Enables management to control the use of the optimum times when customers are at home since it can be programmed to call at these times for each different time zone.*

Predictive dialers have some inherent limitations:

- *The collector loses account "ownership." The next time an account needs to be contacted, the call will go to whichever collector is available.*

- *Dialers work well only on large volumes of accounts with large teams of collectors. For example, a dialer team of 25 collectors can handle more than 16,000 calls a day; with fewer collectors, the dialer begins to lose its predictive ability because the number of accounts it is handling becomes too small.*

Dialer effectiveness is highly dependent upon the production management skill of collection managers. Because of the need to balance the "hit" rate with the number of collectors on hand, a good production manager can have a significant impact on the number of hourly/daily customer contacts by studying detailed production numbers. It requires great skill to analyze how many delinquent customers are actually being contacted at every hour of the day (by region), how long each conversation takes, and then adjusting the speed of the dialer to maximize the collector's time spent actually "collecting."

Dialers can also be used in combination with manual dialing, as in the following example. During part of the day, a collection team might work on the dialer, enjoying its contact production advantages; for the remainder of the day, the collectors might work manually their own assigned accounts, typically those that have been identified as higher risk. It still is possible to use the dialer for this work in what is called the Preview Mode, but many operations revert to manual dialing with these difficult, high risk accounts because of the need to spend more time with them.

In summary, because of the enormous numerical advantage in number of calls placed, dialers are mandatory for a large collections operation—but to function well, they must be managed well. Starting with the length of time for a typical collection call, the manager must manipulate the algorithm so that collectors are not waiting for customers to come on line and customers are not hanging up because no one speaks when they answer the phone.

THE COLLECTION CALL

Collectors are most effective when they reach customers at home (rather than at work), and that makes collections work an off-hours business. Calling a customer at work is best left as a last resort, since calls to businesses take more time (e.g., going through receptionists) or may be prohibited by an employer's policy against personal phone calls.

The following table shows typical at-home-contact success rates during the calling hours permissible by the Fair Debt Collections Practices Act: 8 AM–9 PM in the customer's location (we will cover more on this collections act later in the unit).

Local Time for Customer		Customer Contact as % of Calls Made
Sunday	8 AM–9 PM	14%
Saturday	8 AM–9 PM	12%
Weekday	6 PM–9 PM	10%
Weekday	8 AM–10 AM	8%
Weekday	10 AM–6 PM	<5%

The best calling hours, or "Prime Time," are generally considered to be weekends and after 6 PM on weekdays. This obviously puts tough demands on recruiting and on front-line leadership, but many large lenders now have 70 percent of their paid collector hours during Prime Time. The benefits of converting your operations to Prime Time calling must be balanced with the need to attract and retain quality collectors. This is not a trivial leadership issue.

Once you have the appropriate policies to maximize the "hit rate"—that is, to actually talk to your customers—the essence of a skilled collections operation is the ability to sell on the phone. Today, telemarketing is so prevalent that we all have experienced what poor telemarketing sounds like. First and foremost, good sales skills cannot be scripted. Competent sales demand sincerity, and that cannot be achieved with a pitch that is memorized or read. The same is true for good sales skills for collectors.

"It says, 'Please disregard this reminder if your check is in the mail.'"

EXHIBIT 8-2

The Collection Call

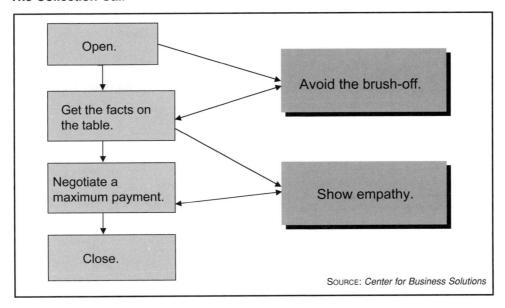

Open.

Get the facts on the table.

Negotiate a maximum payment.

Close.

Avoid the brush-off.

Show empathy.

SOURCE: *Center for Business Solutions*

Exhibit 8-2 is a diagram of six basic sales skills. This widely tested model is currently in use by many collectors in the United States and abroad. There are two keys to this collection sales model. First, collectors must be taught to use the model effectively, and second, the collector must be taught to listen . . . to allow the customer time to talk and to really hear what the customer is saying. If the collector listens effectively, the customer will tell the collector at each step of the call which skill to use next. For instance, if the customer sounds depressed because of financial problems, the collector must show empathy. If he says he's in a hurry and can't talk, the collector must avoid being brushed off. If she says she can only pay X amount, the collector must negotiate to ensure getting the maximum amount the customer can afford.

It is not our purpose here to teach sales skills. Our purpose is to suggest that the following are critical to collector skill:

- *To distinguish your collection efforts from your competitors', the level of sales skill to be mastered is not trivial.*

- *These skills cannot be learned effectively through on-the-job-training, that is by having a new collector sit with and listen to an experienced collector.*

- *Teaching these skills solely via classroom lecture may elicit bright-eyed head-nods but will not result in skill mastery; mastery is assured only when the collector learns by doing, i.e., by practicing and demonstrating the skill in tough simulations.*

- *Skills will be sustained and improved only when first-line supervisors have the call skills themselves, as well as the diagnostic and development skills to improve collector performance.*

In most organizations, collector training consists of a week or two of classroom work, with much attention to how the collection software works, and little attention to specific collection selling skills. The "go sit by Mary and watch what she does" on-the-job training approach is prevalent. There is usually no meaningful call skill development program or periodic testing process. Coaching from supervisors sounds like, "Tom, your results are bad. You've got to do better!" Training is relegated to the training staff, and managers don't view their role as teachers. Yet collector skill is one of the two critical dimensions of collection success (contact production being the other).

Collectors need training on how to make a collection call, and this training must involve many roleplays so that collectors are comfortable handling all phases of the call. As noted earlier, if MIS such as The Roadmap to Payments (Exhibit 8-1) is used after initial training, the supervisor can identify where in the calling process a collector is having problems. Are payments too small? Maybe the collector needs help improving her negotiating skills. Are too few promises taken? Maybe the collector is being brushed off, or has difficulty showing empathy, thereby angering people. By roleplaying with the collector or listening to live calls, the supervisor can identify the specific problem and then work with the collector to improve performance.

ALTERNATE COLLECTION PRACTICES

By now you will have noticed that all the collection activity we describe entails the use of the telephone. While mail is used to bill customers and to notify them of the current status of their account (including any payments past due), the telephone remains the instrument of choice for communicating problems with the account. At least this is true in the United States and other developed countries. In other parts of the world, personal visits are quite common. In one overseas country where I managed a loan portfolio, we would send a collector out Monday morning on a several-hundred-mile route to pick up payments from all the automobile loan customers in his region. On Friday night he would return with whatever payments he had collected and a list of those who had not paid. This trained our customers to make a payment only when personally visited. Of course, the timing of this visit could vary and the customer might not be at home when the collector called—all of which provided a convenient excuse in the event the customer did not wish to pay. It was an expensive way to collect, and I do not recommend personal visits except in the most extraordinary cases, such as repossessing a delinquent auto (as we cover later).

Recently the *Wall Street Journal* reported a most unusual collection practice. The article described a Venezuelan debt collector who visits deadbeat accounts with a hot-rod truck armed with sirens and pulsating dome lights. After the truck pulls up in front of the debtor's house or business office, a hulking man wearing a devil's mask, a woman in a red miniskirt, a four-foot-tall Great Dane, and a business-suited lawyer, all accompanied by a TV news crew, attempt to contact the debtor, shouting out, "You have an appointment with Dr. Diablo." This "Mobile Anti-Deadbeat Crew" is apparently highly effective, but it is used only with delinquents who have already been notified that they are "late," "super late," or "ultra late." I am not recommending this approach, only suggesting that collection practices differ throughout the world. Indeed, in the U.S., the Fair Debt Collection Practices Act specifically forbids the humiliation or harassment of debtors.

SPECIAL COLLECTION TASKS

Next let's cover some special tasks that lie outside the day-to-day routine of collection management.

Skip Tracing

Skip tracing means locating phone numbers and addresses of delinquent customers whom the lender has "lost." Experience shows that up to one-quarter or more of the accounts written off in any month are accounts that the collections operation did not talk to during the preceding sixty days. "Skips" are obviously a serious loss problem.

Prevention is the best solution. It is helpful to design the loan application to capture several phone numbers, including, where possible, those of close family members. Customer service calls also are a good time to confirm current phone numbers and addresses.

A decade ago, the general practice for skip tracing was for a collector or skip tracer to ask contacts at other lenders, sometimes identified through credit bureau reports, if they had a good address or phone number. Naturally, this was a time-consuming endeavor with little hope of success. Many lenders discovered through experience that locating skips is difficult and that a skip, when found, is still unlikely to pay.

The best skip-tracing operations include the following steps:

- *Using the dialer in the very first stages of delinquency to identify accounts that have not been contacted in, say, a week of effort.*

- *Using automated tracing services (including Internet search tools) to locate customers without expensive human intervention.*

- *Using relatively lower-skilled people to search the account opening file or the lender file. Tests have shown that approximately 20 percent of skips can be found in the lender's own files, through another account relationship or through correcting a data entry error.*

- *Sending accounts still not located to collection agencies to collect (not just find) for a contingency fee; do not wait to do this until it is time to write off the account.*

If you find that 30–50% of the high-risk collector workload is skips, this is very bad news. It may indicate that the application process needs revising. Also, a heavy volume of skips in the later stages of delinquency clogs the collector workflow with accounts that, even if found, are extremely unlikely ever to pay. The good news with skips is that those found with the least effort are most apt to pay. Using the easy but effective steps *early* offers a high percentage of payoff at low cost.

Account Rearrangement Options

How much leeway will you give your collectors to negotiate a change in payment terms—for example, to lower monthly payments, to defer payments, and in some cases to accept a lower total repayment—for customers who are *willing*, but *unable* to pay? True hardship cases of a temporary nature (where the customer cannot pay now but has reasonable prospects of beginning to pay again in a few months) can rarely be brought current by repeated calls. In fact continued calls may be counter-productive, irritating the customer with good intentions but no immediate ability to pay. Lenders need a policy regarding hardship accounts; all entail renegotiating the original terms of the loan. The purpose, obviously, is to keep the good customer on the books through a lean or difficult period that is preventing him from making payments.

Any renegotiation must be governed by a written approval policy from the senior management level. The policy should address the types of renegotiation possible, the circumstances under which renegotiation should be considered, what factors the customer must satisfy to qualify for renegotiation, and what supervisory approvals are necessary. In addition, these programs should be closely monitored to avoid abuse.

Some examples of renegotiation programs are:

Rewrites: The rescheduling of a debtor's obligations (usually with lower monthly payments and over a longer term than originally contracted) to allow a better match between the payment due and the debtor's ability to pay.

Extensions: On an installment loan, one or more payments may be deferred until after the original contract has reached term.

Partial payments: To reduce collection expenses, some acceptable percent of the total due (say, 90% of the minimum contracted payment) is considered sufficient to keep an account from moving into a higher stage of delinquency. This practice prevents accounts that may only be a few dollars short (or even a few pennies short) from being dunned needlessly.

Settlements: Every credit business should have a policy that empowers the collector, with specific management approval, to settle for less than the full balance. The policy should define the maximum percentage of debt that can be forgiven and the earliest point in a delinquency when a settlement may be used (e.g., >150 days past due).

Tracking

Renegotiated accounts should be tracked separately, since they are considerably riskier than regular accounts. If not tracked and controlled carefully, they entice collectors to overuse these methods. It is not unusual for as many as 50 percent of renegotiated accounts to become delinquent again after another three or four months. An increase in renegotiated accounts could result from a deliberate policy to reduce collection activity to save money. On the other hand, it could represent a gradual but steady trend toward laxness in collections department procedures, including avoiding writeoffs to meet short-term goals. The latter, of course, only postpones the day of reckoning and is never a legitimate reason for renegotiation.

One other tip for a collections operation: Remove accounts from collections that are several months delinquent but have now made two or three minimum monthly payments in a row (preferably three). Many lenders "re-age" these accounts automatically on their collection system. That is, the system recognizes two or three consecutive payments and returns the account to a current status. Because such accounts have returned to a regular payment pattern, there is no point in retaining them in collections even though they are technically still delinquent; the missed payments simply remain part of the unpaid loan balance, to be paid at a later date.

MANAGING BY ROLL RATES—A WARNING

In the last chapter we described how using net-flow models (the percentage of accounts flowing or rolling from bucket to bucket monthly) helps a lender understand and forecast collection performance and writeoffs. The roll rate, while a good *strategic* measurement, can actually be harmful as an operational performance measure. For example, if the order is given to reduce the roll rate at the collection center or the collector level, the easiest solution is for collectors to ask for minimum monthly payments and no more. Further, they could offer to accept a partial payment. Any payment (minimum or partial) will hold an account in its present stage of delinquency but will not reduce the delinquency workload . . . and in fact will increase the risk for the future. This example of What You Measure Is What You Get can result in collectors telling a customer, "Don't send me $100, just send the minimum monthly payment of $50; we'll need the other $50 next month."

PERSONAL BANKRUPTCY

Bankruptcy has become a major fact of life in the lending business. Some credit card portfolios attribute 40–50% of their writeoffs to bankruptcy, a figure up from the 15–20% range in the early 1980s. The rate on large lines of unsecured credit is even higher, sometimes exceeding 60%. Once written off, bankrupt accounts traditionally offer little chance of recovery since, typically, 75% of consumer bankruptcies are under Chapter 7 of the bankruptcy statute, which essentially sets aside *all* the consumer's debt. The remaining filings, under the Chapter 13 statute, which requires a repayment plan for at least a portion of the debt, usually result in creditors receiving a payment much reduced from the original debt.[1]

Bankruptcy Code

Let's review the current U.S. bankruptcy code. The Bankruptcy Reform Act of 1978 outlines the choices open to creditors and debtors alike. Three chapters of the act, Chapters 7, 11, and 13, apply primarily to consumers.

- *Chapter 7 is for people with few or no assets beyond, say, an automobile or a heavily mortgaged home. The debtor is legally free of his debts except the few that cannot be discharged in bankruptcy (e.g., most taxes due within the past three years, child support, alimony, and most student loans). Certain basic assets can be kept, including a specified amount of equity in a home or car and most IRA and pension savings. Some states are very restrictive on the amount of assets that can be retained, while others (notably Texas and Florida) allow very valuable homes and sometimes land (up to 160 acres) to be kept. The remaining or uncovered assets can be sold to help pay creditors. Typically, creditors recover almost nothing when an account enters Chapter 7 bankruptcy.*

- *Chapter 13 allows people who are overcommitted but have a steady source of income to work out a repayment plan. Typically, the creditors are paid a specified portion of the money owed over a period of time (e.g., 10—20% over three to five years). The agreement is worked out with the aid of lawyers, and a trustee is appointed to administer the plan. Chapter 13 cannot be used if the unsecured debts are over $100,000 and if the secured debts exceed $350,000, in which case a Chapter 11 filing is appropriate.*

- *Chapter 11, long used by businesses, was approved for consumers in 1991. It is similar to Chapter 13 in that the debtor and creditors agree upon a workout plan. However, a Chapter 11 filing is typically more expensive and involved due to the larger assets involved.*

---

1. As this book is going to press, both houses of Congress have passed different versions of a new bankruptcy bill; both versions require more people with identifiable assets to file under Chapter 13. While the final bill may reduce some of the abuses associated with bankruptcy filings in the past, no one can predict what will be included or what the President will sign. (6/02)

Different Rates of Bankruptcy

Going into bankruptcy no longer carries the stigma it once did. It has even become socially acceptable, particularly in certain parts of the country, and lawyers now advertise their expertise in handling bankruptcy. A research project conducted a few years ago by Purdue University's Credit Research Center indicated that nearly 25% of people electing to take bankruptcy could have met their obligations. Although bankruptcy is an accepted fact of life today, there is a wide variance in the rate of bankruptcy by state, by county, and by court jurisdiction. Following is a summary of bankruptcy rates in the ten states with the highest and lowest rates, with the remaining 40 states arrayed between. While the vast majority (71%) of all bankruptcies are administered under Chapter 7, note that states differ in the way that debtors take advantage of the alternatives.

EXHIBIT 8-3
Bankruptcy by State

Bankruptcy Rate/Per 100 Households

High States	2001	Chap. 13	Low States	2001	Chap.13
Tennessee	2.85	53%	New York	.98	18%
Utah	2.78	35	Minnesota	.93	17
Nevada	2.63	25	Connecticut	.92	13
Georgia	2.43	59	Massachusetts	.74	13
Alabama	2.32	55	Vermont	.71	9
National Avg.	1.43	29%			

A 1999 study by SMR Research Corporation finally put to rest some of the conjecture about why there is such variance by state. It pointed out that while there was little correlation between the unemployment rate and debt-to-burden ratios by state, the high bankruptcy states had the following characteristics compared to those with low bankruptcy rates:

- *A higher rate of divorce*
- *A higher rate of gambling*
- *Lower medical insurance coverage*
- *Lower requirements for driver liability insurance*
- *More advertising by lawyers.*

These findings make a good deal of sense and undoubtedly account for most of the variance. While I have no proof, *some* differences in the rate of bankruptcy may result from local court procedures (e.g., whether the court is hard or easy on individuals seeking protection from their creditors) and local acceptance of bankruptcy. After all, if a potential bankrupt sees that neighbors have gone bankrupt but still retain their house, cars, all visible worldly goods, and the same lifestyle, this may influence his view of bankruptcy. But my opinion is merely conjecture.

Given the sizable differences both in the rate of bankruptcy and in the amounts collected under the various chapters, a creditor should be aware of past history when extending credit in a new state.

Handling Bankruptcy

Creditors have responded to the rise in bankruptcies in a number of ways. A few lenders have vowed never to do business with a person who has declared bankruptcy; others have confined their lending to secured home-equity products. Others have restricted credit in certain states where the ratio of bankruptcy to population is particularly high. Most, however, just accept bankruptcy as a cost of doing business and hope that the overall loss rate can be absorbed since many of the bankruptcies would have been writeoffs anyway. . . it's just that the very low rate of recoveries does affect the bottom line.

A creditor can handle a potential bankrupt in various ways. These methods assume that the customer introduces the option of bankruptcy during a collection call or by correspondence (remember, up to 40–50% of those going bankrupt are still current in their payments and their election to take bankruptcy as a way out is a surprise to the lender). If the collector is advised that the customer is considering bankruptcy, he can take the following actions:

1. ***Turn the account over to a specialist.*** *Any collections organization should have one or more collectors trained in handling bankruptcy. These experts should be thoroughly up-to-date in the applicable law, familiar with local court procedures, and able to discuss bankruptcy consequences and alternatives with authority.*

2. ***Explain the negatives.*** *Bankruptcy is not to be taken lightly. The collector should explain the negative side of bankruptcy, of which the customer may be unaware, e.g., there might be no new unsecured credit for a minimum of seven or more years, and all existing credit lines might be canceled.*

3. ***Discuss the alternatives.*** *The collector should be prepared to discuss alternatives to bankruptcy, including reaffirmation of debt. Reaffirmation, under which the customer continues to make payments, normally requires a "carrot" in the form of some continuing extension of credit in the future if certain promises are met. This is an appropriate arrangement only if the agreement is filed with and approved by the bankruptcy court. If the court has not recognized the reaffirmation and the debtor stops paying, the lender is in violation of the bankruptcy laws if it contacts the debtor again. This can be a very expensive mistake for the lender, as some lending institutions have discovered.*

4. ***Try to convert a Chapter 7 to a Chapter 11 or 13 filing.*** *Since a lender has a better chance of regaining some funds under a Chapter 11 or 13 filing, steer the creditor in this direction if you have reason to believe that he has assets and a steady job. As already noted, proposed new legislation (in 2002) is likely to require more bankrupts to file under Chapter 13.*

Another possibility is to discuss nonprofit consumer credit counseling agencies. These agencies, located in most major metropolitan areas, provide advice on bankruptcy for free or at low cost. They may help consumers in temporary difficulty work out a fair solution to their problems by consolidating loans while disciplining personal spending and payment habits.

Legal Action

If a review of the bankrupt's recent credit history reveals any suspicious activity (e.g., a large run-up in new charges), or there is a possibility that the debtor may have chosen bankruptcy when he is capable of repaying his debts (e.g., he lives in an affluent neighborhood), it may be worthwhile to send a representative to attend the creditors' meeting (called a 341 hearing). This meeting offers creditors the opportunity to review the debtor's overall credit record and ask questions. It gives the lender an opportunity to contest, in person, fraudulent or inappropriate actions by a customer. Most usefully, the creditors' legal experts can compare the assets listed on the original application with those actually identified in the bankruptcy filing. Dramatically undervalued assets can be questioned by a creditor, with the prospect of the debtor making larger repayments.

As long as it is relatively easy to declare bankruptcy, abuses will continue. A visit to bankruptcy court is eye-opening. A judge asks a few perfunctory questions, the claimant or the claimant's attorney makes a few statements under oath, and then the debt is wiped out. Most courts process twenty to thirty debtors in less than a hour. Nothing is challenged. Rarely is a creditor representative in attendance, asking even the simplest questions.

The procedure is as easy as that. Only when lenders get together and decide to collectively spend some money to stop the abuses will bankruptcy begin to be controlled.

One objective should be to offset the proliferation of bankruptcy mills, law firms that aggressively advertise their expertise in bankruptcies and sell their services for very low fees. These firms cannot afford to spend much time on any particular client, and if creditors take advantage of all the rights available to them by selectively challenging some applications, they can turn the momentum of the legal apparatus in their favor.

COLLECTION AGENCIES AND RECOVERY— LAST RESORTS

Some final steps can be taken even when the account is written off and/or when your own collection efforts have failed to recover the money. *Recovery* is the name given to collection activity after an account has been declared a loss and written off the books. At this point, accounts are traditionally forwarded to a collection agency for collection on a contingency fee basis. Lenders also use collection attorneys, particularly for large-balance accounts where the customer has assets that can be attached.

The collection agency business has undergone considerable consolidation through acquisition. Currently, there are fewer than ten very large collection agencies, each with over a thousand collectors, and there are, perhaps, thirty to fifty mid-size agencies. In general, lenders should consider the following criteria when selecting collection agencies:

- *Reputation (talk to other lenders).*
- *Financial viability.*
- *Size—can they handle your business/will you be an important client for them?*
- *Sophistication of automated equipment.*
- *Any regulatory constraints for past actions.*
- *Their values—beware, you can be sued for their inappropriate actions.*
- *Other customers—avoid competing with major lenders for the best collection agency resources. Ideally, you want to be an agency's most important customer.*

The number of agencies you use needs careful consideration. One agency is seldom a good number; competition for your business is healthy. More than three is probably excessive, except for the very largest lenders. Using too many agencies complicates management tasks and may result in each agency's receiving too little of your work to make you an important client. You should expect the agency to assign specific collectors and supervisors to handle only your accounts. If you provide too few of them, this expectation is unreasonable.

In measuring agency performance, what is important is the amount of money it has recovered for you on a given *batch* of accounts. This is called a *batch track*. Following is an example of how recoveries typically track on one batch of accounts given to an agency in a month.

EXHIBIT 8-4
Typical Recovery Curve

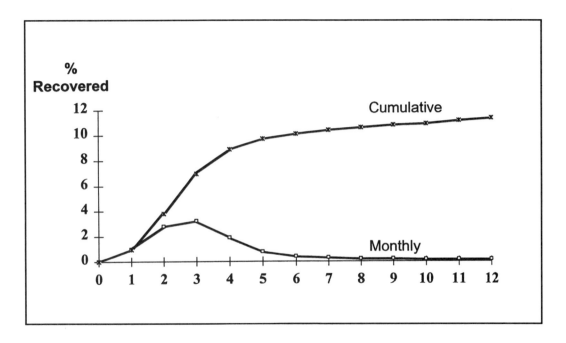

Exhibit 8-4 shows that most recovery success occurs in the first three or four months after a batch of accounts is placed with an agency. This is typical. In this example, after twelve months of effort, about 12% of the dollars have been recovered. Recovery rates will vary by product and by age of the accounts . . . early accounts may be easier to collect. Incidentally, a very high recovery rate is a good indication that you may have performance opportunities in *your* pre-charge-off collections operation, particularly if most of the recoveries occur on accounts shortly after they have been turned over to the agency.

Finally, it is important to encourage competition between several agencies. Comparing agency-to-agency results on similar batches of accounts every month positions the lender to reward good performance with more business. One caveat: make sure all the accounts allocated to each agency are randomly selected from similar portfolios in order to truly compare performance. Following is an example tracking the recovery performance of an agency on a batch of accounts delivered at a point in time.

EXHIBIT 8-5
Comparing Batch Performance

Measuring Effectiveness

	Oct	Nov	Dec	Jan	Feb	Cumulative
Agency 1	1.2%	2.3%	2.2%	1.6%		7.3%
Agency 2	0.9	2.0	1.9	1.8		6.6
Internal	1.5	2.4	1.5	1.0		6.4

Typically, batch track results are shared with agencies to promote competition. As you can see in this example, Agency 1 is performing best after four months of effort. If this continues, they can be rewarded with more accounts.

Since the 1990s, the practice of outsourcing accounts to collection agencies *before* the accounts are written off has become prevalent. In fact most major U.S. lenders use "pre-charge-off outsourcing" to some degree. Typically this work is done on a fee-for-service basis, in contrast to the straight contingency fees for recovery work. Often the outsource agency performs the collection work on the client's collection system, making the agency resemble a branch office and facilitating client control. Lenders gain several advantages from this outsourcing:

- *An* external *benchmark for measuring* internal *performance and costs*
- *The ability to outsource the peaks and valleys of the workload while maintaining a fairly consistent internal staff level*
- *The ability to forward higher-risk accounts to an agency early enough to provide the agency a better collection opportunity*
- *Reduced internal headcount*
- *Some emergency backup capability, in case of a natural disaster or a power outage at one collection location.*

The highly competitive nature of collecting can be enhanced this way. One more point to remember: outside collection activity by third parties is regulated in the U.S. by the Fair Debt Collection Practices Act (FDCPA), a federal statute. Technically the FDCPA does not apply to the collection practices of the lender, but as a practical matter, essentially all major lenders comply with all but one of the FDCPA requirements. The exception is commonly referred to as the "mini-Miranda" clause. In this clause, the FDCPA requires a collection agency to notify all debtors in writing that the agency is attempting to collect a debt and that the debtor has the right to dispute the debt, in which case collection activity will cease until the dispute is resolved.

SUMMARY

Let us summarize some of the steps for a winning approach to collections—the steps that drive good collections results:

1. *Put into place a simple MIS—a one- or two-page report that can make it easy to diagnose contact production and collector skill opportunities.*

2. *Drive up contact production. With the right information about production management and dialer operations, increases in contact production are usually achievable in weeks, not months.*

3. *Teach supervisors to diagnose collector call skill opportunities and to coach and sustain new levels of call skill performance. Try to become the payment of choice: when your collectors are calling a customer, odds are that collectors from several competitors are also calling. Sounding like all the other collectors will not make you the payment of choice. The key is collector relationship-selling skills.*

4. *Focus on contact production and conversion into payments. It is easy to get lost in the many factors of collection operations. The critical dimensions are how many customers you contacted today and what your success rate was in converting these "right-party contacts" into many large payments.*

5. *What you measure is what you get. Collections is a very measurable operation, making it all too easy to get lost in piles of reports. A few correct, simple, "peel-the-onion" tactical measurements that we outlined in the Roadmap to Payments (see Exhibit 8-1 above) make all the difference.*

6. *And finally, demand strong leadership and management. Collections is a people-intensive effort. Results depend heavily on managing processes that drive high customer contact rates and leadership that continually develops and motivates collector sales skill. In collection operations, leadership and management really matter—hands-on, detail-oriented, and with the tenacity to stay heavily engaged every day.*

If a choice must be made, choose strong leadership and management skills over extensive collection experience when hiring collection managers.

This ends the coverage of the credit cycle. In the following chapters, we discuss the unique aspects of secured consumer lending products, with a focus on automobile and home mortgage lending.

The Indirect Lending Business

NDIRECT LENDING IS a very different business from the direct lending business. With direct lending, the loan is initiated by a customer who fills out an application in a branch or is offered credit as a result of a direct-mail offering, cross-sell, and so forth. As the name implies, indirect lending is a business whereby loans are initiated by a third party, typically an automobile dealer, a mortgage broker, a department store, or other retailer, on behalf of the buyer of the goods. This application for credit is then directed by the dealer/broker to the ultimate lender—a bank, a finance company such as GMAC (General Motors Acceptance Corp.), Ford Financial Services or, in the case of a retailer, its own finance company (e.g., Sears) or another financier of its choice such as GE Capital.

Indirect lending is a big business, with great opportunities for those who understand what they are doing. There are more than 17 million new car sales a year in the United States alone and 35 million or more worldwide; 70–80% of these sales are financed. In addition, millions of boats, trucks, recreational vehicles, mobile homes, home appliances, and retail goods are financed this way every year. Financing allows businesses to sell many more units than they would otherwise. Lenders also benefit by having another channel of sales for their finance products. Indirect lending can lead to rapid growth, because once a broker or dealer begins to direct at least a portion of its loan applications to a specific institution, that lender's business grows quickly. In contrast to a direct business, which can be built predictably and steadily over time, an indirect business grows in stair-step fashion: bursts of strong growth occur intermittently. This stair-step growth requires careful management planning in such areas as staffing and building an infrastructure.

Different skills may be required. For example, as a byproduct of doing business with a vehicle dealer, the lender may need to provide services bearing little resemblance to the normal consumer lending business—including financial statement analysis, commercial lending skills, and workout planning and execution—in addition to the normal consumer lending skills. At the upper end of the market, the dealer principals are prime candidates for private banking services.

Because indirect lending is so different, we recommend that it be organized separately from the direct consumer lending business. The purpose of this chapter is to examine the characteristics of indirect lending, especially as they pertain to the two major indirect businesses: vehicle dealers and retailers/department stores.

THE INDIRECT VEHICLE BUSINESS

The steps required to enter and manage an indirect vehicle business are similar to planning any consumer business, except that there are more items to consider. The planning process includes choosing the types of products to finance (e.g., auto—new and used, mobile homes, boats, etc.), selecting the terms and conditions of the financing services to be offered (e.g., pricing, credit criteria, loan-to-value ratios, length of loans), choosing the geographic markets to be entered, and deciding which dealers to establish a relationship with.

PRODUCT DECISION

The differences in the risk/reward relationship of the major products are substantial:

New Autos	Financiers of new cars must contend with highly competitive pricing in the United States, with manufacturers sometimes offering special buy-down financing (e.g., 2% for all Toyotas sold in December) or even "free" financing to boost sales. As in all markets, excellent service and the ability to quickly assess risk are vital to success. Risk varies significantly by product (e.g., sport utility vehicles [SUVs] vs. high-performance or "muscle" cars) and by manufacturer (e.g., Mercedes vs. Hyundai).
Used Autos	More than 36 million used cars are sold annually in the USA. Financing used cars means higher risk, but typically these deals can be priced higher than new-car loans. Lenders should consider when and how to limit financing of used cars, say, six years or older, where the risk becomes even higher. A lender should have a thorough knowledge of the reputation and reliability of the vehicle when financing older cars; the possibility that a car will require extensive repairs just to last through the life of the contract must be assessed. A borrower is more likely to default if the car is a "lemon."

MOBILE HOMES	This is a highly specialized business. Mobile homes are often a marginal product with generally weak dealers and lower-scale buyers. Greentree Acceptance dominated this market until experiencing hard times.[1]
RECREATIONAL VEHICLES (RVs)	RVs are high-ticket items, generally offering solid business, but financing them is highly competitive and highly specialized (do you know which products are marginal, which are top quality?).
BOATS	The high end of the boat market is closer to the private banking business, particularly when considering $1 million yachts. The lower end is closer to auto financing and is just as competitive.

In other words, the first decisions are very fundamental. Which products do you want to finance, which ones can you make money on, and what steps should you take to improve your chances for success? There are other, even more specialized products than those noted above, such as taxi or heavy truck financing, that require a unique knowledge of those industries, but we will not cover these.

What the lender has been financing historically and where its business is located will tend to dictate answers to these questions (e.g., few snowmobiles are financed in Florida or RVs sold in Manhattan). Few financiers have succeeded in breaking into any one of these businesses successfully without careful planning and a long-run approach to the business. Financing should be restricted to only those products the lender understands. The rest should be left to the competition.

This section on vehicles concentrates on the indirect automobile financing business. The principles used to plan, operate, and monitor this business are very much the same as those used in the boat business, for instance, or the mobile home business. The warnings to know the product, the manufacturer, and the dealer are at least as stringent in the other indirect businesses.

In the indirect vehicle business, there is another important decision to make early on: Do you want to be the *primary* or the *secondary* finance source for a dealer?

Primary or Secondary Financier?

The typical auto dealership needs a great deal of funding. In addition to being able to arrange for the financing or leasing of each unit sold, a dealership requires floor-plan financing (i.e., the dealer needs funds to purchase the vehicles that make up

---

1. The late director of the FBI, J. Edgar Hoover, once described mobile home parks as "Dens of vice and corruption, haunted by nomadic prostitutes, hardened criminals, white slaves, and promiscuous college students." Try telling that to the residents of a Florida mobile home retirement community!

its inventory from the manufacturer), working capital loans, facility mortgages, and possibly even financing for a dealer-owned leasing or car rental company. To be the dealer's primary financier, you must be able to provide all these and possibly some private banking services for the dealer and his family. In return for such financing, a primary lender is generally given the opportunity to review and book the best new and used car loan applications.

If you are just entering the market, it is difficult to be the primary financier . . . unless you are willing to deal with the marginal or potentially fraudulent dealers, the ones other financiers are happy to leave behind. The automobile finance business, in particular, is well served today by the major automobile manufacturers. The dealers who sell U.S., European, and Japanese cars typically obtain a large portion of their wholesale inventory, retail, and lease financing from the manufacturer's "captive" finance companies (GMAC, Ford Financial Services, etc.).

The captive finance companies may or may not be the best source of retail financing (that is, providing the best price and the best service), but as the supplier of 70 percent or more of the inventory (floor-plan) financing, they do have an advantage. Just because an automobile manufacturer provides its dealers with this financing, however, does not ensure them control of even a majority of the retail sales financing. Dealers are independent franchisees and, as such, have the final word on who does their financing. A dealer typically makes 70 to 80 percent of his sales on credit, so a dependable source of financing is essential to the health of his business. Consequently, a dealer is unlikely to change his current primary financing source unless a major problem develops with that source or a major advantage is perceived with a new one. So dealers need to be convinced, one by one, that a change in financiers is advantageous for them. An opportunity to gain a dealer's business may come during a credit crunch when some creditors cut back on their lending. Another opportunity may develop when the current lead lender fails to remain competitive in price or service.

The secondary financier typically provides no financial services to the dealer except financing a portion of the retail sales. While the secondary role implies that you will see only the riskier deals (the ones the primary financier rejects), in reality most applications are sent to several finance sources at the same time and the one with the best terms and speediest answer gets the deal. Typically, dealers like having three to four secondary financing sources and expect them to compete on service (application turnaround time), approval rate, price to the customer, and commissions paid. It may take several years of sales effort to secure indirect business from an automobile or mobile home dealer, particularly one that is long established, well financed, and reputable, but persistence can pay off!

If you are going to be either the primary or secondary financier, you had better know a lot about the dealers you are financing and the products they sell. This begins when you select your target market.

Selecting the Target Market— by Manufacturer/Dealer

While your target market is the dealer, selecting a reputable product distributed through a reputable dealer network affects the creditor's exposure. The criteria used to select the manufacturers whose vehicles the lender will finance should include:

- *Stability of the manufacturer*
- *Market acceptance of the product*
- *Service and warranty policy.*

The manufacturer's stability and reputation are important because a low-quality product tends to attract less-reliable customers and because weak manufacturers may not back up their products or their customers. If the consumer feels she has purchased a "lemon" and has no recourse to the dealer or manufacturer, she will more often renege on her loan commitment. In recent years, the Yugo, in particular, and the Hyundai for a while did not perform as well as they should have. Other models, like the Audi, have had temporary quality problems that impacted their reputation and sales appeal.

Finally, it is absolutely essential to select a dealer with a strong franchise and a solid reputation. Even if you are not doing floor-plan financing, you still want to know the character and financial strength of that party. Is this someone you want to do business with over a long period of time?

The number of automobile dealers has been declining as the business consolidates. The growth of large, multi-franchise dealerships such as AutoNation, is a trend that has slowed (at the end of the 1990s, 35% of the 22,000+ auto dealers were part of a chain). Can you deal with these huge organizations that can arrange financing on very competitive terms, or do you want to deal only with the traditional Mom-and-Pop outlets? The degree of commitment on behalf of the lending institution is clearly different. To deal with an AutoNation, you must have a very professional, highly organized approach.

A creditor providing inventory financing, capital loans, and so forth can easily have five to ten times as much money tied up in a dealer's business as the dealer himself does. This can be a real problem when a dealer gets into financial difficulty; in the event of bankruptcy, the creditor often has more to lose than the dealer. The relationship with the dealer must be legally documented and enforceable, with the rights and responsibilities of both parties fully established and understood. The dealer's responsibility might include providing financial data, personal guarantees, insurance to cover floor-plan units, and so forth. Remember you are financing a highly mobile inventory (these are *not* homes), and fraud is always a possibility.

SELECTING THE TARGET MARKET—SUBPRIME LENDING

By selecting the manufacturer, the product, and the dealers you wish to finance, you are already preselecting your customers. A Lincoln buyer in Greenwich Connecticut is inherently different from a Corolla buyer in downtown Chicago. You can make a conscious decision to go after one group of high-risk, presumably high-reward, customers—the subprime market.

In the mid-1990s, certain auto finance companies rushed into this C&D auto finance market. Such companies as Mercury Finance, Jayhawk, and Arcadia Financial were the darlings of Wall Street as they explained to investors how they were going to meet the transportation needs of the people who had either a prior bad credit record or no credit record. Obviously these people needed financing, and the finance companies were going to supply it and make lots of money.

As the larger financiers (e.g., Associates) entered the market, competition intensified. Already loose standards were downgraded, with lower down payments and longer terms made available to poorer-quality customers. The result: major losses reported by these secondary finance sources, and a collapse in their stock prices. The fact that some prior earnings figures had to be adjusted downward (sometimes due to deferring write-offs on repossessed units) did not help. Investors and accountants were even fooled by the old trick of reselling and refinancing repossessed autos . . . repossessing them again and again, thus deferring writing off the loans. These practices will finally catch up with a lender, but for a while it's a great way to mislead your investors. Remember the old saying: "A rolling loan gathers no loss."

The subprime market remains a valid target market, and currently AmeriCredit and some others are doing well in it. But you must be willing not to chase volume for its own sake, as well as to have the proper credit controls, appropriate pricing, and, most important, a good collections and repossession organization (and, of course, a realistic accounting policy) to survive.

Establishing Standard Terms and Conditions

As in any product offering, the core or standard product terms must be set. Since the overall goal of the business is to make a profit, you have to consider the frequency (how many customers go bad) and the severity (how much you lose when a customer does go bad) of any bad loans. The role of scoring and how to control the frequency of losses will be covered later

The following items impact the severity of loss when a customer cannot make his payments. The standard terms include:

- *Maximum/minimum term*
- *Maximum/minimum loan size*
- *Loan-to-value ratios and down payment requirements*
- *Pricing for both dealer and customer*
- *Customer insurance requirements.*

1) Maximum/Minimum Term

What length loans should be financed? Typical auto loans vary from 24 months to a maximum of 72 months, although some will go to 84 months. Very short (<24 mos.) loans may be lower risk but may not be profitable because the costs of putting on the loan can exceed the profit derived from a short earning period. Longer terms can be riskier. All other things being equal, a longer term means a longer time before the customer has any equity in the car, which can mean a higher loss per unit repossessed, as shown in the following chart:.

EXHIBIT 9-1
Impact of Term

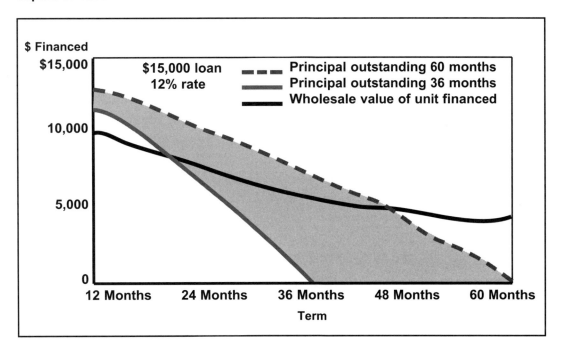

Longer terms also mean there is a longer time frame for the customer to get into trouble (loss of job, bankruptcy, etc.). At one time, the major automotive financiers extended their terms relentlessly (i.e., from 42 months to an average of 55 months) in order to keep the monthly payments down. For instance, the monthly payment on a 60-month loan is about two thirds of the monthly payment on a 36-month loan, at the same interest rate; this can allow the manufacturers and dealers to advertise a much more attractive package *or* sell more car for the same price. When loss rates doubled in the early 1990s, the manufacturers pulled back, but the temptation to extend terms is always there.

Further, the wholesale value over time also varies significantly by *type* of unit financed (e.g., a Mercedes vs. a Ford Focus), so you should know if the vehicles you are financing retain their value or depreciate rapidly. Can the business absorb the added risk of extending terms on a rapidly depreciating car? Only if the lender is getting an offsetting reward by a larger spread—something that has been difficult in the face of aggressive pricing by the captive finance companies.

2) Minimum/Maximum Loan Size

As a rule it makes no sense for a bank to finance any installment loan for less than a minimum amount (e.g., $3,000). The costs of booking are just too high to be·able to make a profit on smaller loans. Conversely, will you finance a $100,000 Porsche? It's a pretty limited market and you might not know enough about the value of the very high-priced cars to take the chance. Set limits and stick to them.

3) Loan-to-Value Ratios and Down Payment Requirements

The old rule used to be: never finance more than 100% of the *wholesale* price of the delivered vehicle, which typically required a down payment of about 20%. This rule is widely flouted today, but you had better understand the risk of doing so. When the loss per unit repossessed approaches $8,000 to $10,000 (as it can with a low-down-payment loan), you need a lot of profitable loans at, say, a profit of $400 to $500 each to offset that amount of loss (a 20:1 ratio!). Also, you must establish which miscellaneous closing and other charges will be included in the amount financed, such as insurance, sales tax, license and title fees, as shown in the following exhibit:

EXHIBIT 9-2
Sample Auto Finance Deal

Selling price (vehicle and options)	$14,300
Less down payment (20%)	(2,860)
Total Car Price Financed	$11,440
Other items financed (optional)	
Insurance	$ 1,200
Dealer-installed equipment	830
Taxes	627
Total Amount Financed	$14,097
Memo: Estimated "quick sale" price of unit (first year)	$ 9,000

The purpose of obtaining as large a down payment as possible, obviously, is to limit the loss per unit repossessed. Remember, the low-risk customer can make a large down payment; the higher-risk customer *needs* to put as little down as possible. As covered earlier, the value of a new unit drops sharply in the first months after delivery. In addition, most of the other items financed in the above example have little or no resale value (although insurance can be canceled in the event of a repossession). Limiting the percent of wholesale or retail price financed minimizes the loss per unit in the event of repossession.

A prudent lender will always make at least a brief check to compare the amount financed to the wholesale value of the automobile as delivered. It is not enough to accept the stated down payment. A dealer can always be tempted to "overfinance" a vehicle by allowing very small down payments from weak customers who are stretched beyond their ability to repay. This is one way to trouble in the indirect business.

4) Pricing

The indirect vehicle business is unique in that it involves several different pricing considerations within one dealer relationship. The *overall relationship* with the dealer must be considered when pricing the cost of financing.

Wholesale and retail sales, new and used vehicles, capital loans, and even leasing transactions may all require separate prices at varying rates of return to arrive at an overall profitable relationship within the dealership. Secondary lenders have to concentrate only on pricing the individual contracts.

Remember that the *net customer revenue* of the indirect business is generally lower than in the direct lending business. The financier is in essence "renting" the dealer's distribution network instead of establishing its own, which means, of course, lower operating costs for the lender.

Pricing is very competitive in the indirect field, and many dealers have enough clout to receive multiple competitive offers on the same deal. Keeping up with competitive prices and pricing strategies is a vitally important job for any indirect financing organization.

Two important factors in determining dealer pricing are commissions and any recourse arrangements.

> **Commissions.** The dealer customarily receives a portion of the finance charge in return for generating the deal. The method of payment and amount are usually set by competition. Typically, the dealer earns all the charges above the amount the lender charges. For example, if the dealer is charged 10.5% for a contract and charges the customer 12.5%, he earns the 2.0% differential. The lender should put a cap on the amount the dealer can charge to keep him from charging a usurious rate.
>
> > If at all possible, the commission should be paid out over the life

of the contract, as it is earned. If commissions are paid up front, there is a problem charging back the dealer for the unearned commission on contracts that are terminated early. And a large number of contracts are paid out early; the standard 48-month automobile loan is on the books on average for only 32 months. Some loans are even paid out after three to four months, as the customer finds a new source of financing. The average actual life of the contract is an important piece of information for the lender to have.

Recourse Arrangements. Today, very few units are financed with the dealer sharing in the financing risk or the disposal of any repossessed unit. It may be possible to get the dealer to guarantee some or all of the loss in the event of a repossession on a very high-risk deal (and where the dealer's profit is proportionally larger), but this arrangement is dictated by competition and local market conditions.

5) Insurance

Because the most likely reason for a car to be repossessed is that a driver with inadequate or no collision insurance sustains major damage to his vehicle, the financier has an interest in requiring the customer to carry minimum levels of collision insurance. The individual states mandate the types of *liability* insurance required to register a vehicle, but no amount of collision insurance is required. It is up to the financier to set a policy requiring collision insurance with as small a deductible as possible.[2] A driver who cannot obtain sufficient collision insurance to cover major damage is not one that a prudent lender should consider financing.

It is relatively easy to enforce this coverage when the vehicle is bought, but most insurance policies are for only six months to one year. How much time and effort can a lender afford to invest in following up on insurance coverage in the second, third, or even fourth year? The answer is not much, but some lenders set up a vast operation to follow each customer relentlessly for proof of insurance. Lenders argue over the cost/benefit of follow-up, and there is no clear answer. If the lender is dealing with the right customers, insurance coverage after the first year is not a problem . . . these customers will continue the coverage automatically, so there is no need for the financier to follow up. For very high-risk customers, it may be worth following up on insurance coverage after the first year, but lenders should analyze the cost/benefit ratio for themselves.

Now that the lender has established the standard terms under which it will accept business, it needs a process in place to review and approve indi-

---

2. Almost all insurance coverage is for the *wholesale* value of the vehicle; in the case of a total wreck, the borrower is still responsible for the total principal owed. This gap can be high in the case of a new contract, and a prudent financier will encourage the purchase of gap insurance.

vidual loan applications. In order to do that, the lender must understand how individual cars are sold and financed.

INDIVIDUAL LOAN DECISIONS

The normal purchase process begins with a prospective customer selecting a particular car on the dealer's lot with the aid of a salesman. After a test drive and some negotiation, they agree on a purchase price and, if required, a down payment (in cash or the trade-in value of the customer's old car). At this point the customer is asked, "How do you plan to pay the remainder of the money you owe?"

If the customer indicates that she could use some help in financing the balance, the salesman introduces the customer to the dealer's financing and insurance specialist (the "F&I"person). The F&I person helps the customer complete a credit application. During this process, the risk/reward value of the customer will be assessed, e.g., is she creditworthy? How much can she pay per month? How stable is her employment? Does she own a home? Based on experience, the F&I person will then suggest possible financing sources. If the customer agrees, the F&I person will then send the application—possibly by Internet or intranet—to several preestablished finance sources that have a relationship with the dealer.

Once the potential lenders receive the information, they review the application, make a decision, and send a reply, often within minutes. As we will cover later, scoring both the application and the credit bureau data is critical to this process.

The winner is the finance company with the quickest and most competitive offer, based on price, flexibility, and the overall relationship between the finance source and the F&I person. If the financier is competitive, the answer can be returned within minutes; slower financiers may not even get consideration unless the first lenders reject the application. The best financiers have the ability to handle this kind of business on weekends, holidays, evenings, if their customers (the dealers) are open at such times. If the competition is lazy, secondary financiers may be able to gain a competitive advantage by offering off-hours service.

The F&I person and the lender may need to negotiate on the financing terms for some units, particularly on the weaker credits. Typically, a dealer has a higher net return on this kind of sale because the customer with a limited or poor credit record is in a weaker bargaining position. Keeping in mind that the objective is to develop a profitable product, the financier must establish rules as to what deals it is willing to accept.

A critical part of managing the business is understanding the ratio of loans, by dealer, that you *book* as a percent of loans *reviewed* by your underwriters ("the booking ratio"). It costs time and money to review each application, enter into negotiations with the F&I person, and communicate the decision back to the dealer. If only a small percentage of these loans are actually booked, your acquisition costs will be too high. As a general rule, if you book less than 25% of applications reviewed, you are in trouble; if you book more than 50%, you are doing well. Following these *booking ratio* numbers gives you the information to terminate or expand a relationship with an individual dealer.

It is essential, then, that the finance source control the approval process tightly, with every request for financing treated in a precise and predictable manner. This is the time to control the *frequency* of loss, which is where scoring comes in, as we will now cover.

Scoring

A validated automobile scoring model is a must for both the primary and the secondary lender. A good credit scoring system allows the creditor to accurately assess the quality of each application reviewed, and then track the percentage of below-average, average, and above-average contracts that he is buying from each dealer, as it is being bought. The following report (which should be available by dealer, by region, by product, etc.) is a powerful record of the quality of the portfolio as it is being bought.

EXHIBIT 9-3
Scoring: Indirect Target Portfolio

Buy the Odds

	Incident* Default Rate	Balance Ratio**	Loss Rate	Target Portfolio Mix
A+ deals	1.7%	.40	.66%	30
A deals	2.0%	.50	1.00%	50
B deals	3.3%	.60	2.00%	15
C deals	5.0%	.75	3.75%	4
D deals	10.0%	.80	8.00%	1
				100%

*Frequency
**Severity

In addition to the incidence of default, which is based on the score system, this report tracks the good/bad balance ratio by score range. Typically, lower-scoring accounts write off at a higher dollar amount than higher-scoring accounts, which may indicate a higher loan-to-value ratio on these loans.

Any automobile credit scoring system will usually take into account the *contract* characteristics (e.g., the loan-to-value ratio, the down payment, the term, and possibly even the model of car), as well as standard *applicant* history as determined from the application and the credit bureau. Youth models are helpful for first-time buyers, and regional models further refine the process where the business is geographically dispersed. Generic scoring models are available for lenders new to the business.

Remember, the financier must be willing to assume some poor deals to get the good ones. Every sale—particularly to a weak customer—is important to the dealer, for the salespeople, the finance manager, the parts business, for repeat sales, and so forth. As in any lending business, the rule is to get sufficient good accounts so the good-bad ratio is acceptable. The lender must be convinced that the dealer is allocating an appropriate portion of the high-quality business before agreeing to accept an appropriate level of D risks. You must have the information to track this.

It is possible to compensate for marginal deals by increasing the down payment, or by moving the buyer down in quality and price (e.g., from new vehicle to used), requiring a second loan guarantor, or stipulating a dealer-recourse agreement. The lender obviously must also stay abreast of what the competition is doing. The dealer is living in a highly competitive world, and a finance source that maintains higher rates or tighter terms than the competition will not book many loans. Turning down a loan in the traditional, direct lending business means losing one customer; turning down a critical loan in the indirect business may mean the lender's losing a large source of business.

Next we will cover what should be done with the small (hopefully) percentage of loans that go bad.

REPOSSESSIONS

Over time, some customers will not meet their obligations. A financier must be prepared to physically repossess delinquent customers' units after a predetermined time; typically, this procedure begins after 60 to 90 days of delinquency, but this period can vary if there are any legal restrictions. An indirect business must have detailed plans outlining when units are to be repossessed, who does it, and how the units will be maintained and sold. The best repossession is a voluntary one, and the lender should encourage this with its borrowers. For instance, if an automobile is critical for the borrower to get to work, there is nothing worse than having his car repossessed in the middle of the night. If he has some warning, presumably he can make alternate arrangements and will deliver the car back to the financier voluntarily.

A good repossession and disposal process is an important part of controlling the severity of loss. Many lenders use professional, outside repossession companies specializing in the business—always with the understanding that anyone representing the lender must abide by all legal restrictions regarding vehicle repossession. It is usually not a good idea to have the lender's own people carry out an involuntary repossession, particularly in a rough neighborhood; the typical lender's employee is simply not equipped to handle such a situation. (See the movie *Repo Man* for a better understanding of the dark side of the repossession process.)

How the units are maintained and sold is also very important. Options for selling them include auctions, through the dealer facility, or through new distribution channels such as the Internet. While the units are in custody, they must be protected from vandalism, theft, and weather; they must also be kept clean and in good working order for resale. A sloppy repossession process is an open invitation to fraud (usually by internal employees). It might also result in higher than necessary losses.

One fundamental rule: Holding a unit for a long period of time is expensive. Keep the inventory down and keep selling. Remember, the first loss is the least loss.

MONITORING THE DEALER RELATIONSHIP

If you are the primary or the secondary financier, you must know where/how your money is being used by the dealer. For the primary financier, as we have already mentioned, you could be providing funds for inventory of new and used units (floor-plan financing), working capital loans, facility mortgages, and any private financing needs. Both the primary and secondary financiers must also understand that a dealer can defraud a lender on retail sales. First let's look at floor plan financing.

The way the automobile business works, the manufacturer (Ford, Toyota, etc.) gets paid for each vehicle on delivery to the dealer; because dealers must carry a large inventory of cars to show prospective customers, there is a time period when these units are sitting on a dealer's lot before being sold. Most dealers have literally hundreds of units in their inventory, worth millions of dollars. And, because few dealers have the funds necessary to buy these units outright, they must finance each unit in their inventory. The rule in floor-plan financing is that each unit financed must be paid off when the unit is sold at retail. If a financially unsound or ethically weak dealer decides not to pay off the lender when the unit is sold, this can cause a major problem for the financier. Obie Kinney, former president of Citicorp Acceptance, with nearly thirty years of experience in the indirect business, uses the following story to illustrate how a dealer in financial or managerial trouble might take desperate steps to stay above water.

> It's Friday afternoon. The accountant comes to her boss, the founder and president of Metro Motors. "Boss," she says, "we can either meet the payroll or we can pay off the bank for those floor-plan units we sold this morning. What do you think we ought to do?"

To the dealer, the answer seems obvious. Keep the doors open, hope some more money will come in over the weekend, and begin to "float" with the lender. Once this subterfuge starts, it is difficult to stop.

Even professionally run finance companies such as General Motors Acceptance Corporation and Ford Financial Services have had franchised dealers who failed to pay their floor-plan financier millions of dollars on units they sold at retail. For example, during the 1990s General Motors was stiffed for more than $650 million by a Long Island dealer in a highly complex, recreational vehicle inventory financing scheme involving overseas financing. The fact that GMAC wrote the book on how to control dealership financing, and had been in the business for over seventy-five years, should serve as a warning to all financiers.

If you are the primary financier, there is no single way to prevent frauds. However, there are a series of steps that a well-managed business can take to minimize these losses. The fundamental requirement is that the business be managed and monitored *by individual dealer,* no matter how small. The quality of the portfolio, the number of customer complaints as recorded, say, by the Better Business Bureau, and so forth provide useful clues to a deteriorating situation. In addition, the following extra steps are necessary.

> *Collateral verification.* The ability to verify that each item of collateral (typically, floor-plan units) exists is vital. Systematic inventory checks should be made at randomly selected dates to assure compliance. At these audits, *every* unit over which the financial institution has a lien must be tracked down, including sample checks of the odometer (there should be very few miles on the odometer of a new car).

> *Organization.* Indirect relationships require a geographically distributed organization, with regular visits to all dealers by the lender's staff. Informal, frequent, on-site inspections are invaluable for monitoring a dealer's financial well-being. Are there changes in lifestyle? Does he take too many trips to gamble at Las Vegas or Atlantic City? These are the types of clues to watch for.

> *Monitoring of wholesale payouts.* A business that has been selling four, five, or ten units a day suddenly stops recording sales. Is this due to a slump in business, or is it the first sign of a failure to pay off on floor-plan units that have been sold?

The lender must be able to move rapidly when a dealer's financial position is obviously weak and formal steps must be taken, early and decisively, to protect its interests. When a dealer showing signs of deterioration has floor-plan or other loans outstanding, there should be some process of highlighting and monitoring the relationship as a potential problem. One effective tool that should be available on a minute's notice is a complete checklist of every step required for a dealer workout. This would include stopping all new financing transactions, checking all recent sales financed, tracking down all floor-plan units, etc., along with all legal forms. Because most dealership failures occur suddenly and the lender must move quickly to protect its interests, this tool can be a real lifesaver.

One more point: a wholesale floor-plan financing arrangement should take into consideration whether or not there is a manufacturer's repurchase agreement. Under a repurchase agreement, if a dealer goes into bankruptcy, the manufacturer will buy back the floor-plan units. It is far easier for the manufacturer to dispose of the dealer's inventory of unsold, current model cars (the only ones a manufacturer will accept) than for the financier.

Dealers can also defraud either a primary or a secondary financier on their *retail* sales. Here are some of the methods used by unscrupulous dealers:

- *False sales contracts are created and the dealer pockets the financier's money for the "sale" of a nonexistent car.*
- *Genuine retail contracts are double- or triple-financed.*
- *Customer data are falsified to improve the credit approval rate.*
- *The terms of a deal (e.g., down payment or value of trade-in) are misstated.*

Again, there is no single way to prevent dealer fraud, but one step is the regular, statistically meaningful telephone sampling of retail customers to determine that 1) the customer exists, 2) a car was purchased, and 3) the financing terms are as stated in the contract. At *any* sign of deviation from standard procedures, *all* contracts should be audited. With a highly reputable dealer this can be done on a small percent of the deals (say, 10–20%), unless some discrepancies are found, in which case the percentage should be sharply increased. But with a new or possibly suspect dealer, sampling should be performed on every contract.

MANAGEMENT INFORMATION

In the indirect business, each individual dealer, no matter how small, should be managed and monitored separately. Information should be gathered both for primary and secondary financing relationships for management to review and analyze. Factors to analyze include:

For both primary and secondary financiers:

- *Volume and type of retail paper (the number of applications for new, used, and leased vehicles)*
- *Accounts booked as a percentage of applications received (very important!)*
- *Credit score (the distribution, by score, of each month's sales)*
- *Customer complaints (the number and severity of complaints)*
- *Retail audit performance (did the customers exist and were the contracts correct as stated?)*
- *Delinquencies, repossessions, and writeoffs*
- *Frequency and severity of loss per unit repossessed.*

For primary financiers only:

- *Line limits and those dealers who repeatedly go over their limits*
- *Wholesale audits (reports on floor-plan units sold by the dealer but not paid off on time)*
- *Age of units in stock*
- *Payment record (late payments, bounced checks)*
- *Financial strength (financial statement analysis).*

It is helpful to follow these key performance indicators, grading each dealer in terms of potential risk. A below-standard rating alerts the financier to structure the credit conditions to correspond with the risk involved. Where detailed financial data are available in a common format for a large group of dealers, the data should be used to build a dealer scoring system. The U.S. domestic auto manufacturers can do this with their captive finance companies because a standard financial reporting system is available. However, most dealer financial data—particularly with the lower-volume marine or mobile home dealers—are not standardized enough to allow this.

Dealer financial statements are often unreliable; they are not always audited, and even when audited by a small, local accounting firm, they may still be unreliable. Consequently, financial analysis must look beyond the cash flow or the numbers on a statement. As we have already noted, common sense, or informal signals—such as number of salespeople laid off, increasing/deceasing levels of inventory, rundown premises, poor local reputation, or taking too many vacations—probably provide a better early warning system.

AUTOMOBILE LEASING

Another option for basic business is the market in leased vehicles. You need to decide whether to finance only new and used retail autos or whether you are willing to offer *lease* financing as well. Leasing now accounts for 25 to 30 percent of all units "sold" in the United States, so it is a big business. Leasing used to be confined to businesses, especially small business customers, who could write off the monthly lease payments, but now any qualified customer is targeted for leasing.

How does leasing work? The basic premise is that the person leasing the car does not own it; the leasing company, which could be Ford Credit, the dealer's leasing company, or an independent leasing company, owns the car and rents it out to the driver for a stipulated period of time. The lessor (the financier) and the lessee (the customer) agree on the initial sales price, the monthly payment due to cover interest and amortization of principal, the length of the payback period, mileage limitations, maintenance and insurance requirements, and, most important, the agreed-on buyback price at the end of the lease . . . the residual value. This residual value is the key to the business. The way it works is this:

> A leased unit does not amortize fully. The residual value is the estimated value of the car at the end of the lease; the difference between the purchase price and the residual value is the amount that is amortized. Monthly lease payments are therefore less than typical purchase payments where the full purchase price is amortized. This is the main benefit of leasing for the customer. The higher the residual value, the smaller the amount that is to be paid off—hence, lower monthly payments.

Setting the correct residual value is critical. Typically, the customer (the lessee) has the right to buy back the car at the predetermined residual value. If the car is worth more than the residual value at the end of the contract, the lessee can buy the vehicle outright and resell it at the higher price. If it is worth less, he can just walk away from the contract. In addition, if the residual value is set too low, the monthly payments may be too high to be competitive; if it is set too high, the monthly payments are lowered, but the automobile may not be worth the amount estimated at the end of the lease, and the lessor takes the loss.

Most leases are sold on a low-monthly-payment basis, so the leasing company is under great pressure to set the residual value as high as possible. Newspapers carry ads such as "Lease a Toyota for $269/month" or "Lease a Taurus for only $312/mo." Today even the Mercedes is advertised with "Low, affordable monthly payments of $500 or $600/month." The customer must read the fine print to learn about the down payment and any hidden charges, but this is the way leasing is sold.

With leasing, the financier has to project the future value of the car as accurately as possible. Many leasing companies, however, particularly the manufacturer's leasing companies, are willing to gamble that the value of the used car (in two, three, or four years) will remain sufficiently high to keep monthly payments down to a very attractive level. Competitive leasing companies, however, must recognize that on every unit sold, the automobile manufacturers make a profit (which can be several thousand dollars) that outside lenders do not.[3] Following is an example of the impact of the loss per unit at varying levels of depreciation:

---

3. Outside lenders do, however, have the same tax advantage as any corporation: they can deduct expenses and they are able to depreciate the vehicle (a deductible, non-cash tax writeoff).

EXAMPLE: $21,000 auto

Approximate gain/loss if resale value is:

      40% of original price – ($2100)

      45% of original price – ($1050)

      50% of original price – 0

In 1999, the *New York Times* reported that lessors absorbed an estimated $1,300 average loss per leased car returned in 1998. It is difficult to believe that each lease finance deal makes sufficient profit to sustain that size loss. The lesson: the financier of leases is in the *used car price prediction and disposal* business. While resale price insurance is available, it is expensive, and you need to be sure of the financial strength of the insurer in the event of a collapse in used car prices.

In theory, residual value can be set based on the historical rate of depreciation of a particular model. In the past, many models have depreciated predictably: a Cadillac or Ford would be worth 50 percent after three years, a Mercedes 58 percent, and a Nissan or Honda 45 percent. These prices are impacted by the type of equipment installed at the factory (engine size, air bags, air conditioning, leather seats, stereo systems, etc.), which can be taken into account. There are, however, also very unpredictable factors (e.g., the price of gasoline and its impact on gas-guzzler cars such as SUVs), unexpected quality problems (e.g., the Audis with mechanical problems), and the fickle nature of styling and public acceptance—these can cause big surprises.

The financier had better decide whether it is in the finance business or the used car business before offering a leasing product. It takes a lot of expertise and guts to bet on the market for used cars in three, four, or even five years. Few lenders have this expertise, and only those who have it or can hire it should enter the business.

One more point to consider before entering the leasing business: how will you re-market the vehicles returned to you by the lessee? Normally, approximately 50 percent are returned and 50 percent are purchased or re-leased by the lessee, but the percent returned could go to 80, 90 percent or more if used car prices are down. Can you handle the volume? If you can't, you shouldn't be in the business.

As the market has become more and more competitive, financiers have tended to stretch their terms to meet market demands, but not always with a thorough understanding of the business. Any financier entering a leasing program should do so with great care.

Next we cover another indirect specialty finance business, namely the financing of department store and retailer's credit sales. While there are some similarities, there are major differences between the automobile financing business we have covered thus far and the retailer's finance business.

The Indirect Retail Business

Retailers have traditionally considered credit sales a very important part of their business (as do auto dealers, boat dealers, or whatever). In the absence of any manufacturer's finance companies, the first question that a retailer has to answer is: Do I want to run the credit business myself or do I want to have it handled by an outside professional? The original retailing giants—such as Sears, J. C. Penney, and the late Montgomery Ward—all have had well-managed credit card operations virtually since they opened. The basic assumption is that the "private label" card buyer is a loyal store customer. It used to be estimated that a private label card customer would buy three to five times as much store merchandise annually as a non-card customer, but this figure has plummeted as essentially all retailers today accept Visa, MasterCard, Discover, American Express, etc. Not surprisingly, however, retailers still consider their large lists of card customers extremely valuable because these customers presumably spend more and can be contacted directly about special sales and promotions. The concept that a private label card is worth more to the retailer than a mass credit card is still very much alive, and retailers do everything they can to protect and nurture this source of profitable business.

Following is a comparison of some of the major differences between the indirect auto and private label businesses:

Vehicle Dealer	Private Label
• Installment product	• Revolving product
• 70–80% of sales are on credit.	• 20–30% of sales are on private label cards; balance on bank/T&E cards or cash.
• Balance financed is large (> than $15,000).	• Balance financed is small ($20 to $500 per charge; sometimes higher on electronic items, appliances, or furniture.
• Dealer gets a commission on every unit financed.	• Retailer may pay a fee per account for financing.
• Additional financing is often provided (wholesale, capital loan, and so forth).	• Other financing is typically not involved.
• Each consumer transaction is negotiated individually; lender may require a higher down payment or second endorsement to approve riskier deals.	• Credit application and authorization decisions are made on an actuarial basis or by judgmental rules, with overall acceptance level negotiated.
• Pricing is very competitive.	• High prices are charged on revolvers.

If you're a retailer, the problem with having your own consumer finance business is that it is time-consuming, absorbs large amounts of cash, and requires very good management to control and run a large portfolio of small-average-balance accounts. Understanding the degree of risk and profitability of thousands, hundreds of thousands, or millions of accounts is not easy (as any reader of this book will quickly understand). This is particularly true for smaller or medium-size retailers, but even the giants have not always managed their portfolios with precision.

Sometimes retailers face a cash drain if their store operations are unprofitable or money becomes tight. Hard times may force it to sell *all* of its receivables—as well as the management of its receivables—to a financing specialist. Luckily an alternative exists, because third-party financiers such as GE Capital, Citigroup, and others have built businesses specifically dedicated to the management of retailers' portfolios. In fact, GE Capital has become the giant in this business, with nearly 40 million active private label accounts, followed by Citigroup (15 million accounts) and Household with over 7 million. This business has become possible only because the financiers have shown they meet retailers' needs by providing a highly competitive level of credit sales while running a tightly controlled, predictable, and profitable credit card operation. Turning over their credit program allows retailers to concentrate on their main business, the retailing of goods and services, and to leave the running of the credit sales to specialists. In the past, however, retailers have sold their receivables reluctantly, for fear that the lender is interested only in profit and will dismiss the marketing needs of the retailer and the service needs of its customers.

In theory, a retailer can afford to take a loss on its private label financing if it can make an incremental profit by selling more of its merchandise. An outside financing specialist has to understand the importance of every sale to the merchant, yet it must also make a profit. For this reason the retailer and the financier need an up-front understanding regarding such critical items as the following:

> **New accounts.** The day-to-day acceptance/rejection of new card customers should normally be within the lender's full control, but because of the importance of each sale to the merchant, there should be a clear understanding of what scoring systems will be in place and what approval level will yield an acceptable writeoff rate. Also, the retailer should be kept aware of any changes in policy that could impact anticipated acceptance rates (e.g., a new scoring system or a change in cutoff score). There should be *no* surprises in something as important as the rate of acceptance of new card customers.

> **Individual purchases.** Individual transaction decisions should be made automatically, with virtually no negotiations. Again, however, the two par-

ties should be in agreement on the authorization process, including whatever scoring or judgmental system is in place and what over-limit exceptions (if any) will be allowed. It is easy to stop *all* purchases exceeding the credit limit to control losses, but the credit limit must be balanced with the retailer's need to make the sale. This strategy should also be worked out and documented in advance.

Pricing. The base price and/or any risk-adjusted pricing levels should be established for revolving accounts, along with such details as the grace period, any penalty fees for late payments, over-limit charges, et cetera.

Collections and customer service. The merchant must know the lender's overall strategic collection decisions, such as when and how the customer is to be contacted, when the account is to be cut off, how behavior scoring will be used, etc. Because of their desire to protect their relationship with long-standing customers who might be mildly delinquent, many retailers use softer collections tactics than professional creditors would feel comfortable with. This strategy should be worked out and documented in advance.

These details must be decided upon with the merchant in advance in a careful, well-documented agreement. Retailers are highly individual in the products they sell and in their customer base. For this reason, private label retail financing is typically a product tailored for a specific merchant.

MANAGING THE CONVERSION

At some point a retailer decides to turn over his receivables to a new supplier of credit. This is more than just passing a check, because now the whole credit sales process passes to the hands of a third party. This step is very significant for both the retailer and the financier. Once this transfer has taken place, as a practical matter the merchant seldom reassumes control of the process. Few alternate sources of financing and processing are available, and reestablishing its own operations is very expensive and time-consuming. For this reason, most contracts are for four- or five-year periods, and all the mechanics for possible termination are very carefully spelled out. In addition, it is important to make arrangements for how to handle the existing portfolio.

A typical new financing package might allow for all receivables over 90 days past due to stay with the merchant for about nine months to one year so that the merchant can attempt to collect or write them off. It takes time to understand the details of a portfolio and for the acquirer's own processes to work well. After that takeover period, financial accountability (e.g., writeoffs and collection costs) typically is assumed by the decision-making authority (i.e., the one who controls the approval process); some contracts, however, may stipulate that the merchant will absorb all accounts >90 days old. If so, this situation should be carefully defined and priced.

The lender should always consult counsel on whether an appropriate lien has been or can be filed against the receivables to obtain security. This should be done regardless of whether the contract says that the lender is making a loan against the receivables or purchasing them outright. There are many tests of ownership and, as a practical matter, the lender may not really know if it owns receivables until the bankruptcy court makes a ruling.

LESSONS LEARNED

No matter how good the intentions, a conversion from one system to another is fraught with peril. The lessons that lenders have learned over time include:

- *A conversion is always difficult. Don't rush it. Take plenty of time to make sure the billing process is working correctly, to understand the flow of payments, to train collectors, to set up an authorizations process. The lender should not convert from the existing merchant system until it is absolutely certain its system is working flawlessly.*

- *Never convert a merchant prior to a peak period. Many merchants do 30 percent or more of their annual business near Christmas, and any change at this time, or even 90 days before, invites disaster.*

- *Introduce change slowly. If scoring is to be introduced, credit limits changed, or floor-authorizations procedures changed, these changes must be done with care and with the agreement of the merchant.*

- *Some customers routinely make payments on their accounts in the merchant's store. Plans should be made to handle these, once the merchant's receivables system has been converted.*

As I suggested in an earlier book written for Citicorp:

There is no more embarrassing moment than facing an enraged retailer and explaining that a conversion has been botched. They will know immediately by the impact on their sales, on their customers, and finally on their profits. The key to a well-run indirect private label business is proper planning, an open, up-front relationship with the retailer, and a thorough understanding of his concern for his customers, who are, after all, the lifeblood of his business.

About the time these words were written, Citicorp was completing plans to take over the financing of a major retailer's accounts. The proposal had even gone to the Citicorp board of directors and been approved. Never had a consumer deal reached so lofty a level; never was there such a textbook disaster. Everything that could go wrong, went wrong. Lenders, live and learn.

The Home Mortgage Business 10

PREVIOUS CHAPTERS HAVE FOCUSED on higher-volume consumer products such as credit cards, revolving loans, retailers' cards, and the secured automobile and related products. In this chapter we will cover the unique characteristics of the various home mortgage products (e.g., first or second, closed-end or revolving mortgages). Home mortgages (along with automobile loans) are among the oldest consumer loan products, allowing people to improve their standard of living by spreading out the loan repayments over many years. For most consumers their home represents their largest single asset and their largest single debt. Buying and moving into one's first house or apartment, typically with the aid of a mortgage, can be one of the more memorable events in one's life.

Because first mortgages are usually large (>$200,000) and can run for a long time (up to 30 years), they require a particularly careful review of the borrower as well as the value of the collateral and the amount that can be lent against this collateral. For lenders it is, traditionally, a low-risk business because homes have retained their value and consumers will work hard to avoid losing their homes; it is after all their shelter from the world. But it remains a complex business because of the variable length of the loan (a purported 30-year loan can last only one to two years) and the need to understand the impact of changing interest rates over time. We will cover these points in this chapter.

Single family, 1–4 family, and vacation homes as well as apartment (cooperative and condominium) mortgages represent the largest single source of business for lenders, with more than $5.0 trillion dollars in mortgage loans outstanding in the United States. Although lenders make fewer mortgage loans than other types of loans, the amounts are far larger. Thus a lender can afford few mistakes in assessing risk. There is an additional significant risk as well: when customers default on a credit card, they risk losing the card; when they default on their mortgage, they can lose their home. Foreclosure, covered later in this chapter, is unpleasant and costly for the customer as well as the lending institution.

For many years the home mortgage business was low-risk, predictable, and sometimes downright boring. Most Americans believe, even today, that everyone has an inherent birthright to buy a home that will increase in value every year. There are, of course, periods during which home prices decrease, but overall, home prices do rise. For instance, in 1975 the median selling price for a house was under $25,000, in 1990 it was $84,000; currently at the turn of the century it is over $133,000 ($165,000 for a new home).

Home mortgages have traditionally provided banks with large dollar profits (the loans are large, the risk is low), although they have a narrow profit margin, resulting in a lower return on assets than, say, credit card products. With the right credit processes and careful attention to detail, the home mortgage business should continue to be profitable for lenders; however, the business has become more complex, and the old days of 3-6-3 (i.e., pay your depositors 3 percent, charge them 6 percent for a mortgage, and be on the golf course by 3 PM) are gone forever.

Let's review how the home mortgage business works:

EXHIBIT 10-1
Home Mortgage Business Overview

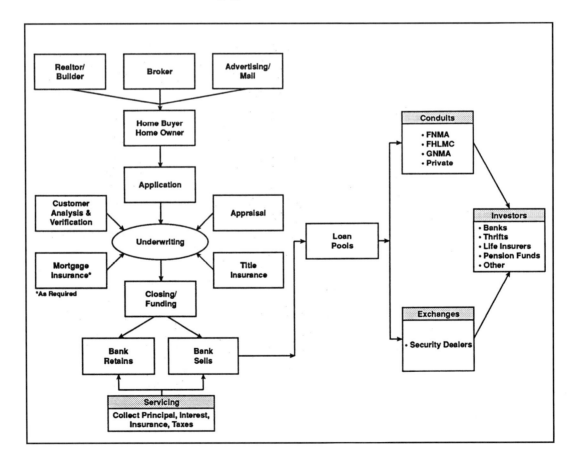

The process starts when someone needs to borrow funds to buy real estate—a house, an apartment, a vacation home, or investment property. He contacts a mortgage broker, his own bank, an Internet source, or whatever, and obtains an application form to fill in. The completed application goes through a very rigorous underwriting process, including an analysis and verification of the customer's information (scoring is now an important part of this process), an appraisal of the value of the property, and a review of the insurance requirements. Once approved, the customer typically attends a formal closing where the paperwork is completed, the funds are released, and the customer receives a key to the property. The whole process can take one to two months or more, depending on the complexity of the deal; however, the customer can obtain at least oral approval in a very short time if an automated underwriting process (AU), covered later, is followed.

Once the bank completes the deal, it can retain the loan or package and sell it in the secondary market. By selling to the secondary market, a lender can obtain funds to initiate more loans.

A bank can make a profit on home mortgage loans in three ways. It can:

- *Originate loans and hold them*
- *Originate loans and sell them in the secondary markets*
- *Service the loans generated by others.*

There are risks and opportunities with each "business."

Originate and hold. If you originate 15- or 30-year fixed mortgages and hold them, funding becomes a real problem, particularly in a rising rate environment. Unless you have matched your funding terms to your loan portfolio, you risk what happened to many savings-and-loan institutions in the 1980s. At that time, the S&Ls (and many other financial institutions) borrowed money at the low, short-term rates then prevailing and lent it out for long-term mortgages at the competitive, long-term rates of 7–8% (then perceived as being high—but not for long). When short-term interest rates rose above 20%, these lenders got killed. If you hold long-term fixed mortgages, you must match the funding terms by borrowing funds in line with the expected life of the fixed portfolio.

Originate and sell. There are two main buyers of mortgage loans: a) the government-sponsored entities, e.g., Fannie Mae and Freddie Mac, for loans that meet their exacting guidelines, and b) a private market for loans that do not meet these guidelines, called nonconforming loans. A lender's selling of a mortgage is invisible to the customer because the monthly payments are typically sent to the same electronic or mail address. As funds are received, they are directed to the current owner of the loan by a loan-servicing organization. If you follow this route, you must understand that you will probably incur more costs to approve and book the loan than you can charge the customer, and that your true profit comes from the sale of the asset. You also must include in your calculation of profit the gain or loss that comes from rising/falling rates during the warehousing period until you actually sell the loan.

Servicing mortgage loans. Servicing loans—the act of billing and collecting the funds monthly—is a very specialized business. It requires a high degree of automation, a very precise control of the paperwork, plus an understanding of the real term of the loans you are servicing, as opposed to the contractual term. Since home owners tend to refinance their mortgages when rates drop, your business can decrease sharply when/if customers refinance their loans with another institution; conversely, a heavy refinance period can also be an opportunity to pick up business.

Because the actual life of a mortgage loan is critical to the business, let's review the forces that impact that term.

ACTUAL VS. CONTRACTUAL LIFE OF A MORTGAGE

Although different contractual terms are offered (e.g., 15 and 30 years), these terms are only directional in nature. An individual initial 15-year loan can stay on the books for 10 or 12 years, while an individual 30-year loan can stay on for only 2 to 3 years. Since lenders do not know what to expect from individual loans, all they can do is estimate the actual life of a mortgage portfolio on the basis of experience. Two major factors enter into this calculation:

People Move

The average American moves every four or five years. People graduate from school, move away from their parents, get a job, get married, have children, get a divorce, change jobs, and, yes, some die. Some people may move from place to place only within their hometown; others move around the country or the world in pursuit of a career. Any of these events can change where a person resides and cause them to buy or sell a home, usually with a mortgage.

Interest Rates Go Up and Down

Changes in the cost of money—the interest rate that people pay for a mortgage and that lenders pay for funds—have a profound effect on the mortgage industry. In times of prosperity, the Federal Reserve Bank tends to raise interest rates to slow down inflation; conversely, during recessions, the Fed cuts rates (sometimes too late). During a high-rate period, people take out adjustable-rate mortgages, which usually have lower initial rates than fixed-term mortgages. (And people usually plan to refinance with a fixed-rate loan when rates fall in the future.) In a rising-rate environment, people tend to hold onto their existing fixed-rate mortgages. When interest rates are falling, however, people take advantage and refinance their existing higher-rate mortgages. For instance, in the years 1992 and 1993 and again in 1998 and 2001, there was a flood of refinancings and prepayments as falling rates induced high-fixed-rate borrowers to move to lower-rate mortgages, as shown in the following chart:

EXHIBIT 10-2

Refinancings—Percent of New Mortgages

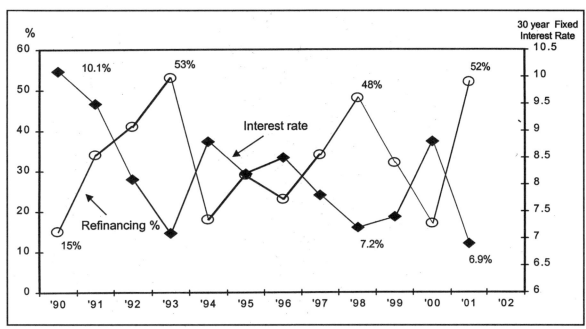

The period of falling rates was a win for consumers because they ended up with substantially lower monthly mortgage payments, although they had to endure the sometimes difficult and time-consuming application and review process. Many lenders and loan servicers, however, suffered as they lost their more profitable accounts.

PREPAYMENTS

While a prepayment penalty—a fee that a lender charges if the loan is paid off early—is one way to slow down refinancings, these fees have all but disappeared in the conventional mortgage financing market. This is not true today in the subprime market, however. According to a Standard & Poor's survey quoted in the *Wall Street Journal* in August 2001, about 80% of mortgages in the subprime market carried prepayment penalties in 2000. While conventional home owners have been able to save hundreds of dollars a month by refinancing as rates dropped, subprime borrowers are finding that if they want to pay off their loans within the first three to five years—for whatever reason—they are first required to pay thousands of dollars in fees (up to 5% of the total loan). Government regulators and legislators have been investigating to see if these penalties should be limited.

The net result of these personal and economic forces is that the contractual term of a loan is, as we said earlier, only directional in nature. Following are some typical actual terms of loans in different economic environments:

	AVERAGE ACTUAL TERM		
	"Normal"	Rising Rates	Falling Rates
Original Term			
15 years	4.5	5.8	3.2
30 years	10.4	12.5	3.0

One final point: because of the size of the loans and their generally longer terms, economic cycles (inflation/deflation) potentially have a major impact on the mortgage market:

1) *Inflation brings rising wages and rising home prices, both of which benefit current homeowners (the value of their homes goes up), but inflation causes difficulties for a first-time buyer (e.g., a higher down payment and larger monthly payments). One piece of good news: a period of economic inflation solves almost all of a lender's risk problems. If the customer defaults on the loan, the lender can almost always get its money out when the customer (or lender) sells the house.*

2) *A flat economy or deflation, on the other hand, brings stable or lower home prices, but also higher unemployment and small changes in wages, and of course, a surge of prepayments. A recession brings higher defaults and a longer selling time for foreclosed properties.*

A lender should understand the implications of each stage of the economic cycle.

PLANNING THE PRODUCT

Most of the steps in planning mortgage products are similar to the planning steps for other consumer products: the target market and sources of customers must be identified, and the product terms and conditions must be detailed. There are, however, additional and unique steps necessary to the mortgage business. For mortgages, a lender must also qualify appraisers, select attorneys and title companies, and prepare for possible foreclosures.

The planning process for mortgage products begins by identifying the target market.

Target Market—Geographic and Demographic

The two most important decisions the lender must make regarding the target market involve the geographic territory it wishes to cover and the type of customer it wishes to attract. Lenders, typically S&Ls, have gotten into trouble expanding beyond their natural markets—for example, financing vacation homes in exotic settings with no understanding of the market and little knowledge of the risks. As a rule, it makes sense for a lender to stick to the markets and customers it knows. As we have already covered, some lenders suffered severe losses by entering the subprime automobile market; while no similar rash of losses has yet occurred in the home mortgage business, the possibility always exists in the future as lenders pursue profits from new sources. At the end of 2000, nearly 3% of subprime mortgages were delinquent more than 90 days, ten times the rate of delinquency on conventional mortgages, so the risk is there.

Sources of Customers

Traditionally most mortgages were sourced through branch offices and existing customer referrals; today the Internet is growing in importance as a source of business, and *indirect* sources, such as real estate brokers, attorneys, accountants, builders, and mortgage brokers, now account for nearly half of the loans generated. Mortgage lending shares several similarities with indirect auto lending. Just as the auto lender must be completely familiar with the auto dealer, the mortgage lender must be completely familiar with the broker. As with auto dealers, you must have a process in place to track the performance of your brokers over time. And again, it is vitally important to cultivate only reputable sources of accounts.

The lender must take care not to let in bad referrals in a drive for volume. There are always marginal or unscrupulous loan brokers who will go to any extreme to get an application approved. Some will even create false information to make the candidate appear more acceptable.

Product Terms and Conditions

The days of a single product offering in the home mortgage business (i.e., a 30-year, fixed-rate, amortizing loan) are long gone. Today, lenders have developed multiple products to cater to customers requiring first or second mortgages for many different needs. There are eight or nine major product variations based on the following three characteristics:

- *A fixed or variable term*
- *A fixed or variable rate*
- *A fixed or variable payment schedule*

The products that can be assembled from this mix include the following:

1. An adjustable rate mortgage (ARM) where the rate varies monthly, semi-annually, or annually, the monthly payment varies, and the term is fixed.

2.. An ARM where the rate and the term vary, but the payment is fixed; if rates rise, the term typically lengthens to avoid negative amortization.

3. A graduated payment first mortgage, where the rate and the term are fixed but the payment increases regularly over time. This product is designed for first-time or young buyers who must stretch to buy their home. These young buyers make an excellent target market. Only 36% of 25- to 29-year-old household heads own their own homes vs. 52% of those aged 30 to 34. By contrast, 80% of household heads age 55 to 64 own their own homes.

These are just samples of the multiple products available. If you bring in the different indexes (the prime rate, the 90-day T-bill rate, etc.) that drive the rates, along with the alternative of capping or not capping rates, plus the possibility of a balloon payment required at the end for loans that do not amortize all the way to zero, the alternatives for the lender and borrower become, in fact, almost infinite. Each permutation has its own unique set of financing risks.

The following items should be considered when designing mortgage products:

	RISK	REWARD
1. Long terms	• Funding risk • Life-event risk • Slow equity buildup (very slow on 30-year)	• Steady stream of income • Lower payments— attracts customers • Longer amortization of acquisition costs
2. Fixed rates	• Funding risk	• Predictable payments— attracts customers
3. Minimum or no amortization/interest only	• Little or no equity buildup	• Lower payments— attracts customers
4. Variable rate indexes subject to rapid changes	• Customers hurt in high-rate environment	• Lower funding risk
5. Rate caps	• Some funding risk	• Better customer relations

Rate caps generally allow a lifetime increase over the initial rate of 5 to 6 points, depending on competitive pressures and a lender's desire to keep its customers happy. Rate increases are usually restricted to no more than 1 to 3 percentage points a year. Indexes selected may change rapidly (monthly), or more slowly (6 months or even annually), depending on a lender's ability to either control the funding risk or willingness to absorb a temporary negative spread. In an inflationary environment, obviously, a slow-changing index benefits the customer and a fast-changing one benefits the lender.

UNDERWRITING PROCESS

The basic standards and guidelines for the entire mortgage underwriting process are set by the quasi-government secondary-market financiers, the Federal National Mortgage Association (Fannie Mae) and the Federal Home Loan Mortgage Corp. (Freddie Mac). They cover:

- *Maximum loan size and loan purpose*
- *Creditworthiness (including scoring)*
- *Debt burden and asset analysis*
- *Verification steps*
- *Loan-to-value standards and appraisals*
- *Mortgage and title insurance.*

Nonconforming markets exist for lenders who wish to package and sell mortgages that do not meet these guidelines and of course, you can always set your own guidelines for mortgages you wish to hold. The secondary markets, however, exert a powerful influence over the standard underwriting processes. The following sections discuss these guidelines in greater detail.

Loan Size and Loan Purpose

Fannie Mae and Freddie Mac currently (2002) allow a maximum loan size for the secondary market they control of $300,700 for first mortgages. The maximum has been increased over time and presumably will continue to rise in the future, so this limit should be reviewed each year. With the median prices of houses varying from a high of $375,000 in Hawaii to a low of $56,000 in Des Moines, there is obviously a wide diversity in the need for large loans. In Kansas City a large loan might be $150,000, but in San Diego $350,000 might buy only a two-bedroom ranch house and the mandatory swimming pool.

As a result of the inflation in housing prices, the rise in the stock market, and the strong economy (at least until 2000), the number of people who have the resources to buy more expensive homes with jumbo loans has increased substantially. So where resources are available and the value of the house is appropriate, an excellent market for larger loans exists. A lender faces obvious risks in concentrating a large dollar amount in any one loan, but the rewards are also obvious (i.e., it costs no more to service a large loan than a small one, and the profit per account should be higher). Any financial institution willing to understand the dynamics of making larger (e.g., >$300,700) or jumbo loans, as they are called, should be prepared to use all the underwriting techniques we describe with some caution and good human judgment. No statistical method that I am aware of can evaluate a $2 million, $3 million (or more) loan to build a "starter castle" for a twenty-nine-year-old Internet entrepreneur. That takes expertise and judgment beyond the boundaries of this book.

Consumer first mortgages are typically limited to owner-occupied first and second (vacation) houses and to the smaller investment properties (1 to 4 units). Many smaller investment properties are owned by people who live in one unit and rent out the other two or three. Larger mortgage loans for investors with extensive holdings are a different, specialized market and aren't considered *consumer* lending.

Applying for the Loan

At the consumer lending seminars we run, we often ask participants: "Which would you rather do—fill out an application for a home mortgage or have your dentist give you a root canal without anesthetic?"

Almost always the answer is the root canal. Applying for a mortgage can be time-consuming, exasperating, and intrusive. The last time I refinanced a mortgage, my wife and I had to sign our names 39 times on 39 different documents and the total package included 51 pages of documentation, weighing over 3 pounds! But this is beginning to change. Only a few years ago, it was estimated that financial institutions lost $1,100 in acquisition costs for each loan booked, which included an average cost of $2,600 to review the application, partially offset by an average of $1,500 charged to the customer. (The costs include the time and money spent on loan applications submitted and later withdrawn as well as those that the bank declines.) Most lenders charge an up-front fee for processing an application, or charge points (e.g., 1–2 % of the loan amount) to cover some of these costs; these fees and points, however, are sometimes waived as part of a promotional campaign to acquire new accounts. Today, using an automated loan underwriting process, many institutions are giving speedy approvals and booking home mortgages at the lowest cost consistent with managing the risk. One major mortgage lender now estimates it costs $600-$700 to book a conventional first mortgage loan (even less for a second mortgage loan) using an automated loan process.

The underwriting process begins with the customer's completing an application, either in the financial institution's offices or submitted online or through a broker. Presumably you will have a well-trained underwriter (or broker, if the application is coming through a broker) interview each applicant to determine if the loan being requested meets your minimum standards; in the event of an online application, a reviewer would be looking for the same information. Here are the questions you want answers to:

1) *Is this the type of loan you want to make?*

2) *Is the value of the property sufficient security for the mortgage amount requested?*

3) *Has the borrower been meeting his obligations in the past?*

4) *Is the borrower able to meet the monthly payments?*

If the loan being sought is appropriate and the applicant meets your minimum requirements, a full application is then filled out.

A well-trained reviewer can eliminate some applicants quickly—those who obviously will not qualify—and then make sure the best ones get special/speedy service. While most applications will fall in the middle, this triaging process can save time and money and keep your good customers happier.

Automated/Desktop Application and Review Process

After the application is taken, the underwriting can be done manually using a traditional, intensive human review process; however, because of the need to keep costs down and to improve the statistical reliability of the mortgage review process, we will concentrate on the automated underwriting process used by most lenders today. The drive to speed up and automate the home mortgage underwriting process has been given a strong boost by the secondary market lenders, Fannie Mae and Freddie Mac. For instance, Fannie Mae's *Desktop Underwriter Guide* outlines a method of assessing mortgage risk quickly to tailor specific loan terms based on an individual's risk profile; Freddie Mac uses a similar process called Loan Prospector. These automated underwriting (AU) systems evaluate a combination of risk factors—including the property type, the size and purpose of the loan, the loan-to-value (LTV) ratio, debt-to-burden ratios (either housing or total expense ratios), available assets, each borrower's credit history, employment status—in order to direct the underwriting process, including the amount and depth of information required to be obtained in order to give a speedy reply. According to Freddie Mac, the automated underwriting process can reduce processing time by 20 to 30 days and will probably also improve the lender's ability to extend mortgages to borrowers with less traditional credit profiles.

Based on the data submitted, the AU programs guide a lender through the whole application process, including when to use streamlined documentation and appraisals, when mortgage insurance is required, and when expanded loan-to-value ratios can be applied. If their procedures are followed and you are a lender recognized by Fannie and Freddie, they can review and give provisional approval (or preliminary rejection) to an application in a matter of minutes. These automated systems, of course, depend heavily on the use of scoring to accelerate the process. With over 75 percent of mortgage applications scored today, it is my opinion that the most successful lenders of tomorrow will be putting a great deal of energy into automating and speeding up the mortgage application review process.

Following are the steps a lender should take in underwriting a mortgage loan.

1) Describing and Valuing the Property

The process begins with the underwriter obtaining enough information from the applicant to be able to determine the price of the property being purchased or refinanced, the amount of the loan being sought, where any down payment will come from, along with a description of the property. It is very important, early on, to determine if the property being purchased is a new or used single-family home, vacation home, apartment or condominium unit, investor-owned property, or whatever. A lender might not make every type of loan, so the applicant can be directed elsewhere if the loan seems "out of scope."

If the underwriter is sufficiently experienced, she will know approximately what similar properties in the area have sold for recently and will either accept what the applicant reports or ask for further proof of the pending sale. The whole process of valuing the property is just as important as determining the customer's ability to pay, because it represents a second way out of the loan if the customer fails to meet his obligations (although, as we discuss later, foreclosure is a nasty business). After getting a complete description of the property and estimating its value, the next step is to determine how large a loan you can make.

2) Loan-to-Value Ratios

You must determine whether you can make a loan of the size being requested. There are industry standards for the loan-to-value ratio for each of the major loan categories (owner-occupied, vacation home, investor, etc.), and you have to determine if the loan will meet these standards or if you are willing to make an exception. We have already said that currently the conforming markets will finance homes with a value up to $300,700; the nonconforming markets can finance much larger loans, and your own institution can go anywhere it wants. The basic starting point, or standard allowable loan-to-value ratio for an owner-occupied-home first mortgage, is usually 80%. In other words, most lenders will advance 80% of the value of the property, calculated as follows:

First mortgage

Value of home[1]	$100,000
Allowable advance	80%
Maximum loan	$ 80,000

---

1. Based on the sale price or the appraised value, whichever is less.

Many lenders are now going up to a 90–95% ratio, theoretically only on the stronger, fully qualified applications or where private mortgage insurance (PMI) is obtained (see below), but the 80% standard is a good starting point. Although 80% is the typical allowable loan-to-value ratio on owner-occupied first mortgages, these ratios typically decline as the loan sizes increase and the purpose of the loan changes, as follows:

EXHIBIT 10-3
Sample Loan-to-Value Ratios

Type	Agency ≥$300,700	<$300,000	Non-Agency $300,000 - $400,000	>$400,000
Owner Occupied	95% (PMI) 80% (no PMI) 80/15/5*	95% (PMI) 80% (no PMI) 80/15/5*	90% (PMI) 80% (no PMI) 80/15/5*	80% (no PMI) 80/15/5*
Vacation/ Second Home	95% (PMI) 80% (no PMI) 80/15/5*	80%	70%	60%
Investor	90% (PMI) 80% (no PMI) 80/10/10*	80%	70%	60%
Second Mortgage	Combined first and second mortgages up to 95% (some lenders up to 125%) for owner occupied; 90% for vacation/second home. Combined LTV decreases as loan amount increases. FICO score generally applies.			

*First mortgage/second mortgage/down payment

For customers who cannot raise the minimum 20% down payment, there are some alternatives:

a) The borrower can obtain (and pay for) private mortgage insurance (PMI) to cover the "missing" share of the down payment, or

b) Some lenders offer an "80/15/5" or sometimes an "80/10/10" product; this requires only a 5–10% down payment with the remaining 15–10% balance financed with an additional loan priced at a higher, or second mortgage rate. This can benefit both the borrower and the lender:

- *For the borrower*—The cost of the higher interest rate for a portion of the loan can be less than the cost of private mortgage insurance.

- *For the lender*—The higher rate aligns the risk with the reward.

Loans to individuals to purchase a property or refinance a property they are already living in tend to carry the lowest risk of all mortgage loans, and it is appropriate that they have the higher loan-to-value ratios. Owner-occupied second homes or vacation homes have also proven to be low risk. Units purchased by *investors* tend to be higher risk. Speculative purchases of housing units—typically concentrations of high-rise vacation homes in booming markets—can be even riskier. It is prudent for a lender to limit the number of units owned by any one investor and to lower the loan-to-value ratio to the 60–80% range or below for these units, particularly the more expensive ones.

In addition, it might be wise to limit advances in very hot markets (such as Silicon Valley in the late 1990s), preferably in advance of a sharp pullback in values. Home values that rise at extraordinary rates (e.g., 2–3% a month) could be a warning sign of future problems. Also, markets entering a regional recession (such as that experienced by some of the farm markets in the 1990s) would normally call for reducing loan-to-value ratios for a while unless the appraisals are extremely realistic. Further exceptions might be made for marginal properties—those in very poor condition or in rural areas with limited marketability.

Once you have determined that the loan amount and loan-to-value ratios are appropriate (at least on paper; the actual verification of these figures comes later), the next step is to determine the creditworthiness of the applicant(s).

3) Borrower Creditworthiness

The applicant's credit score is obtained as part of the AU process and will be a strong guide as to what further steps are necessary; a credit score should be requested for every applicant. The predictive power of scoring was discovered by the secondary mortgage markets a few years ago, and today lenders are encouraged to use the Fair, Isaac (FICO) or other validated scores to rank-order applications. If cost justified (and remember, mortgages typically are large loans so it usually is worth spending the money), lenders should request a merged credit report based on information contained in the three credit bureaus (the Equifax Beacon score, the TransUnion Empirica score, and the Experían/Fair, Isaac model at Experían). If the borrower does not have a credit history or a score, the application must be processed outside of the normal, automated format (a judgmental review).

4) Income and Debt-to-Burden Ratios

Another key element of the application process is to obtain information on the amount and source of each applicant's income (or total family income in the event of a joint application) and what assets (liquid or property) he holds. The financing institution has to know how the applicant(s) plans to pay for the mortgage, including where the down payment is coming from. This asset/income information should be checked for any obvious discrepancies (does a plumber make $250,000/year? . . . a shipping clerk $90,000?) and to determine if there is enough money for the down payment as well as enough resources to see them through a few months of unemployment or hardship (e.g., do they have a retirement account? an IRA?).

Once income has been established, the lender must perform a debt-burden analysis, that is, examine the ratio of monthly income to the monthly cost of carrying the loan. Earlier we covered the problems associated with determining the value of debt-burden ratios as well as the difficulty in obtaining complete and accurate data. However, even though statistical verification of the predictive power of such analysis may be lacking, the size of these loans makes it appropriate to perform a debt-burden analysis on every mortgage transaction, particularly on loans for sale in any secondary market where the guidelines require it.

The two most common ways to establish debt-burden ratios are:

- **Total monthly housing payment method.** *Here the monthly mortgage principal plus interest, hazard insurance, real estate taxes, mortgage insurance (if required), and homeowner association dues should be within the following ratios:*

  Typical % of Stable Monthly Income

  Conforming = 28–33%

  Nonconforming = 30–35%

- **Total monthly debt method**. *Monthly housing payment plus monthly payments on revolving, installment, and other loans should be within the following ratios:*

  Typical % of Stable Monthly Income

  Conforming = 36–42%

  Nonconforming = Up to 45%

These guidelines are fairly typical; a lender could, however, take local conditions into account. For example, housing is typically a very high proportion of a young person's expenditures in major metropolitan areas. A lender may want to go up to 50% for a first-time urban buyer with good prospects for the future; this level makes less sense in rural or less populous areas. Guidelines make a good starting point for underwriters and suffice for most applicants, but rigid adherence to guidelines can restrict good business.

The first debt-to-burden ratio is relatively easy to calculate because you can obtain the monthly principal, interest, taxes, and insurance payments (PITI) with some accuracy, and presumably you have some idea of stable income. The second calculation, total monthly debt as a percent of stable income, entails estimating monthly payments on *total debt* outstanding. This is more difficult to determine because:

1. *You may have inaccurate information on the total debt outstanding, due to incomplete or misreported credit bureau information.*

2) *The customer can obtain new revolving lines or loans at any time, with the potential for a large increase in monthly payments.*

Either event can substantially alter the monthly debt payment calculation.

Calculate monthly debt payment only when you need a very complete analysis of the applicant, say, when there is a lower score and evidence of heavy outside debt. In view of the problems of debt-burden analysis (covered throughout this book), some lenders are instead relying on analyzing available assets, including stocks and bonds, IRAs, 401(k) plans, etc., where these can be verified. While it is true that assets can "disappear" (even as income can change at any time), the very existence of even moderate savings indicates that the homeowner has some discipline, and they can help carry a borrower through some hard times.

Preliminary Decision

After the loan-application information is submitted for analysis (e.g., on Fannie's Desktop Underwriter, Freddie's Loan Prospector, or your own processing system), the system will make a recommendation and suggest next steps to verify and implement the decision. Recommendations can range from:

- *Approval—The suggested loan meets the credit risk and eligibility requirements.*
- *Cautious approval—The loan does not appear to meet the risk or eligibility requirements; further information must be obtained before it can be approved.*
- *Outright rejection—The application can still be resubmitted if new information is obtained.*

Once the lender receives the recommendation, it must decide whether to accept the application, or in the case of rejection, to try to obtain new information. Further, if the loan does not meet the eligibility requirements of the secondary markets, a lender might still choose to keep the loan on its books (say, in the case of a jumbo loan).

NEXT STEPS

If the decision is to approve the loan, the AU process will guide the lender through the final steps of verification of the applicant's information and whatever appraisal of the property is required.

1) Verification of the Applicant's Income and Assets

Depending on the degree of risk determined through this underwriting process, some verification of the applicant's income and assets may be required. Some information can be readily determined; for instance, income from a regular job can easily be checked with a copy of the tax-withholding form from the employer (the W-2), but income from self-employment, a second job, overtime, bonuses, commissions, or fees can be tricky to evaluate. Other income, say from interest and dividends, or from outside investments, trust funds, alimony, or rental property, also may be difficult to prove/verify. Obviously, the verification process should be more rigorous for a self-employed applicant. At a minimum, a knowledgeable underwriter must review one or two years of business tax returns. Because preparing a small business tax return entails many nuances, the underwriter should fully understand the underlying stability and reliability of the data.

The secondary market manuals (such as the *Fannie Mae Servicing Manual*) provide great detail on how to analyze income from alternate sources (and every other aspect of the underwriting process), but a good automated process can help underwriters decide which income item or assets must be verified and when assertions can be accepted without confirmation. While I recommend the use of an automated process, the manuals can serve as a resource in the event of any exceptional applications.

2) Appraising the Property

As we have said, obtaining an accurate, well-documented property valuation is a key element in ensuring a prudent underwriting of mortgage loans. The objective of the property appraisal process is to establish a value for the home or apartment based upon whatever information is available. This can include recent sales of comparable properties, tax records, or the cost to replace the property at today's building prices. Valuation is simple in the case of tract homes or apartments where there is a lot of turnover; however, it can be highly complex in the case of a unique, architect-designed, expensive home or a home in a rural area where there have been few sales. Further, since appraisals are based solely on past information, the lender must bear in mind that a sharp rise or fall in a market's home values will cause old valuations to become unreliable. There are always some appraisers and appraisal firms that do a better job than others over the long run, and appraiser performance must be monitored over time to see which ones do the best work (appraise the appraisers!). While the lender is responsible for ensuring that the process is accurate and reliable, the actual appraisal is usually done by an outside appraiser. Thus selecting the right appraiser is critical.

The appraiser's task is to give the lender a complete, accurate description of the property and an accurate, adequately supported estimate of its value. Depending on the size of the loan, the loan-to-value ratios, the applicant's score, and the underlying riskiness of the property, appraisals can range from 1) an automated or electronic review of similar properties derived from multiple listing services, property tax and assessment records, prior inspections, etc.; 2) an exterior-only property inspection (a "drive-by") to check the current condition of the property; to 3) a full on-site review.

With a full appraisal, the appraiser personally examines the property to determine its age, size (land and building), type of construction, location, as well as condition of the building and neighborhood. Measurements might be obtained for each room. The appraiser will also identify any features that might make the property unique, including all additions (e.g., a garage, gazebo, pool, hot tub) that might add or subtract value.

Appraisal costs range from $35, for an electronic review, up to several hundred dollars for a full appraisal. Selecting the appraisal method most appropriate to the risk is very important, and here again a well-developed automated process can keep costs down and speed up the process.

THE VALUE OF PROPERTY TAX RECORDS

Some real estate appraisals rely heavily on state or county property tax records, which can give an accurate idea of the true value of a property. Typically, each year local tax authorities bill property owners an amount to cover local government expenses including school, police and fire protection, road maintenance, etc. This tax is computed by assessing each homeowner a standard percentage of the home's value. In some regions this method is very fair and appropriate. In Minnesota and Florida, for example, property values are regularly updated on the basis of current sales and the local tax bills are constantly revised. In this case, tax records add considerable weight in estimating the value of the property.

In other regions (e.g., Nassau County on Long Island), property valuations (and taxes) are rarely updated;[2] in California, tax records and thus property valuations can be updated only upon the sale of the property. Under this system, the new homeowners eventually end up paying a higher and higher share of the total taxes. How does this happen? Here's an example: A house purchased in 1998 cost $250,000; the exact same house next door was purchased in 1950 for $25,000. If well maintained, both are worth the same amount if resold in 2001, but the taxes on the house bought in 1950 remain 10% of the house purchased in 1998. It's called the "welcome stranger" method of taxing property. So property tax records in each region must be researched to see if they are of any use.

3) Insurance Requirements—Mortgage, Title, and Fire Insurance

Before closing, the owner must demonstrate that he has obtained the required hazard and liability insurance to cover the mortgaged property. This includes proof of the standard fire, casualty, and liability insurance on the home, with the lender named as the lien holder. Title insurance is another requirement. Title insurance covers the validity of the underlying deed to the property and assures the buyer that the property will not be repossessed due to incorrect registration of

---

2. In 2001, Nassau County embarked on a three-year revision of its residential property tax assessments, which had not been updated since 1938.

the deed whenever the property was previously transferred (this could be, say, in the year 1632 for some old, eastern properties). Flood insurance may also be required for homeowners who live in a federally designated flood zone, and earthquake-prone areas may require special insurance.

In the world we have been living in, one where housing prices are strong and have been increasing, it may be advisable to accept a customer with a small down payment (e.g., 10%) but require private mortgage insurance. For a fee, certain private institutions will insure the first 10–30% of a bank's loss in the event of foreclosure or sale of a property. As with any insurance arrangement, however, the lender must know the value or worth of the insurer. Is the insuring company strong enough to survive a major turndown in the market and extensive losses? The rates charged are small (typically 1% or less), but the exposure can be large, so the insurance may run out just when a lender needs it most, such as in a major recession or a downturn in the market. One warning: a lender should have a process for eliminating this added monthly fee if/when the customer builds up sufficient equity in the house so that it is no longer required. In the United States, new legislation makes it illegal to continue charging this added fee once the homeowner has built up the appropriate equity; its impact is yet to be determined.

Closing and Legal Process

After conducting its credit review, a lender must complete the legal and audit process before releasing the funds and actually booking a mortgage loan. A closing is a very precise operation undertaken only after the lender is certain that all the paperwork has been completed and a lawyer has reviewed the legal details. For instance, a search must be made to assure the borrower (and lender) that all taxes due on the property have been paid and prior liens are satisfied. Even such a mundane item as the water bill must be checked or the new owner could be unpleasantly surprised to find himself owing a large amount incurred by the previous owner.

At the closing, a home buyer faces several costs, which must be carefully explained in advance. The pre-closing explanation of costs is not only common sense but is also a legal requirement. In addition to the insurance fees covered above, there may be mortgage registration fees, appraisal costs, legal fees, and usually one or two exotic transfer fees or taxes devised by the federal, state, or local governments. (Some counties/local authorities now also charge a transfer fee, typically 1%, to cover such worthy causes as buying wetlands or open land for environmental protection.) These fees can shock a first-time buyer, and it is the responsibility of the bank to keep the customer fully aware of these and all other costs *before* the closing. Unless the purchase is quite modest, these miscellaneous fees can add up to thousands of dollars. The old rule, "Bring a checkbook to the closing," will probably go on forever!

HOME EQUITY LOANS/SECOND MORTGAGES

Second mortgages are one of the fastest-growing areas of financing in the United States. Just to review, a second mortgage refers to a loan made to a property owner who already has a first mortgage; in the event the loan goes into default, the first mortgage holder must be paid in full before the second mortgage holder can receive any payment. With the vast buildup in the equity of existing houses, the elimination of tax benefits for interest paid on any loan other than a first or second mortgage,[3] and the ever-increasing number of attractive new mortgage products, second mortgages have become a very normal way of meeting one's individual financial needs. Lenders are constantly soliciting second mortgage business by mail and on television, and on television in particular, they target high-interest-paying, credit card debtors.

Borrowers take out a second mortgage for many purposes. They provide a convenient way for consumers to pay off credit card and other short-term debt, to finance home improvements, to buy a vacation home, to pay for almost any sizable expense. There are two basic products, either of which can be priced with fixed or variable rates:

- *Fixed balance, term installment loans*
- *Revolving loans, typically accessed by check (usually called a HELOC, or a home-equity line of credit).*

Either loan may be amortizing on a regular basis or non-amortizing for a period of time (typically five years' interest only), then amortizing over a fixed period. Few second mortgages are made for periods exceeding 20 years, although there are exceptions.

From a lender's point of view, a second mortgage loan, while obviously not as well secured as a first mortgage, does provide some degree of protection from a writeoff. The fact that a lien is placed over the property when a second mortgage is taken out can be a powerful incentive for a borrower to meet this credit obligation. But lenders should recognize that, in many cases, foreclosing on the house may not be worthwhile, unless the first mortgage holder has already taken such action. Some lenders look at second mortgages as "unsecured" loans, regardless of the lien on the property. Previous chapters have covered the effect of the growth of bankruptcy on the American consumer loan market, and how much unsecured debt can be wiped out this way; it is not as easy to remove secured debt.

Lenders typically charge an annual rate of 2–4% more for a second mortgage than a first mortgage, reflecting the added risk plus the smaller loan sizes with its higher relative operating costs. Loss rates on second mortgages have been higher than on first mortgages (30–40 basis points vs. 20–30 bps), but they are still low, reflecting the fact that the loan is secured by a home.

---

3. Currently limited to interest paid on a maximum of $100,000 for a second mortgage loan.

Dinner at the Mortgage Restaurant

Ever seen a meal you fell in love with but simply _couldn't_ afford?

Well, at the Mortgage Restaurant you can afford just about anything.

Every table comes with not only a waiter but an accountant and a lawyer, all of whom would love to be of service.

Here's how it works: Let's say you want the baby lamb chops with baby potatoes and baby vegetables listed on our menu for $185.00.

For as little as $18.50 you can have that meal brought right to your table.

And in only 20 years you can call it your own.

R. Chast

Lenders, however, are constantly devising new and presumably riskier variations of products to tap this second mortgage market. The subprime market is solicited; borrowers with little equity in their homes are targeted with "high loan-to-value" (e.g., 125%) loans. The riskiest target market I have heard of encourages borrowers to take out a second mortgage on their home and then invest the proceeds in the stock market. Borrowers are encouraged to day-trade their way to millions of dollars on borrowed money! It would be acceptable if the market went up forever, but it doesn't, as the dramatic fall in tech stocks and other parts of the market in 2000 and 2001 showed many investors. Does it make sense to get into these businesses? You had better know what you are doing. There will be a time of reckoning for these extreme lenders.

Second Mortgage Underwriting Process

A prudent business should follow the same credit underwriting process for second mortgages as it does for first mortgages, but it must control the time and money spent in this review. These loans are much smaller on average than a first mortgage (typically in the $25,000–$40,000 range), so you must control the acquisition costs. Also, borrowers expect not to pay large closing costs. I recommend that the basic account approval process fall somewhere in between the high-volume approval process (e.g., for credit cards, which relies very heavily on scoring and does an absolute minimum of debt-burden analysis and verification) and the home first mortgage process (which entails a more detailed property valuation and human review process, in addition to scoring).

In other words, the approval process should include a reasonably short application, scoring, a simple debt-burden and loan-to-value analysis, and a briefer appraisal process. For a small second mortgage, an electronic check of the property records, and possibly a drive-by, would be a sufficient check on the value of the property. This is particularly true if the first mortgage is new (obtained, say, in the past three to four years), in which case the appraisal made by the first mortgage holder would be of more value. If you have reason to believe the borrower's home is in an area on the decline, a more thorough property appraisal would be called for.

Some Final, Common-Sense Thoughts on Mortgage Lending

1. Because many second mortgage loans are used for debt consolidation, some lenders go to great lengths to ensure that the borrower really has paid off his old loans, even tearing up all credit cards at the closing. A lender, however, has no way to keep a borrower from getting new lines of credit the day after the closing. A debt consolidation loan may really be a way to launch a new credit binge. The danger for the borrower is that a life event or crisis such as the loss of a job may cause a future default, but now the home is at stake.

2. If you could choose, assuming a limit of an 80% loan-to-value (first and second mortgage combined) ratio, which loan would you rather make as the second mortgage lender?

	ALTERNATE 1	ALTERNATE 2
Appraised Value of Home	$100,000	$100,000
Less: Outstanding 1st Mortgage	(60,000)	(40,000)
"Available" equity	$ 40,000	$ 60,000
Maximum 2nd Mortgage Loan Allowed	20,000	40,000
Total 1st + 2nd Mortgage allowed	80%	80%

Many lenders would say the $20,000 loan (Alternate 1) is the more conservative, since the loan is smaller; however, Alternate 2 is probably less risky, because you only have to pay off a $40,000 first mortgage before you have some equity.

3. A second mortgage lender should understand the terms and conditions of the first mortgage and any other prior lien. For instance, a lender should be more conservative if there is a variable-rate first

mortgage when making a second mortgage. Two unrestricted variable-rate mortgages (i.e., first and second mortgage loans) can easily double the burden on a borrower in a time of rising interest rates, thereby increasing the chance of a default. Further, a variable-rate first mortgage may go through a period of minimal or even negative amortization, which can erode the equity underpinning the second mortgage. For this reason, some lenders refuse to fund a second mortgage behind a variable-rate first loan. A business should carefully spell out its policy on when variable-rate first and second mortgage loans can be given to one borrower.

4. Beware of predatory pricing as a solution to high-risk or subprime home mortgage lending. Predatory pricing is the term applied to charging unusually high rates, adding hidden costs, setting huge prepayment penalties, and in general taking advantage of unsophisticated borrowers wherever possible. When a home is involved, this can be a very poor way to offset the risk of subprime lending. The unfavorable reaction from the press, the regulators, and the community can quickly put a greedy lender out of business.

5. One last warning: during the early 1990s a few banks tried to cut some corners. Not only did they put on combined high loan-to-value and high debt-burden loans, they exacerbated this by accepting these applications from brokers (sometimes less than reputable brokers) and by sharply limiting the loan documentation required ("short-doc" loans). This "quadruple whammy" process is reputed to have contributed to Citicorp's reporting a writeoff rate of 1.31% on domestic home mortgages in 1995 . . . nearly ten times the national average. So much for cutting too many corners.

This concludes our review of the home mortgage application and review process. Despite all your precautions, some of your accounts will get into trouble and you will need to have a collections and foreclosure process in place to handle these.

COLLECTIONS

The collection process for home loans is quite different from the rest of the consumer lending business. Here, the whole thrust of the collection effort is to have an intelligent process in place to distinguish between the many who want to bring their accounts current and those few who cannot or will not. Because of the size of the loan, the cost of foreclosure, and the importance of a home to a customer's family, this distinction is easier to make.

For most customers, a brief reminder notice and the imposition of late fees whenever some slippage occurs are sufficient to bring the account current. The threat of beginning a foreclosure is always available as a final reminder. The problem is identifying and moving rapidly with people who are beginning to get into trouble. For these customers, it is worth spending money on a personalized collection procedure.

When a customer gets into a financial bind severe enough to risk losing his house, the lender should take the time and trouble to understand what has gone wrong. It should explore, together with the customer, every possible alternative to keep the customer current and avoid the foreclosure process. While many of the procedures covered in the chapters on Collections still apply, I advocate a dedicated home mortgage collections organization. This unit is trained to listen to customers and is given the resources to be able to take the time to really talk with them. I recommend only a few, very few, quickie "Have you forgotten to send in your payment" calls. I even question the need for a behavior scoring system for a mortgage collections unit. Save your money. All late mortgage payments are serious; remember the customer's priority of payment.

FORECLOSURES

Inevitably, a time will come when all collection efforts have failed and an account cannot be brought current. A lender must then have a well-defined process in place to handle the foreclosure process. This area is highly regulated, not only in the U.S., but throughout the world. The image and reality of a financial institution dispossessing a family from its home is all too familiar with regulators and the public. A lender who ignores the prevailing sentiment does so at its peril. For those who have never seen the impact of a foreclosure, I recommend seeing the classic movie *Roger and Me*. The movie follows a foreclosure representative as he moves families out of their homes in the town of Flint, Michigan, during the mid-1980s, when this area was going through hard times after the downsizing of the U.S. automobile business.

Further, foreclosure is expensive and should be avoided if any reasonable alternative exists. Thankfully, most foreclosures do not reach a forced sale of the property; typically, customers sell the house on their own and then settle with the bank. If the problem appears to be temporary, the lender should make every attempt to allow a period of reduced or interest-only payments. Recent articles in the press (2002) indicate that mortgage lenders are indeed attempting to work out arrangements with customers during this period of economic recession, as evidenced by a continuing low rate of writeoff on mortgage loans, despite higher rates of deliquency. Of course, with the strong housing market currently, there is an incentive for borrowers to try and retain their home (or else sell it at a profit).

Finally, if the customer repeatedly fails to meet her obligations and there is no alternative, a decision to foreclose may then be made. The legal process varies by country and state, so the time it takes to foreclose varies greatly. In this difficult and unpleasant situation, it is essential to have a very precise process in place to handle the property during the legal steps of foreclosure, taking title to the property, and finally, disposing of the house.

During this period, it is important that a lender take steps to maintain the property and preserve its resale value. This may require hiring people to provide rudimentary services. Nothing is more discouraging to a potential buyer than seeing a house for sale with an unmown lawn, broken windows, and a generally shabby exterior. An estimate of the potential costs of carrying a specific home for a period of time should be prepared. Selling it may take months, or only a few weeks. Costs include the monthly carrying costs, such as local taxes, maintenance, utilities, and ultimately, the broker's commission on the sale. There are also one-time foreclosure costs such as legal and closing fees. Following is a sample worksheet for calculating the costs of foreclosure.

EXHIBIT 10-4
Foreclosure Carrying Costs Worksheet

Cost Items	One-Time Charge	Monthly Payment	Total Costs at the End of		
			4 months	8 months	12 months
First Mortgage					
Second Mortgage					
Maintenance & repairs					
Security					
Utilities					
Taxes					
Insurance					
Appraisal					
Closing & Legal					
Sales Commission					
Total Costs					

	Current	+4 mos.	+8 mos.	+12 mos.
Loan Balance + Carrying Costs	_____	_____	_____	_____
Quick Sale Price	_____	_____	_____	_____

As with automobile repossessions, a good rule of thumb is still "First loss is the least lost." Do a simple break-even analysis to compare the carrying costs over time with any bids in hand.

Providing below-cost financing to a potential buyer (i.e., offering a lower interest, subsidized rate) is one way to attract buyers for a distressed property. Although this tactic is a perfectly appropriate way to move a unit, a lender should keep very careful track of how often such loans are made. The cost of below-cost financing goes on for years, whereas a one-time capital loss on the property is recorded immediately. A lender also must ensure that proper accounting rules are followed. It is easy for a local manager to look good in the short term by keeping his property-in-inventory down while the true loss impact is concealed.

This ends the discussion of the home lending business, a very important and excellent business for those who do it well.

Profit Analysis for Consumer Products

T HE PURPOSE OF business is to make a profit, and thus it is vital for every business to fully understand how its profitability is derived. By understanding the components of profitability, management can better control each phase of the operations and alter the process to improve profits. In other words, with the right information, you can make better decisions. The questions to keep asking are:

- *Is the level of profit appropriate for the risk inherent in each product?*

- *Which products should be expanded and which products should be restricted or eliminated from the marketplace?*

- *Is the spread (i.e., the difference between the price charged the customer and the cost of funds) adequate?*

- *For which products do expenses appear high, and where should costs be cut to meet targeted profit levels?*

- *When should competitive pricing cuts be matched and when not?*

- *When should price increases lead the competition if a product is unprofitable or only marginally profitable, even at the expense of volume?*

These are hard, practical questions. Understanding profitability is not a theoretical exercise but the heart of the business itself. Not every product must be profitable at all times. Sometimes a product will be offered as a loss leader to promote the overall objectives of the organization. For instance, new credit card accounts may not be profitable for two or more years because of their low initial balances and high acquisition costs, and so the organization must be prepared to absorb the initial costs because these accounts can become very profitable over time. The sum total of all products, however, should generate sufficient profit to meet the corporate goals. Only by knowing the components of profitability, in detail, can a lender make the common-sense decisions necessary for survival.

This chapter outlines a methodology for analyzing and understanding profitability for the typical consumer financial services business. Our level of detail will not satisfy most accountants; for instance, we do not tell you whether to measure profits by return on assets (ROA), return on equity (ROE), shareholder value added (SVA), earnings contribution, risk-adjusted return on capital, or any of the other measures used by financial gurus. In fact, we have even skipped over some of the finer points, including when/how to allocate fixed charges, the calculation of present value, and other nuances of the business; we leave coverage of those subjects to other experts.

What we want to do is to outline the fundamental concepts that underlie profitability analysis in the consumer lending businesses and to give you tools to at least understand how to compute profitability by product. We also briefly review the one item not covered in detail anywhere else in this book—namely, funding. Proper funding is a special world, but it is critical to profitability in the consumer lending business. We merely outline a few principles of good management and leave the rest to your Treasury experts.

To begin, let's cover the fundamental concept that profits must be calculated over several years . . . a product's lifetime.

LIFETIME, SINGLE-LOAN PROFITABILITY ANALYSIS

The key to understanding profitability in the consumer lending business is to determine the flow of income and expenses for each product (i.e., its profitability) *over its lifetime.* Let's review what we mean by product (covered briefly in Chapter 1) and how you determine "lifetime."

Profitability by Product

The goal of analyzing consumer loan profitability is to determine the profitability of every group of loans acquired with the same *standard terms and conditions*, which means that they all have virtually the same revenue, risk, and operating costs. We refer to these groups of loans as products or subproducts throughout this book, including first mortgages, second mortgages, classic credit cards,[1] premium credit cards, student credit cards, new automobile loans, used automobile loans, etc. Since it makes no sense to follow the profitability of each individual loan, we group similar accounts into product/subproduct categories, and these groups are what should be analyzed. While most products have standard prices, if you use risk-adjusted pricing, the revenue and the loss rate (and

---

1. We cover the handling of revolver vs. convenience users later in this chapter.

thus the profitability) could vary from loan to loan. The best way to track these loans is to estimate the mix of loans by range of profitability—say, 30% high-risk, 60% medium-risk, and 10% low-risk, for the total product—and then track the actual mix of business booked versus the estimated mix to see if your estimates are realistic.

Lifetime

The next goal is to establish a normal lifetime for each product. The average actual lifetime varies significantly by product. Let's begin by looking at the two major loan categories: installment and revolving products.

Installment Loans

Calculating the lifetime of an installment loan starts by determining the fixed period which the borrower has selected. For example, with automobiles, the standard loan is booked for three to four years; leased units tend to be booked initially for a shorter period, say two to three years. First mortgages, on the other hand, are typically booked for fifteen to thirty years. But early payouts on both these products can be significant, as we have already covered in Chapters 9 and 10 on secured products. As many as 20–30% of all auto loans pay out early (often in the first few months) as borrowers find they can get a lower interest rate with another financier (e.g., their credit union) or the unit is wrecked, repossessed, etc. Mortgages are refinanced regularly as customers move and interest rates change. Consequently, while the normal lifetime for a 15-year loan is 4.5 years, this can range from 3.2 years in a falling rate environment to 5.8 years in a rising rate one. Thus a lender must build in a factor for the early payout of installment loans, with particular attention to the cost of reviewing the application and booking the loan.

Revolving Products

For revolving products, you should build a model using your best estimate of the revenue and costs for the next few years for each product. I typically use four or five years for a credit card product, based on the assumption that it is difficult to predict the customers' usage of your card, the buildup of balances, the cost of funds, etc., for more than a few years ahead. This is not perfect, but it is a start. A one- or two-year lifetime model would provide misleading information; a ten-year lifetime model is way too long (things change too much!). First let's see what happens if you look at just one year's results. The following chart shows information that a simplified profit-reporting system might include (assuming that such product detail were even available in an unsophisticated business) for a given year.

EXHIBIT 11-1

Sample Profit Model —Traditional

($ Millions)

	Product A	Product B	Product C	Total
Income				
Revenue	$ 5.0	$ 9.0	$ 10.0	$24.0
Fees		1.0	---	1.0
Cost of funds	(2.3)	(5.0)	(4.7)	(12.0)
Net Income	$ 2.7	$ 5.0	$ 5.3	$13.0
Expenses				
Acquisition	0.5	0.1	2.0	2.6
Delivery	0.6	0.3	0.2	1.1
Maintenance	0.8	0.4	0.4	1.6
Collection	1.3	0.2	1.2	2.7
Writeoffs	1.0	0.0	1.0	2.0
Total Expenses	$ 4.2	$ 1.0	$ 4.8	$ 10.0
Net Profit Contribution	($ 1.5)	$ 4.0	$ 0.5	$3.0

Obviously, this report provides important data required for the accounting records, annual reports, tax statements, senior management reports, and so forth. The report, however, does *not* provide the necessary detail to really understand the performance of a portfolio. By looking at only the aggregate results, the following points are missed:

- *Marketing and acquisition expenses precede the booking of revenue.*
- *Some accounts are never booked but still incur all the costs of acquisition, including the initial investigation costs.*
- *The method of income recognition can vary from product to product.*
- *Over time, net customer interest income decreases on installment products and increases on credit cards.*
- *Collection costs and writeoffs vary over the life of the account.*
  - *They are minimal at first on a new revolving account, then build over time.*
  - *Installment loans incur these costs early, typically in the first year.*
- *Recoveries from collection activity come in months or years after an account is written off.*

Accounting conventions can soften some of the impact of these facts (say, by writing off acquisition costs over time), but refining the accounting methods alone cannot entirely solve the problem of misleading information. In short, there are many variables to understand in looking at the profitability of a product, *particularly in a fast-growing or rapidly declining business.* The solution is to look at each product (and subproduct, if significant) over its lifetime.

Once the appropriate lifetimes for a revolving or an installment product have been determined, the lender should project what will happen to one typical loan over its lifetime. This is done by estimating as carefully as possible the normal income, costs, and profits (e.g., average balance, interest, fee income, cost of funds, acquisition, processing, collections costs) for a typical account for each month (or possibly quarter) over the estimated lifetime.[2] This one-loan projection is used as a surrogate for how the entire portfolio of similar accounts would perform.

EXHIBIT 11-2
Credit Card Profit Model

	Year 1	Year 2	Year 3	Year 4	Year 5	5-year average
Avg. balance	$1200	$1500	$1800	$1950	$2100	$1710
Income						
Gross revenue	119	282	338	367	395	
Cost of funds	(66)	(83)	(99)	(107)	(116)	
Net revenue	$ 53	$ 199	$ 239	$ 260	$ 279	$ 206
Expenses						
Marketing	60	25	15	15	15	
Maintenance	35	40	45	45	44	
Collection	10	25	30	34	34	
Writeoffs	15	61	80	103	100	
Total	$ 120	$ 151	$ 178	$ 196	$ 210	$ 171
Net Contribution	$ (67)	$ 48	$ 61	$ 64	$ 69	$ 35

This is an example of a revolving card customer building up a balance over time. As shown, the credit card product may not be profitable for a year or so until the customer starts really using the card and building up a balance. By the third or fourth year the model indicates that the product is very profitable, the kind you would like to keep forever. But this is just one sample product. The profit model can differ sharply, say, if the customer is acquired by a balance transfer program, typically at a low introductory price. In that case the balances outstanding, and most of the expenses, would all start at a high level, but profits might be low or nonexistent because of the low initial price. Further, there probably will be a higher rate of attrition with balance transfer accounts, reducing the number of accounts that will stay with you.

---

2. A monthly model is usually most accurate, but sometimes a quarterly analysis may suffice.

As we have indicated, these models merely project the lifetime profitability of one typical account, in this case a credit card. A similar projection for an installment loan would show a very different pattern of revenues and costs, e.g., profits are typically high at the beginning of the loan because the outstanding balance is high, while profits are marginal or nonexistent at the end of the loan term as the outstanding principal is paid down.

The next step in profit analysis is to estimate how many accounts, revolving and installment, you will have in each stage of its lifetime. The following chart shows this calculation, on an annualized basis, for a growing credit card business (in this example, adding 200,000 accounts per year). The example shows one year's profit for each of five years.

EXHIBIT 11-3
Total Profit Contribution

	Year 1	Year 2	Year 3	Year 4	Year 5	5-year average
Avg. balance	$ 1200	$ 1500	$ 1800	$ 1950	$ 2100	$ 1038
Accts. - new (000's)	200.0	200.0	200.0	200.0	200.0	
1 year old		180.0	180.0	180.0	180.0	
2 years old			160.0	160.0	160.0	
3 years old				150.0	150.0	
4 years old					140.0	
Cards (total)	200.0	380.0	540.0	690.0	830.0	
Profits/loss/acct./yr. Year 1-5	$ (67)	$ 48	$ 61	$ 64	$ 69	$ 35/ card
Profit loss - new ($M)	(13.4)	(13.4)	(13.4)	(13.4)	(13.4)	
1 year old		8.6	8.6	8.6	8.6	
2 years old			9.7	9.7	9.7	
3 years old				9.6	9.6	
4 years old					9.7	
Annual Contribution	$ (13.4)	$ (4.8)	$ 4.9	$ 14.5	$ 24.2	$ 5.1

5-Year Total $25.4

The model shown above reveals that the total card business loses $13.4 million in the first year, loses $4.8 million in the second year, makes a slight profit in the third year, and then becomes truly profitable as the profitability of older accounts begins to more than offset the losses on the newer accounts.

This model illustrates a number of points regarding profitability of a credit card:

1) It takes time for a new business to become profitable.

2) There is attrition among customers as some business put on in the first year begins to migrate away and some is written off.

3) The faster a lender builds a business, the more time it takes to become profitable, at least on a cash flow basis (although accounting rules can alter this, say, by allocating the cost of new accounts over time). To keep things simple, we have only shown a cash flow analysis of profits over time.

The model above, which is reasonably appropriate for a standard United States credit card, shows the importance of understanding lifetime profitability. It allows you to understand the dynamics of the business and to explain to senior management what will occur over time. For example, a lender entering the credit card market will probably lose money for at least two years. Are you willing to tell your management? Would it reassure them to know that the business will actually make money on the vintage of first-year cards during their second year on the books, and a lot more in their third year? If a lender can't describe its portfolio this way, then it doesn't belong in the business.

Thus, profit modeling helps a lender ensure that there will be no surprises when it enters a new market or delivers a new product. The longer-term goal can be kept in sight despite losses in the first years. A manager has to understand how a growing or shrinking portfolio will impact the bottom line and most important, whether a product is profitable over an estimated lifetime.

In order for this lifetime profitability analysis to be fully effective, it must be developed in detail for each product and each distinct subproduct. For instance, new auto loans, used auto loans, auto loans for used autos over five years old, all have very different profit models. One more detail; within the revolving portfolio, there are essentially two different types of customers—those who actually revolve, and those who don't. Although we covered this briefly in Chapter 1 (Planning), it is worthwhile reexamining this important aspect of the credit card business.

The non-revolvers use the card as a convenience and pay off their balances every month; the revolvers pay either the minimum amount due or some other portion of the total balance (including interest at their predetermined rate of 9.9%, 15%, or 19.8%, and so forth). Some borrowers get used to budgeting a monthly payment of, say, $200, $300 or more a month and allow the balance to go up and down with their spending.

The profitability analyses included in this chapter assume an estimated mix of revolving and convenience accounts. Accordingly, the average balances on which interest is received have been lowered to reflect the fact that some percentage of accounts are convenience accounts only.

You can also have a separate profit model for each type of customer (convenience and revolving); the convenience or non-revolving accounts may be unprofitable, while the high-balance, slightly slow-paying revolvers can be very profitable. The only source of income for the card issuer from an account that religiously pays off its balance within the typical 20- to 25-day grace period comes from its share of the merchant discount fee (for example, 1.25% of the sales volume); occasionally, there is also income from an annual fee. Some card issuers compute that it takes more than $500 a month ($6,000/year) in new charges to gain enough revenue from the merchant discount to break even on a no-fee convenience account. Carrying a lot of low-usage, no-annual-fee, convenience customers on the books may explain a lower rate of return. The point is that management should know and understand this relationship.

Other Considerations

Additional considerations can make the modeling process more accurate and useful.

- *Annual returns can be discounted to obtain the present value (future profits are worth less than today's).*

- *The model should be validated as carefully as possible to ensure accuracy. This can be done by summing the total results projected (per loan multiplied by the number of accounts) and comparing these results with actual year-end totals. In other words, if you are estimating that it costs $18 to process an average loan application, does the total cost of all loans processed last year equal the actual costs incurred by the underwriting department?*

- *The model can be truncated to show only the contribution to profit, with overhead calculated separately. It may be impossible to accurately allocate overhead by product or sub-product in great detail.*

- *Once validated, a lifetime model such as we have shown need not be updated more than once per year (or even less often), provided there is no significant change in the product offering, in customer behavior, or in the underlying economy.*

The end result—a net profit (or loss) for every one of your products, for a month, for a quarter, a year, or over its lifetime—allows management to know whether it is worthwhile to maintain, modify aspects of, expand, or abandon a business. These decisions can be made rationally along with intelligent pricing decisions, cost-cutting analyses, and so forth. To ignore this modeling is to court disaster in the competitive world of consumer finance in the new millennium.

Allocating Revenues and Costs by Product

The next step is to begin allocating the total revenues and costs in detail, following accepted accounting principles. Cost allocations can be done by a common-sense review of each of the major steps in the credit cycle including account acquisition, account maintenance (including customer service), collections, and writeoffs.

These costs, which I have defined as variable since they are incurred on a per account basis, must be analyzed in some detail. Ask yourself:

- *Does it cost more to process an application for a Gold Card line of credit than for a Classic Card, and is this reflected in the per-unit cost of processing?*
- *What is the booking rate for an automobile or home mortgage loan? How much money is spent approving loans that are never booked or underwriting and then rejecting applicants?*
- *Are delinquencies higher on one product than another? Is this fact taken into account in the allocation of collection expense?*
- *Are there more customer service calls for one product over another? Are they easier or harder to handle for one product or another?*

A typical headcount or cost analysis will provide specific information, such as the cost of an account's being booked, and the cost of maintaining it each month. This calculation is made by carefully reviewing the process, checking in detail the time and amount spent on each function, and then dividing these costs by the number of accounts booked or the number of active accounts. All this information can be used to modify the processes if necessary.

Finally, the fixed costs—costs that remain fixed regardless of how many accounts are booked—should be examined, including managerial expenses, office space and furniture, corporate management allocations, computers and operating equipment, and all other allocated overhead expenses (e.g., accounting). And don't forget the chairman's airplane.

Fixed costs should be allocated by normal accounting methods, using common sense wherever specific rules do not apply. Standard methods of allocation include breaking down these costs by headcount, asset size, revenue contribution, variable costs, or a mix of these methods. Some costs, such as the cost of political contributions, or the costs for your lobbying efforts in Washington, D.C., may not be worth allocating. Another approach is to just calculate the contribution-to-profit figure by product; this means that you summarize only the direct revenues and expenses associated with the product and the fixed costs are absorbed by the business in total. As long as this approach is clearly stated, it may resolve the dilemma of some unallocatable expenses.

The underlying idea is that common sense and logic should be used to develop product profitability. In total, the products should tie to recognizable numbers. For instance, the sum total of the profit by individual product should add up to the financial results for the total business for a given time period. It is far more important for the lender to ensure that the numbers are logical and can be verified in total than to worry about the fine points of cost allocation among the individual products.

Summary Profitability by Product

The following chart summarizes examples of lifetime profitability for some key consumer lending products. While the numbers can, and will, vary substantially by financial institution and country, they are directionally correct. These lifetime summaries represent a good way to think about the risk/reward of each product.

EXHIBIT 11-4
Profitability by Product – Sample Lifetime Model

% Return on Assets

| | Bank Cards | | Unsecured | Retailer Credit | | Home Mortgage | | Sub |
	Classic	Premium	LOC	Cards	Auto	2nd	1st	Prime
Interest Income	14.8	13.9	11.0	21.0	7.5	9.0	7.0	23.4
Fee & Other Income	4.1	3.8	2.5	2.5	0.5	(0.5)	(0.5)	4.8
Total Revenue	18.9	17.7	13.5	23.5	8.0	8.5	6.5	28.2
Less: Cost of Funds	5.6	5.5	5.7	6.5	5.2	6.0	5.0	7.5
Net Revenue	13.3	12.2	7.8	17.0	2.8	2.5	1.5	20.7
Operating Expenses	4.0	3.8	2.3	5.5	1.5	0.3	0.1	6.0
Write-Offs	6.5	5.2	4.5	9.5	0.6	0.5	0.2	10.5
Total Expenses	10.5	9.0	6.8	15.0	2.1	0.8	0.3	16.5
Pre-Tax Profit	2.8	3.2	1.0	2.0	0.7	1.7	1.2	4.2
After Tax -ROA	2.1	2.4	0.8	1.5	0.5	1.3	0.9	3.2

With a quick glance at the model, you see the very high return (3.2% ROA) which can (and should) be achieved with a high risk sub-prime revolving product, you see the lower return, lower risk home mortgage products, and the risk/reward of every product in between. Risk is just one factor in these profitability numbers; note there are wide variations in the interest income, cost of funds, fee income, and operating expenses by product, and these too should be understood.

I recommend that managers carry their own version of these lifetime profitability numbers in their heads (and in their computers), obviously adjusted to reflect their own target market, product mix, etc. These profit summaries are also useful guides to the numbers you should be following to understand and control your business.

FUNDING

A bank or financial services company typically goes out of business in one of two ways: by making too many bad loans, or by improper funding in relation to the pricing. Proper management techniques are vital to control risk. Funding is just as important but has not been covered extensively in this book because it is generally left to the Treasury experts to raise the funds. The typical business manager is usually allocated funds from a central pool, and her results are measured on how well she does by keeping a tight control over operating costs, building volume, and controlling losses.

Financial institutions normally raise funds from customer deposits, savings accounts, certificates of deposit, borrowing from other banks, securitizing and selling the accounts (see below), issuing debt instruments (including the whole panoply of subordinated and senior debt), and, of course, from its own capital.

As a general rule, the cost of money increases with time; in other words, the investor is supposed to be rewarded for lending money for a longer time period because of the higher risk of not being able to get his money back and the increased chance of inflation. Typically, customer and small business deposits in checking accounts are the least expensive source of money, since the only cost incurred is the cost of managing the account (e.g., having branch offices, hiring tellers, sending out statements, and so forth). However, they also have the shortest maturity, since they can be withdrawn at any time; this is not a good way to finance a thirty-year mortgage. Other debt instruments, such as CDs, bonds, etc., and customer savings accounts all have defined maturities ranging from overnight to 6 months, 10, 20, or 30 years, and the rates paid are clearly spelled out in advance.

Since loan products all have differing maturities, the key decision the lender must make in funding is how much risk to take in *matching* or *not matching* the term of the money needed to fund the business with the term of the loans it is making. If all loans can be funded with short-term funds, a great deal of money can be saved.

This approach, however, incurs two significant risks: 1) that the cost of short-term money will go through the roof (when the Federal Reserve decides to raise rates to dampen inflation), and 2) that depositors and short-term investors will withdraw their money precipitously or, in any event, before the lender can get its funds back through a normal liquidation of assets. This type of "run on the bank" crash has not occurred for many years in the U.S. (since deposits up to $100,000 are guaranteed by the FDIC), but it has occurred in some overseas banking systems.

To avoid such problems, a bank normally matches its borrowing terms *approximately* to its lending terms. Thus, credit card lending is matched with more short and medium funds, automobile loans with more medium-term funds, and home mortgages with some medium- and longer-term funds. The word *gapping* is used to describe the degree of risk that a management is willing to take in funding short and lending long. Alternatively, the loans can be packaged and sold through a securitization process, removing the risk of funding.

Securitization (an alternate way to fund your portfolios)

In recent years, organizations with large consumer portfolios have begun to package and sell (i.e., securitize) portions of these portfolios as another way to raise money (or, more correctly, as a way to eliminate the need for raising money in the traditional ways). As banks have come under continual pressure from the regulatory agencies, they have sought to raise their capital/asset ratios. One way to do this is to remove assets from the books by selling and securitizing them. Citicorp, Sears, the monoline banks, and the other major card issuers have been strong proponents of this form of fund-raising.

This concept is not new. For years, banks have packaged and sold first mortgage instruments through government-sponsored agencies such as Fannie Mae and Freddie Mac (see Chapter 10, The Home Mortgage Business). What has not been around for as long is the trend toward collateralizing and selling portfolios of credit card, automobile, home-equity, and even mobile home loans. This trend has created a completely different multibillion-dollar market for securitized instruments.

A sale of a credit card or other portfolio of consumer loans begins with the creation of a trust. The selling institution puts a fixed amount of receivables in the trust, with about 70 percent designated as the investor share or interest. The security thus created is then sold as a registered offering in the public markets. Receivables for the entire trust vary as payments and new charges are made. The seller's share varies while the investor's share is kept constant.

The typical credit card transaction lasts about four years. Usually, the selling institution makes interest-only payments to the trust for the first two years, and repays principal and interest for the next two years. The securities are typically priced at a margin above Treasury notes of a similar maturity. These premiums have ranged from 50 to 100 basis points, but may be heading higher. The cost is comparable for most banks to the cost of a certificate of deposit.

Securitization offers a number of advantages for a bank:

- *Issuing a security backed by a consumer loan portfolio is treated as a sale of receivables, but the control of the accounts never leaves the issuing bank. The debt held by the trust frees up the bank's capital and allows the bank to either grow more with the same capital or restores the capital/loan ratio to a healthier condition.*

- *The bank receives the net income from servicing the accounts, plus the net excess yield, which results in a high return on equity (because most of the assets have been removed from the bank's books).*

- *Securitization provides an alternate way of funding receivables growth for a fixed maturity at a highly competitive cost.*

In short, banks love this source of funds, the public markets love it (because of the higher rate of return with minimum risk), and the investment bankers who often put these sales together love it (because of the fees involved). It's a win-win situation.

SUMMARY

To summarize, let us review the varying levels of sophistication that financial institutions employ in understanding and managing profitability. Here I describe four different levels of profit knowledge. You may want to treat this as a test to discover where you are today and where you want to be in the future if you are not happy residing at one of the lower levels of expertise.

Level 1

Revenues, costs, and profits for all consumer products are combined in one total. Year-to-year and year-to-date comparisons versus budget are made, but only the major reasons for variance can be identified. Prices are changed to meet or beat competition with little analysis performed. Risk management goals are set to minimize losses. Income and cost items are casually analyzed.

Level 2

Same as above, except that the profitability for each major product is known in a general sense. Income recognition is standardized, cost analyses are performed with major reasons for variance identified. Variable, semi-variable, and fixed costs are known. Funding decisions are made without a complete understanding of term matching.

Level 3

The lifetime profitability of each major product is known. Product and pricing decisions are made on the basis of careful analysis. Profits are optimized with higher risks taken on high-return products; unprofitable products are eliminated. Long-term investments are made in potentially high-yield products, even if they are unprofitable in the short run. Costs are analyzed and controlled in detail. Funding decisions accurately reflect product terms and outstandings. Gap risks are taken only with a full knowledge of the consequences of unexpected rate swings.

Level 4

Same as above, except that the lifetime profitability of each product by vintage and/or subproduct (e.g., five-year-old used cars), by source, by revolving vs. convenience, etc., is known. Where scoring is employed, the profitability by score range is known, and cutoff decisions are made to maximize profits, not minimize risk. Extensive control and test groups are used to understand the effectiveness of marketing programs and to control collections and other costs.

The objective for any corporation serious about staying in the consumer business in today's highly competitive world is to move up the ladder of sophistication in profit analysis toward the highest level of professionalism.

Management Information

T HIS CHAPTER DISCUSSES the key concepts of management information (sometimes called metrics or MIS) that a consumer lending organization needs to understand what is going on in the business. The basic method of conveying information about every aspect of the business—including operations, marketing, finance, risk management, etc.—is through standardized reports containing the daily, weekly, monthly, or even annual numbers needed to understand what is happening. These reports must be carefully balanced. Too much data and the manager is swamped; too little and he is out of touch. The temptation today is to provide too much detail and not enough analysis. The computer is partially to blame for this. It has no sense of judgment, discretion, or understanding of the limitations of the human mind. It will spew out numbers endlessly, and it has always been easier to reward quantity than quality.

The purpose of this chapter is to review some of the guidelines for reporting. I focus on seven selected rules of good management reporting.

1. *Report the* trend *of the business over time; management needs to see the progress of the business.*

2. *Compare the actual results with a forecast of what you expected would happen.*

3. *Summarize the important data; leave the supporting detail for the technical people to follow.*

4. *Disaggregate data wherever there is reason to believe that there will be differences in the performance of the business over time; for instance, the performance of accounts may vary by the way they were acquired (e.g., by mailing, by dealer, by merchant, region vs. region, etc.), and this would be important to track.*

5. *One picture is worth a thousand words; present the key results graphically.*

6. *Tell a story—make the report interesting with precise words that support the numbers.*

7. *Never, never lie with the numbers or omit information that might be embarrassing.*

Let's review these points one by one.

1) Report the Trend

I have seen too many reports showing nothing more than a snapshot of the business at the end of one day, one week, or one month, but a report that does not show the *trend* of performance over time violates almost every rule of good reporting. Sometimes snapshot reporting is the only source of information about an institution's lending business, and some good information may be presented (say, for example, the current account-approval percentages), but reporting that gives *no* indication of any trends is incomplete. Are the account approval percentages going up or down? Is the business growing or shrinking? Is delinquency up or down?

In contrast, the *trend* of a rising problem in one bank's record of credit cards reported lost or stolen is seen in the chart below:

EXHIBIT 12-1
Account Maintenance—Fraud Indicators

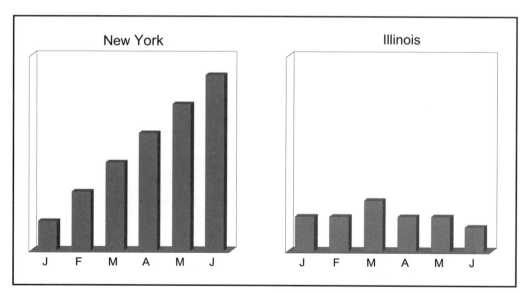

Something is going wrong here. A bad, new trend of possible fraud appears in the New York area, but fraud does not seem to be a universal problem since the Illinois results are stable. You don't need much experience to know that the New York figures must be investigated. Has there been a change in the mailing procedure? Is this happening to other card issuers or just to us? This report raises questions, it doesn't give answers, but this type of information must be produced and seen before you know what to ask or can get any answers.

2) Use Standards or Norms

A series of standards or norms allows a business to measure performance over time versus what was expected. In the following chart, management forecasted a certain performance in a scored portfolio as it was being acquired.

EXHIBIT 12-2
Management Information

Monthly Activity Summary
Date: August 30
Product: Auto

	Forecast	Aug	Jul	Jun	Ytd
# Applications	1850	1491	1602	2424	15068
# Approved	1400	1085	1141	1658	10849
% Approved	76	73	71	68	72
% Scored	100	98	98	94	97
Score Range					
% A	34	41	36	31	39
% B	58	55	61	58	51
% C	4	1	3	9	5
Average Score	124	127	124	119	129
% Low Override (D)	4	3	0	2	5
% Score Errors	3	0	0	6	2
% Hi Overrides	9	8	10	12	6

The number of applications, accounts scored and approved, the score range, and the number of exceptions are all shown month by month, versus the forecasted or budgeted numbers. Two figures, the percent of high-side and low-side overrides versus the forecast, are particularly important to follow. If these figures are significantly higher than you projected, it could indicate a real problem with 1) your scoring system or 2) the ability and training of your underwriters. This report shows that high-side overrides were rising above budget but appear to be under control as of the last month.

Many other operational goals or standards have been covered throughout this book, including standards such as the ratio of accounts booked/accounts reviewed in the automobile business, the net flow of accounts from one stage of delinquency to the next, key customer service standards (e.g., number of rings before the phone is answered), and so forth. Set the standards and then follow the actuals over time. Remember, the final measurements of overall performance—the key norms such as profitability, return on assets, or return on equity—have usually been clearly defined by senior management and by the Wall Street analysts who follow your stock. You will be quickly rewarded/penalized for results versus those forecasts.

3) Summarize the Data

Time management is vital for a manager. A senior manager should mercilessly reduce the number of reports she reads *regularly* to the ten or fifteen most important subjects, including the key indicators of marketing, sales, risk, and operational performance which we have covered throughout this book. For example, it doesn't take very long to understand that a very high average balance of written-off accounts can be a key indicator of problems in the credit card business. A manager can learn a lot about the average balance size at each stage of delinquency by glancing at the following report:

EXHIBIT 12-3
Managing Current Accounts

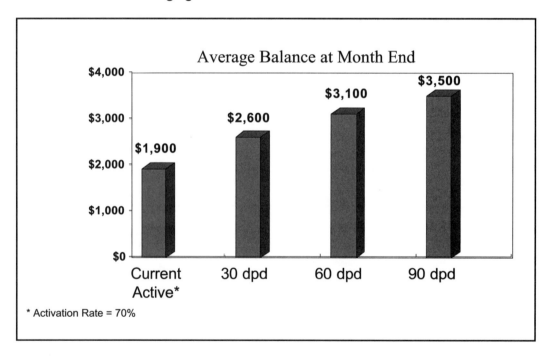

Of course, more detailed reports should be available within the organization, but Exhibit 12-3 is a good start. A manager should be able to request the latest results of a test mailing, the performance of different collection strategies, and the results of the latest sales promotion. However, requiring management to read the Southwestern region's monthly performance for used autos by score range (how did the 210s perform, the 220s, etc.) and by dealer, on a regular basis, tests the limits of human endurance.

4) Disaggregate the Data

The term *peel the onion* is often used to describe the process of disaggregating the portfolio. Disaggregating is how organizations are able to define what is the problem and what is *not* the problem. Or better yet, where the opportunity is and where it is not.

If a business is booking the same number of accounts, the same way, month after month, there may be little need to disaggregate the portfolio. Few lenders, however, operate this way. For fast-growing portfolios, the need for fast feedback is vital. For instance, if delinquency is increasing in total, is it a general problem, or can it be attributed to one particular mailing? While we have already seen this chart in Chapter 5, Direct Mail, this information is so important that we have reused it to illustrate the importance of understanding the source of a problem. In this case, an unfavorable trend of higher writeoffs in each successive mailing suggests trouble:

EXHIBIT 12-4
Gross Writeoffs by Mailing

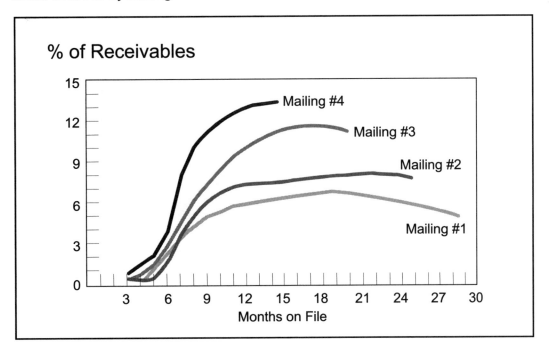

The next question to ask is: Why the increase in writeoffs in each mailing? Is it caused by lower average scores, one or more lifestyle selector codes, one geographic area, or is it general? This chart merely raises questions. By disaggregating the data of each mailing, you can see if there is a problem with the target market, the screening process, the geographic sourcing of the accounts, or whatever. The point is that you now have the information to start addressing the problem, and the evidence to *ask* the right questions and to get the answers. Ultimately, answers allow you to take the appropriate actions. Many careers have foundered over the manager's inability to answer the one simple, obvious question.

5) Present the Data Graphically

There is no excuse for presenting senior or even middle management with masses of data in the form of rows of numbers. The cliché that one picture is worth a thousand words really does apply to the task of presenting the trends and issues of the consumer business. Is the scoring system working? When you see the following chart, it takes only a quick glance to see that the score system appears to be working:

Exhibit 12-5
Auto Loan Portfolio—W/O's By Score Range

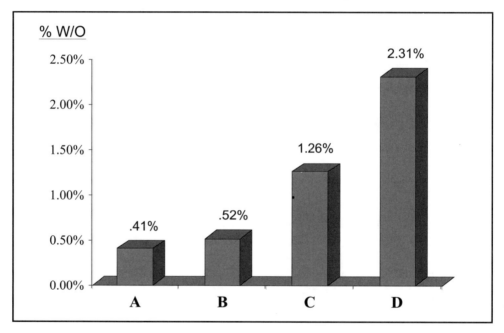

Although only a mathematician can prove statistically that the system is discriminating the way it was designed to, one visual chart can instantly tell a manager that low scorers have higher writeoffs than high scorers.

6) Tell a Story

Many statistical reports are boring; an entire book of business statistics can be mind-numbing. No task is more formidable than plowing through a 35- to 45-page report each day, week, or month, searching through the thousands of numbers for the item or items in need of management action. The key is for the analysts to wade through the detail on their own, to isolate the important data in the report, and to tell that story in a way that focuses the attention of the manager on the important data.

There usually is a story to tell. For instance:

- *The Southern region's booked/approval rate is down to 43% on the home-equity product. The product is not profitable with a booking rate below 53% and does not hit the targeted profit level until 60%. The region is reviewing its list of brokers to cull those with below-par performance and has set a target of 50% booked/approval rate for the month of May and 60% by August. The new targets have been charted and performance will be measured monthly.*

- *The July promotional program on Gold Card accounts scoring above 250 appears to be going well. The average charge volume is up 23% (vs. 3% for the control group), while the average balances have increased by 18% (vs. a decline of 4% percent for the control group). An additional 32,000 accounts will be reviewed for a similar promotion in the month of January.*

THE QUIET MAN

David Halberstam's *The Reckoning* is a brilliant book on the rise of the Japanese automobile industry and the decline of its American counterpart from 1950 to 1970, as evidenced by two companies—Nissan and Ford. One chapter, "The Quiet Man," covers one of the best business reporters of all time, Ford's Executive Vice President for Finance, Ed Lundy, and his impact on the organization.

In monthly meetings with Henry Ford 2nd (the "deuce"), Ford's senior management, and the board of directors, Ed Lundy summarized the worldwide performance of the Ford Motor Company in carefully crafted detail. Brazil's manufacturing performance was noted ("over budget by more than 12 percent for the third month in a row"); the Ford Division's sales results versus objectives were praised ("but the sales incentive allowance has been exceeded by 13 percent"); and the new Asia-Pacific Operations were finally rewarded by receiving honorable mention for beating their budget by $11.2 million or 12 percent.

Nothing escaped this monthly review, which summarized the operations of the company in 30 or so carefully developed and totally objective pages. Rather, nothing beat the ingenuity of the dozen or more analysts (including one of the authors of this book) who pored over the details of the company, trying to 1) locate the story and then 2) summarize it in crisp enough fashion to gain the Lundy approval. The individual review pages consisted of a precise graph or numerical chart up top ("the slide"), supported by very carefully written text ("the script"). Instructions on preparing these pages were handed down from analyst to analyst and finally encoded in a memorandum that ran more than 50 pages. To err was to risk disaster, firing, or, worse yet, a transfer to the Ford plant in Outer Mongolia; to succeed was to move on to a senior job in Finance or elsewhere.

This monthly report, the Financial Review, because it was so rigorously prepared, focusing on accuracy as well as incisive communication, became one of the most powerful tools for Ed Lundy and his Ford Finance staff in helping senior management understand a complex business that was changing rapidly.

Both of these stories are worth telling. They give a clear statement about an important trend and back it up with figures, then describe the actions taken in response to the figures. The first paragraph imparts bad news. It is expensive to review home-equity lines of credit, that is, to go through the whole application analysis and then not book the account. However, if the reporting system is routine, objective, and standardized, no one will be offended by bad news. Good managers will appreciate the objectivity with which it is presented (along with a plan of action). And they will be delighted when rewarded with good news, such as that conveyed in the second example.

The goal for the report preparers (as guided by their managers) is to ferret out the news—good or bad—and to report it in a factual, non-emotional fashion. It is exactly the same process that a good newspaper reporter goes through in digging out the news, except that the internal reporters, who are often in the finance or risk management departments, are all part of the same team. There should be no adversarial role, although sometimes animosity exists, human nature being what it is. By avoiding editorializing and attempts to place blame, and by stressing good news whenever possible, a reporting organization can play a vital role in the success of a business.

7) Never Lie with the Numbers

Despite the old cliché that "figures don't lie, but liars figure," the use of the word *lie* is alarmist. Few people in reputable organizations deliberately lie. Certain management pressures, however, sometimes encourage half-truths in the typical reporting environment. We mentioned earlier how one major credit card issuer suffered a humiliating setback when forced to announce that earnings would be severely impacted by a special $70 million writeoff on its portfolio to reflect bad loans that, essentially, had been hidden. The stock took a big hit. The full-scale investigation that followed revealed that line managers had devised ingenious ways to meet unrealistic writeoff targets assigned from on high with no regard to the quality of the accounts being booked. But "lying" can take other forms as well, such as:

- *Overestimating the value of properties in foreclosure or that are owned, and minimizing the potential write-downs still to be taken*
- *Forecasting unrealistically low writeoffs because of anticipated hyper-collections activity on a distressed portfolio*
- *Failing to disaggregate a portfolio to identify the problem accounts; that is, using the good accounts to cover up the bad ones.*

Business reporters should always avoid this temptation. The real truth will inevitably come out and such evasion could cost the manager his job. Also, such subterfuge wastes precious time that would be better spent identifying and solving the underlying problems.

Another, more subtle, type of problem in reporting is when the truth is casually concealed because of ignorance. This situation is best evidenced by the problem of calculating the delinquency and writeoff percentages on a fast-growing portfolio.

As covered in Chapter 7, Collection Strategies, it takes time for a surge of new accounts to become delinquent and ultimately to be written off. In the meanwhile, the new receivables are in the divisor and the normal portfolio ratios can be distorted. Delinquency and writeoff percentages may actually *decline* during a period of fast growth. When this growth is combined with the failure to disaggregate the data, say, by vintage, the results can be disastrous. Reports that do not account for these factors can easily deceive people unfamiliar with the business. Let's look at a sample report, lagged and unlagged, and by vintage:

EXHIBIT 12-6
Kwik Kash—Portfolio and Vintage W/O's

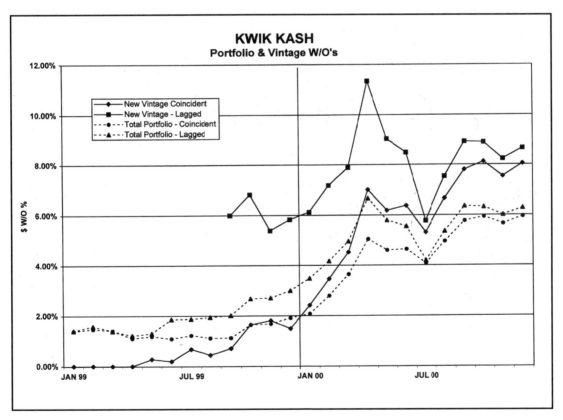

Exhibit 12-6 shows the actual writeoffs over two years for an unsecured line of credit portfolio (which we call Kwik Kash to protect the guilty): If you just look at the coincident (or unlagged) writeoff rate of the *total* Kwik Kash portfolio, you would be hard pressed to say anything was wrong—it just reaches the 2% level at the end of 1999 (see the lower dotted line). On a lagged basis, too, the numbers are not alarming, as the writeoff (W/O) rate hits slightly over 3% at the same time period.

Now let's disaggregate the portfolio to reflect the performance of the rapidly growing new vintage of business, which added $250 million in new balances in the first year, effectively doubling the size of the business. Again, taking a look at the coincident numbers for the new vintage of business (the lower solid line), the numbers are not alarming: writeoffs reach a rate of less than 2% by year end as rapid growth conceals the problem. It is only when you *both* disaggregate the business *and* lag the numbers that the truth comes out. The new portfolio is really writing off at a rate of 6% (the top solid line). This is the truth, the whole truth, and nothing but the truth! A management team with a chart that disaggregates information like this would be taking immediate action to find out what is going on here (Was it forecasted? Is the problem in collections, operations, the mailing target? Can the portfolio be profitable, ever, with a writeoff rate of 8% or more?). The point is that good MIS can be a terrific tool; bad MIS is a disaster.

SUMMARY

Each manager must decide how much detail he can absorb. Every person is different and some managers have the discipline to work with immense detail while others live more by the seat of their pants (in which case they had better have a good staff of analysts sifting through and summarizing the essential facts). An annual review of all reports can also help focus attention on which reports to expand, eliminate, or maintain, which in turn may help to control the tendency of reports to proliferate (left unchecked, they breed like rabbits). An annual review process by senior management can also help make the essential reports more visual and useful.

Organization and Management 13

ORGANIZING THE MANAGEMENT of a consumer lending business can be done in many ways. Financial institutions have both thrived and failed with highly centralized management structures, with decentralized ones, with delegated profit responsibility, with little or no identification of profit responsibility, and with complete chaos.

Rumor has long held that human resource departments and organizational consultants survive by first decentralizing an organization, then five years later, recentralizing it. Each move requires lots of study, late-night meetings, lengthy planning sessions, and great expense, before finally being announced as the solution for all existing or perceived problems. Some organizations indeed do well on this type of continuing confusion, but obviously too much can be harmful.

On the whole, I have found that organizations work best when:

- *Authority is clearly delegated, along with responsibility.*
- *People have clear, realistic, attainable goals.*
- *Rewards are in line with actual results.*

In this chapter, we will address some ways of organizing a consumer lending organization.

MANAGEMENT STRUCTURES

There are two principal ways to structure a business into a well-managed organization; these are a *functional* management structure and a *product* management structure.

Functional management, basically a centralized approach to managing a business, is organized around the concept of having highly efficient, specialist operations, such as marketing, finance, collections, etc., provide their services for many different products. Managing by *product*, on the other hand, is a decentralized approach, with each product having its own functional experts. There are advantages and disadvantages to both types of organization, and of course, different businesses use many variations and refinements of the basic models (e.g., organizing by geographic region). In both alternatives, the head of the consumer business is clearly identified. I don't see how a business can operate without such an individual; consumer products (both assets and liabilities) are so different from the traditional commercial bank products as well as the newer investment bank products that the consumer business should be separate, with its senior management reporting to the highest level of the organization (i.e., the chief operating officer [COO] or the chief executive officer [CEO]).[1] In addition, small business lending is becoming more and more statistically based and that business could easily fit into a consumer operation.

Let's look at some of the pros and cons of both organizations, product and functional management.

Product Management Structure

In this alternative, a clearly defined product manager has the staff, organization, and authority to enable her to implement every decision regarding her products. Ideally, this includes all the necessary authority to impact the bottom line so that the product's profitability is clearly one person's and one organization's responsibility. The necessary staff includes operations, sales, marketing, systems/technology, risk management, finance, audit, human resources, and sometimes a management information (MIS) manager, all of whom report directly to the product manager. If the organization is large or complex, there might even be an additional layer of management; Exhibit 13-1 is illustrative only.

This organization works particularly well with a clearly defined lending product, such as a credit card, an indirect automobile business, or any of the home-equity or mortgage products. In addition, there could be a separate subproduct manager and further product divisions, such as Premium and Classic cards within the credit card area; Internet banking could be organized separately because of the unique requirements of running that type of business, although some financial institutions currently do not see the need for separate organizations.

A variation of this form of organization may be appropriate where the business is so large that it must be separated by geographic region. In this case, there may be several regional managers reporting to the business manager. This makes sense when the business requires hands-on local management, as in the indirect automobile business, where you have to deal with large numbers of dealers. The credit card business typically can be highly centralized because of the ease with which data can be moved around the country (and the world). The concept remains, however, that one person is responsible for the success (or failure) of any individual consumer product.

---

1. An exception could be made when an organization is so small that there is no need for separate organizations.

EXHIBIT 13-1
Product Management Organization

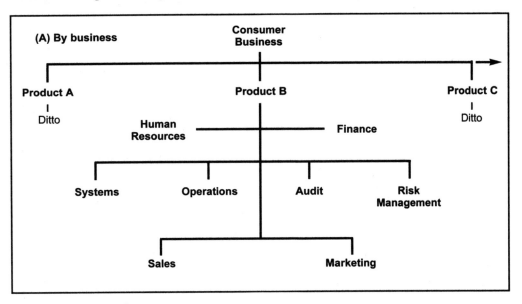

One potential problem arises here. Does the product manager have complete responsibility for all aspects of the products he is managing? Does he have control over funding costs, marketing decisions, risk management, and operations, or are some of these functions handled elsewhere? Further, does he have any control over allocated overhead expenses? Certain allocated costs will always be beyond a manager's control (e.g., corporate headquarters expense, the chairman's winter office in Aspen, and so forth), but the costs allocated should at least be in reasonable proportion to the potential earning power of the product. For instance, it would be impossible for a product manager of a first mortgage product to absorb 200 to 300 basis points of allocated cost.

If these items can be resolved, the product management approach makes great sense. The advantages are:

- *Authority and responsibility are clearly defined. There is no need for finger-pointing or assessing blame when things go wrong; conversely, there is a way to clearly define (and reward) success.*

- *Decisions can be made where they should be—close to the line organization.*

- *The scale of operations is small enough so that human beings can truly understand it; bureaucracy can be kept to a minimum.*

- *This type of organization encourages and promotes the development of the entrepreneurial manager. The approach may stimulate new and innovative ways of doing business.*

One major disadvantage is that operational and personnel expenses may be higher than with the alternate functional organization.

WHO'S RESPONSIBLE FOR A BUSINESS'S PROFITS?

In the early days of building a consumer business, Citicorp operated under the concept that funding costs were allocated from a central pool of Treasury funds. Thus, managers had no direct control over how their products were funded. They actually believed that they were not responsible for the cost of funds, surely one of the most important, if not the single most important, item affecting profitability of mortgage products!

All other items of revenue and expense—pricing, fees charged, account acquisition costs, collections, customer service, writeoffs, and almost all of the indirect costs such as office space, equipment, and so forth—were considered controllable, but the cost of money was "someone else's" business, specifically the Treasury department, whoever they were.

The business plan for 1980 looked great, with an allocated and very theoretical 8% cost of funds. A problem arose that year . . . the cost of overnight money went as high as 21%, and the 12% ceiling that regulators allowed lenders to charge their customers at that time covered only part of the actual cost of money, much less the rather large operating costs and writeoffs the bank was trying to absorb. Other fixed-rate products suffered similarly.

The result was a bloodbath. Managers learned that they were indeed held responsible for all items affecting the bottom line, and they took charge of their own funding. From then on, terms like *gap* management (i.e., managing the term of *borrowing* with the term of *lending*) became part of Citicorp's management processes.

Functional Management

Following is a sample functional organization.

EXHIBIT 13-2
Functional Management Organization

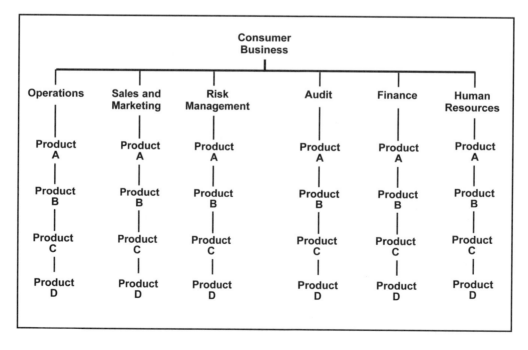

The advantages of a functional management are clear. It is possible to save costs with this type of organization. The disadvantages are more nebulous and difficult to define clearly. Basically, they are the opposite of the advantages of the more entrepreneurial product management organization:

- *It is difficult to accurately allocate costs and thus define profitability by product with this type of organization.*

- *Because profit responsibility resides at such a senior level, it is difficult to balance risk and reward. Operations may be interested only in cutting costs, because that is the way they are rewarded. Who then assures that service goals are met? Who balances the two conflicting goals? Is marketing rewarded for new accounts generated, regardless of quality? Can the risk manager be compensated for contributing to profit, or is she rewarded only for minimizing losses?*

Because of the difficulty in resolving these questions, a product management type organization may be preferred. Although costs may not be minimized and there may be duplications, the ability to identify (and reward) the right end goal—overall profitability—makes this type of organization attractive.

Sometimes organizations may combine elements of both basic ways of organizing. For example, a product manager type of organization may allow the manager to "contract" for operational support from an in-house processing shop, or to go outside if the in-house processor is more costly or less efficient.

Each consumer lending manager should elect the type of organization he feels most comfortable with and that fits into the corporate culture. It is not easy to build an entrepreneurial spirit in an organization that has always been bureaucratic, and vice versa.

POSITIONS AND DUTIES

This section defines in more detail the jobs performed by the key managers within the two types of organization. The functions remain essentially the same for the key managers under either structure; only the scope of the job differs.

Business or Product Manager

The business or product manager is responsible for the overall profitability of all consumer products within his span of control. He determines the tactical approaches and organizes available resources to meet major problems and opportunities. He selects key managers, assigns goals, and rewards achievement appropriately. He approves all key product terms and conditions as well as works with senior management (the president and board of directors) to determine the strategic goals. Finally, he is responsible for selecting the key management information reports required to oversee the management of the business and for establishing a process for the regular review of these reports.

Operations Manager

The operations manager administers the day-to-day internal operations, including account acquisition, customer service, payment processing, and, typically, collections and agency management (sometimes the last two functions are under a risk manager). She selects the specific department managers and sets their operational and service goals in conjunction with them. She is responsible for managing major systems projects as well as installing and updating systems as required. She oversees the effectiveness and efficiency of the operations through the appropriate MIS and provides operations input on all product decisions.

Sales and Marketing Manager

The sales and marketing manager (which may be either combined in one position or divided into two) runs the distribution system (typically the branches, but it could include all forms of product delivery). In addition, he is responsible for competitive analyses and makes recommendations regarding the consumer lending and liability products to be offered, along with their appropriate terms and conditions, the method of distribution (direct or indirect), and pricing. In conjunction with the business manager, he develops the strategic plan for the growth of the business. He defines the target markets geographically and demographically as well as oversees both the planning and execution of all advertising and promotions, including any direct mail account acquisition campaigns.

Finance Manager

In conjunction with the individual functional managers, the finance manager prepares the annual budgets, summarizes them, and presents them to senior management. He identifies areas for cost reduction and cost control. He regularly (i.e., daily, weekly, or monthly) reports actual results against approved budgets. He develops the profit models, reporting actual performance as required, and participates in pricing decisions. He supervises the accounting departments and assists in providing financial results for all internal and external reports, along with outside auditors. He either oversees or runs the Treasury function, which includes funding and money management.

Risk Manager

The risk manager develops credit policy. As a key member of management, he helps evaluate the degree of risk and reward in each major product decision and provides a balance to marketing, finance, and operations recommendations. He works with internal resources and outside vendors to introduce and validate all the scoring systems (acquisition, authorizations, collections, etc.). Finally, he analyzes the financial results (with special attention to the major items of risk and reward, including revenue, collections, and writeoffs) and reports on the effectiveness of all major programs. He works closely with the management information manager to develop a complete senior management reporting system (or develops one himself if there is no MIS manager).

Management Information Systems (MIS)/Metrics Manager

With the aid of the various functional managers, the MIS manager defines the key information (sometimes called the metrics) required by senior managers and prepares them on a daily, weekly or monthly basis. A good MIS manager will make sure that the format is appropriate for senior management review (trends summarized, performance changes noted, etc.). He also provides the resources (computers, software developers, etc.) to assist the various functional areas in preparing their detailed operating reports.

Human Resources Manager

The human resources manager assists the business manager and functional managers in defining their organizations; her duties include developing specific key job descriptions and assisting the line managers in recruiting the best-qualified personnel to fill these posts (either from inside or outside the company). This person analyzes competitive wage and benefit packages to ensure that the compensation structure remains in line with the market. She provides in-house counseling and makes sure that all equal opportunity commitments are being met. She oversees all in-house personnel communications and advises senior managers of any problems with morale. In addition, identifying the need for and running any corporate training programs (in-house and with outside vendors) are often key human resource goals.

Auditor

The auditor reviews finance, credit, marketing, and operational results to ensure compliance with approved policy and procedures. He regularly prepares formal reports to management that rate all key functional areas and note all exceptions to policy. The reports also include management's plan for corrective action. The auditor stays current with technological and procedural advances that affect his duties and provides judgment on the practicality of the policies and procedures as adopted.

CREATING A CREDIT CULTURE

How does an organization go about creating a climate where the management of risk is woven so tightly into the corporate culture that risk and reward are always weighed equally? Should risk management be assigned to a specific individual (e.g., the credit manager or risk manager), or can it really be shared by all?

In an ideal consumer lending operation, a separate risk management specialist would be unnecessary because responsibility for controlling risk would be spread among all the managers. Marketing managers would focus on obtaining the most creditworthy customers in the least expensive manner; operations experts would make continual adjustments to systems to control the risk of accounts as they process a greater volume of loan applications; and finance specialists would make projections of profitability and initiate cost-control measurements to help reach common profit goals. Everyone would work in harmony under an enlightened business manager. In such a world, the role of a risk manager—if one existed at all—would be organizing the Wednesday afternoon golf games.

In the real world it hasn't worked that way. Typically, the directive to grow the business comes down from some senior level. Marketing managers concentrate almost exclusively on building the account base—no matter what the cost. Operations executives spend their time designing systems primarily to hold down costs rather than to allow for better management of growth. Both types of managers increasingly have overlooked the careful management of risk that was built into the mind-set of the generalists who previously ran the business.

It has been a recipe for disaster at some organizations. When the disaster came in the form of burgeoning bad-debt losses, managers responded by cutting operating costs, which made matters still worse. The drive for increased volume was accompanied by insufficient investment in personnel and systems to resolve billing and collection problems. The controls that were in place became compromised by the pursuit of short-term sales and profits.

Businesses learned the necessity for assigning risk management at a senior corporate level to a single high-level executive and for each major business or product manager below that level having his own risk manager. The large credit card organizations, including American Express, Bank of America, Chase, Citigroup, Discover, Wells Fargo and US Bank (among others), have developed a strong risk management culture throughout the business. This includes supporting the training of all functional areas to work together in the management of risk; this is one part of building a credit culture. In fact, our program, *Consumer Credit: Managing Risk & Reward*, has been delivered at each of these organizations (sometimes many times). We will describe this program later.

RISK MANAGERS—SOME UNIQUE PROBLEMS

What are the unique problems faced by a risk manager, and what are the characteristics of people who take these jobs? It is tempting to be the "Dr. No" of the consumer lending organization, the person who "just says no" to taking on any added risk. While at times it may be appropriate to say no, the job is far more complex.

The Policymaking Role

While specific assignments vary from one financial institution to the next, in most cases the consumer credit risk manager plays several key policymaking roles. The most obvious is to provide the organization with a formal definition of the balance between acceptable risks and desired rewards. Thus, the power of the risk manager is most clearly visible in his authority to approve revisions to existing consumer credit product programs and the adoption of any new products or programs.

That authority is not merely a mandate to minimize losses. It has to be tempered with the wisdom to encourage profitability. To do so, the risk manager must be involved in the analysis of program revisions and expansions from the beginning. She should help identify new markets and prospects from the standpoint of her risk/reward analyses. That minimizes the tendency to view the risk manager only as someone to be sold on any program, or as someone called in only when mistakes in targeting markets and screening customers show up in the form of heavy credit losses.

Line or Staff Position?

It is always a possibility for the line operations (e.g., account acquisition processors, collectors, and customer service representatives) to report to the risk manager. Most lending institutions that have appointed credit management specialists in recent years, however, have defined the job as a staff position.

Introducing New Technology

The risk manager can also be the catalyst who introduces new analytic techniques to the business. He is likely to be the organization's repository of knowledge on the latest analytical tools available in the consumer lending industry, including bankruptcy-scoring models, mail solicitation models, neural nets, and behavior-scoring models. The importance of using statistical control techniques in managing the high-volume consumer business cannot be overemphasized, but it is the risk manager who is responsible for constantly testing new methods and for making sure that the most effective models are being implemented throughout the organization.

By distributing the new analytical tools through on-site visits, professional seminars, and written communications, a risk manager can help maintain standards of credit analysis throughout a large financial service organization.

Management Information

One absolutely vital role . . . the risk manager should be intimately involved in providing top management with the critical statistical reports needed to assess risk. Hopefully, by working closely with the finance people, this risk will be assessed in relation to the reward of a product, and not simply toward the goal of "lowest writeoffs." The lending business is a business of tracking details, and it is the risk manager's responsibility (sometimes working with an MIS manager) to design MIS reports that allow top managers to analyze and act upon them to control the business. However, the risk manager should use his position to ensure that MIS remains a tool for top managers, not an excuse to abrogate their decision-making authority. As in any well-managed organization, common sense must prevail over management by the numbers.

Protecting the Messenger

Finally, a good part of the credit risk manager's job relates to setting norms or standards, and then tracking performance against them. In all consumer businesses, a number of key decisions must be made on standards—from setting the cutoff scores for credit applications, to forming and monitoring policies that override those standards in special circumstances, to possibly even establishing the appropriate ratio of collectors to accounts. Because of the importance of such standards in controlling credit risk, the risk manager must be heavily involved in determining that such standards are appropriate from a risk/reward standpoint.

Given the nature of her assignment, the risk manager is in danger of being criticized within the organization as the numbers cruncher who always delivers the bad news. Even when she approaches her job with growth and profitability in mind, her decisions will not always be popular.

Thus, one vital element of the risk manager position is that it have the continuing support of senior management. Of course, top management need not side with the risk manager all the time. The business manager may well decide to take an excessive risk and thus disregard the suggestions of the risk manager. In this case it is the job of the risk manager to make sure that the results are forecast early and to try and persuade top management to change if the business is not profitable.

Finally, there must be a way of supporting the risk manager, who literally puts his job on the line when standing toe to toe with his peers and his boss. In larger organizations, this can be handled by allowing the risk manager to report directly (or indirectly) to a functional or matrix boss, such as a group credit executive or an independent credit policy committee. Both of these organizational entities should be senior enough to absorb the heat from the line organization for a negative decision by the risk manager.

Nothing can insulate the risk manager more than her own conviction of the importance of her position and her unflinching dedication to it. If the risk manager stays abreast of the latest analytical tools, has command of all facts affecting credit risk, and presents them clearly to management, her views will earn the respect they deserve and the organization will reach a consensus that incorporates her input. In a period of high bad-debt losses, it cannot afford not to.

Thus, it is vital that the risk manager be highly regarded by senior management, by his peers, and by his subordinates. Senior management can help attain this high regard by appointing a risk manager who is fully grounded in the consumer credit business and has the intelligence, work habits, and personal integrity to gain the confidence of the organization.

RISK MANAGEMENT TRAINING

Consumer lending requires relatively new disciplines. While college courses and graduate degrees are available in marketing, finance, data processing, general management, auditing, and so on, opportunities for training in the academic world in the latest consumer lending skills, particularly risk management, are limited. For many organizations, developing the specific skills is typically left to on-the-job training. Experiencing one or two failures is often the only way someone can learn the idiosyncrasies of the job. There are obvious disadvantages to this approach.

Any bank or financial services company should consider the pros and cons of requiring all high-potential employees to complete a formal training program in order to advance to a senior management position.

The major purposes of training are to:

- *Help an organization avoid reinventing the wheel every five years or so . . . to learn from and not repeat prior mistakes. Case studies based on past failures (fictionalized to protect the guilty) can be a powerful way to describe what went wrong and what can be done to prevent such errors from recurring. Training also imparts the minimum technical skills required in the organization.*

- *Encourage the cross-cultivation of skills throughout the organization. A commercial lending officer or an insurance executive may decide to transfer to the consumer side of the business in mid-career, and with training he can learn the business much faster than he would by asking his boss, his peers, or his employees for help.*

- *Allow managers to get away from their business for a few days and benefit from a mind-expanding, shared group experience.*

Training can be obtained from trade associations, such as the American Banking Association (ABA), which offer specialized courses, and from industry professionals like Fair, Isaac, Inc., the scoring developers, who run workshops on the intricacies of scoring. Some of the largest banks and financial institutions develop their own risk management courses and deliver them multiple times to their own employees. Admittedly, this type of program can be expensive, and only larger organizations can afford to do them on their own.

Some financial institutions avoid training altogether by hiring experienced people from other organizations. The major financial institutions have all been raided, particularly those with a reputation for developing good managers (in some cases, of course, they have been the raider). Hiring from the competition is an easy way to avoid developing and operating an in-house training program. It is, however, very expensive. According to Nancy Griffiths, head of her own New York–based executive recruiting firm, "A bank normally will have to pay a premium of 25 to 40 percent over the going market rate to attract a seasoned professional, and that premium gets built into the hiring institution's structure forever because it has to be paid year after year. Also, others already in the organization will be looking for similar raises to match the newly hired expert."

CONSUMER CREDIT TRAINING—THE LAST HOLDOUT

When Phillip L. started his banking career several years ago, he did so as a management trainee at a major commercial lending bank in New York City. For ten months he spent every day attending the bank's own training school to learn the craft of commercial lending. Day after day he worked with a group of highly motivated, professional instructors who taught a wide range of advanced courses on such subjects as accounting, cash flow analysis, statement spreading, and report writing. Only after this initiation process was he ready for an assignment as a "banker."

At about the same time, Mary P. joined a different major New York financial institution, also as a management trainee, but in her case, in the consumer lending end of the bank. Her initiation was considerably different from Phillip's. After she was shown her desk, the location of the washroom, and introduced to her neighbors, she was handed a policy manual on how to make good loans and told to start making decisions on consumer lending. It was classic on-the-job training. Her decisions, of course, were reviewed by senior underwriters, but she essentially learned the business by doing it. Many lending institutions have a long history of teaching their commercial lenders but very few have that same dedication to training for their consumer lenders. On-the-job training can be expensive in that bad lending habits are handed down from generation to generation.

One alternative used by financial institutions is to run internal offerings of commercial courses that teach basic and advanced consumer lending skills. Our own program, for example, *Consumer Credit: Managing Risk & Reward,* has been run over 250 times for many of the major banks and finance companies here in the U.S. as well as abroad. *Consumer Credit* is a survey course, teaching the basic principles of managing risk to consumer lenders at all levels of management, including the complete credit cycle we talk about in this book (planning, acquiring, maintaining, and collecting accounts). There is also heavy emphasis on the statistical management techniques we cover here.

Developing Training Programs

Training can be accomplished by sending people to attend outside seminars or by developing in-house programs. There are advantages and disadvantages to both.

External Programs

- *Outside courses can be inexpensive. Key people can be sent to highly specialized outside programs to develop their skills for a few thousand dollars or less per session.*

- *People who put together outside seminars or courses must stay abreast of the latest technology and ideas or the seminars fail; further, there is no internal bureaucracy interested in perpetuating a stale course.*

- *Outside courses tend to be taught by highly professional people who are leaders in their industry and typically have a lot of instructional experience; people within an institution may know their business but are not necessarily good teachers.*

- *Finally, with outside courses, the institution can be highly selective in whom it sends and when it sends them; there is no fixed schedule as there may be for internal courses.*

One warning: An outside course may not be appropriate for all levels of management (e.g., it may be over the head of a trainee, or too simplistic for an experienced manager), so it is important to learn what the course is all about first. It may pay to send one or two people to gain an understanding of the program and its target market before sending many people.

In-House Programs

- *Once developed, an in-house program can be repeated again and again for qualified personnel, thus lowering the cost to a reasonable figure per attendee.*

- *An outside course may not reflect the institution's own corporate culture. Management philosophy can be more clearly articulated and transmitted to the appropriate target audience through an in-house training program (although many externally developed programs can be run internally and customized to better reflect the institution's culture and methods).*

- *Finally, teaching is good experience for the development of any manager. In fact, the teacher usually learns more than his students, at least at first. Letting others train your employees does nothing to stretch your own managers.*

There is no one right way to go. The best and the brightest organizations will recognize the rewards of training and be willing to pay the costs. Those who fail to follow with at least some training will do so at their own peril. I find it puzzling that an institution will increase its allowance for writeoffs by $10 million without qualms while rejecting the expenditure of $100,000, $250,000 (or even $25,000) to train people to help control losses in future years. This approach is simply short-sighted.

Managing in a Recession

A WHOLE GENERATION OF LENDERS has grown up thinking that the economy (and the stock market) would go up forever. None of them remembered much about recessions, especially a serious one—a recession was something your boss might have lived through years ago, but why waste time on history?

At the time this book is being finalized (March 2002), there is talk that the United States may be ending one of the shortest and mildest recessions recorded, after experiencing the longest period of economic expansion in its history. But what is a recession? The simplest definition is "two consecutive quarters of decline in the GDP (gross domestic product)." Although a more sophisticated measurement records the trend of employment, industrial production, real income, and sales activity, the press responds to the GDP figures.

A lender has to be prepared to handle the impact of recession on the consumer lending industry. It is conventional wisdom that business will suffer during a recession, but is this necessarily the end of the world for the manager of a consumer business? Should he push alarm buttons, stop all new business, reduce existing credit lines, and double collection activity? Specifically, what steps should a consumer lender take when a national recession has arrived?

Ultimately, he should change very little of what he has been doing all along, as long as he has been managing the business intelligently (i.e., using all the tools available today to control portfolio risk). For a well-managed business, a recession can represent an opportunity to grow a business, particularly when other lenders pull back. If, however, a manager has been blindly following faddish competitive practices or expanding beyond his ability to control the business, then he should watch out; a recession can exacerbate his weaknesses.

PAST RECESSIONS

Recessions have been part of the U.S. economic scene ever since records have been kept. The unemployment rate, a key indicator of recession, went over 7% in the short, sharp recession of 1980 and over 9% in the very deep and painful recession of 1982; in contrast, during good economic times it can be as low as 4% (as it was at the turn of the century). The major problem during a recessionary period is unemployment, and more, the *fear* of unemployment. Consumers pull back their spending and borrowing, and the effects travel like a wave through the economy. But not everything that happens during a recession is bad. Following is a summary of the major trends in consumer credit, both negative and positive, that emerged during past recessions:

- *There is a slowdown in the growth of total consumer credit card sales volume, as well as outstandings.*

- *There is a decline in the volume of automobile, home mortgage, boat, recreational vehicle, and other retail sales–based credit. Second mortgage and home-equity loans remained steady through the 1990–92 recession; they have since grown to record highs. We will see what happens to these newer products in this recession.*

- *Collection efforts must be increased to recover the same number of dollars.*

- *The total quality of accounts accepted declines, and writeoffs increase in hard-hit areas. However, the decline is not as consistent and general as widely believed.*

- *Subprime lenders are hit hard.*

- *Automotive dealers and retail merchants fail at a higher rate.*

- *The cost of funds declines as general interest rates go down; this assumes that the Federal Reserve finally admits it is more interested in fighting recession than inflation. For lenders charging a fixed rate of interest, the spread increases; for those with a variable rate, there may be a limited benefit (e.g., the cost of money could decline faster than the customer's index). Lenders with a variable rate but with a floor (i.e., a rate tied to a variable index but with a predetermined bottom price) can also benefit.*

- *Management focuses on control (sometimes too late, but better late than never).*

- *Late fees and other miscellaneous charges may increase.*

- *Well-developed scoring systems continue to discriminate, but losses typically are higher at every score level so the cutoff scores should be carefully reviewed as overall loss rates rise (we will cover this later).*

One final point: income, at least credit card income, has remained remarkably steady through good times and bad. After rising significantly in the early 1980s as price restrictions were eliminated, credit card income has remained between 17-19% for the past sixteen years. While you assume that revenue would decline as interest rates go down during a recession (since most rates charged are variable today), there are other factors that impact income (e.g., late fees, interchange fees) so that the overall revenue has remained remarkably constant. Here is the average income on credit cards versus the short-term cost of funds over the past twenty-five years:

EXHIBIT 14-1

Credit Cards: Total Income and Cost of Funds

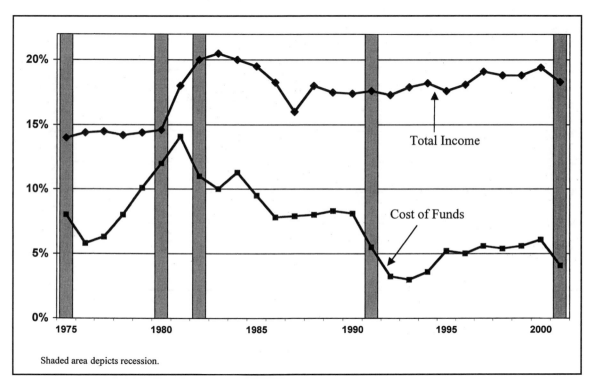

Shaded area depicts recession.

This apparent "price stability" as the cost of funds changes does not hold as true on some other consumer loan products (e.g., auto loans and home mortgage loans) where rates are very visible and a larger percentage of the total income. Rates, particularly home mortgage rates, receive an enormous amount of publicity with every twist of the Federal Reserve bank. You can hear the following comments on television every night as rates decline: "Mortgage rates have declined to a 23-month low of 6.75% as the Fed continues to lower rates to offset the recession." And, of course, the reverse is true during a time of rising rates. In the credit card business, then, a recession may help profits, or at least offset some of the rise in writeoff rates that occurs. Let's see.

Writeoff Rates over Time

Many factors influence writeoff rates, and recession is only one of them. Let's look at what happened to these rates during the 1980–82 recession, the 1991–92 recession, the 2001 recession, and during the good times between.

EXHIBIT 14-2
Credit Cards—% Writeoffs

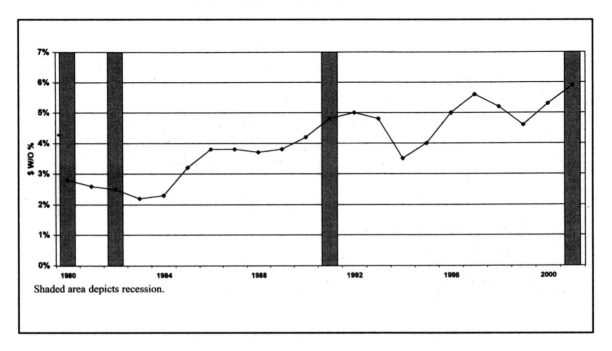

Shaded area depicts recession.

THE 1980 AND 1981–82 RECESSIONS

Writeoff rates, after rising sharply just prior to and during the recession period of 1980, *declined* during the actual recession period of 1981–82. Further, the same pattern of declining writeoff rates was seen in the portfolios of the major automobile credit companies (e.g., Ford Motor Credit Company and General Motors Acceptance Corp.), the major finance companies (e.g., Household International and Beneficial Finance), and at the major retailers (e.g., Penney's, Montgomery Ward's, and Sears, Roebuck), among others. What is the meaning of the *decrease* in writeoffs during the recession of 1981–82? Does this trend mean that risk managers should pray for a recession to help them work out their problem portfolios?

Several unique factors were at work during this period:

- *The pre-1980 rise in writeoffs might be explained by the very heavy mailing and expansion of the credit card business during 1978 and 1979. The writeoffs came later—in 1979 and 1980.*

- *The period from 1981 to 1983 was a time of retrenchment for the big card issuers as the high cost of funds and the caps placed on interest rates restricted (and in some cases eliminated) profits.*

- *The substantial rise in writeoff rates after 1984 (when the recession was over) reflects both an increase in the rate of bankruptcy and the return to an expansionist mode by card issuers as the spreads increased substantially. Some of these marketing programs had very low standards of screening.*

THE 1991–92 RECESSION

The story is different when you look at the 1991–92 recession: writeoff rates went up. This recession apparently hit the middle managers and clerical staff hardest, not the blue-collar workers who had borne the brunt of prior recessions. Industries that boomed during Ronald Reagan's presidency, such as defense, were cut back. Customers who got into trouble included many who were the target market of the boom years of the late 1980s, and their ability to pay (not their willingness to pay) was now a problem. The object of a good screening process is to identify the *ability* as well as the *willingness* of applicants to pay. Credit bureau reports increasingly were used during the 1990s, and at the time credit was extended, borrowers appeared to be good candidates by any past standard. Financial situations, however, change over time. A 1991 MasterCard study of bankruptcy showed that the typical customer filing for bankruptcy averaged seven loans or lines of credit ("trade lines") at the time of application, and eighteen six years later when the bankruptcy occurred. Presumably, these borrowers must have been performing well for those six years, meeting their obligations, otherwise they would not have been given all those new lines. There is no evidence of unwillingness to pay. Thus, some life event or crisis must have sharply reduced their ability to pay. Most typically this is caused by a job loss (either by one or both wage earners in a family), and presumably this is what happened during the 1991–92 recession.[1]

THE GOOD TIMES—THE 1990S

How then to explain the rise in writeoffs that occurred during the years 1995 through 1998, before finally turning down in 1999 and 2000? These were economic boom times, with some of the lowest unemployment rates ever in the USA. The most likely cause of rising writeoffs during this period has been the increasing acceptance of personal bankruptcy as a way of life. Here is the history of personal bankruptcies over time:

---

1. It is too early to interpret what is happening during the 2001–02 recession but writeoffs have been rising.

Exhibit 14-3
New Bankruptcy Petitions Filed (Consumer)

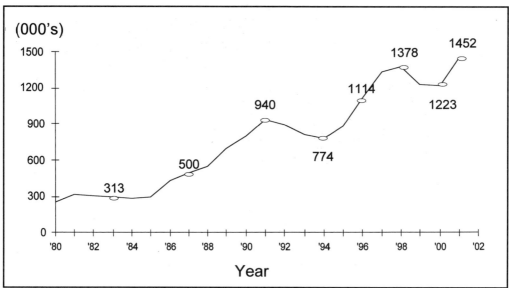

Since credit card debt was easy to incur (via mass mailings) and easy to wipe out (through bankruptcy), the impact of bankruptcy on card portfolio writeoffs was severe during this period. The secured products—automobiles and home mortgages—did not experience the same kind of increases in writeoffs, which can be explained by the fact that autos can be repossessed and homes foreclosed on, reducing the impact of bankruptcy on those products.

Managing in a National Recession

The truth is that the national economy is just *one* of many factors that impact a business's quality. Let's not forget the importance of good management. Other key factors that influence portfolio quality are:

- *The accuracy and thoroughness of the account acquisition process. A statistically derived and validated screening system is vital in this process. Some credit card portfolios have a writeoff rate of 15% (on 18-month-old accounts), but some similarly aged accounts have a writeoff rate of less than 3–4% (at a very conservative institution). The target market, the screens, and the screening processes were vastly different.*

- *Practices that encourage your good customers to use your card. These include retention marketing programs, support for their activity with well-managed operations, and good customer service.*

- *A well-run, well-staffed collections shop. Collections should use the latest scoring systems to direct the flow of work to those accounts most likely to pay with collection contact.*

- *The average age of the portfolio. New accounts tend to be riskier than those on the books for a while, and this can impact the bottom line.*

- *The geographic distribution of the portfolio. There are wide differences in the underlying economics and the fundamental bankruptcy rates by state, as we covered in Chapter 8, Collection Tactics.*

- *The maintenance of standards: avoiding stretching the terms, lowering down payments, and accepting marginal customers for the automobile and second mortgage portfolios. With lowered standards, losses on units repossessed can soar from 50 bps to 150 bps and home mortgage writeoffs can exceed 100 bps.*

Consumers generally try to discipline themselves. They get scared during hard times, they cut back on discretionary purchases, and they try to meet their obligations. If they did not, the whole system would fail because no collection activity could work in an environment where customers are irresponsible. In other words, success in the consumer lending business comes from careful attention to the details of the business and strict adherence to the principles covered in this book. It is always easy to give away credit through sloppy lending practices and by following the latest fad.

The first priority for a manager of a consumer business is to have the correct processes in place to maintain control over his operations. Anticipating a national recession is just one of those processes, and it may not even be the most important.

REGIONAL RECESSIONS

Let's not forget the importance of the health of the underlying regional economies. Although national recessions have been infrequent, regional dislocations have occurred throughout the last twenty years. These have included:

- *Low/high oil prices impacting the Southwest and other oil producing states*
- *Problems with the Rust-Belt economies of the Midwest as manufacturing jobs went abroad or were automated*
- *The short, sharp stock market crashes of 1987 and 1989 (which hit New York City hard)*
- *Lower farm prices, severe droughts, crop freezes, etc., which impact states with farm-dependent economies*
- *High energy costs, as in California in 2000.*

In short, a portfolio heavily concentrated in states undergoing a regional recession may have problems for a while, or conversely may enjoy good times. We strongly recommend that you follow the economic figures for your regional economies closely; the national figures get all the attention, but regional economic strengths and weaknesses may have more impact on your portfolio's performance, over the years, than the national figures.

RECESSION PLANNING AND ACTION PROGRAMS

Despite our contention that recessions are just a part of the management challenge, certain prudent steps can be taken when the economy (national or regional) turns down. Senior managers will wish to err on the side of caution and tell the board of directors that they are indeed taking action to prepare for economic hard times.

The following suggested process may help "routinize" the management of a consumer lending business during a national or a regional recession.

1) Defining the Problem

The first step is defining the problem by reviewing key national and regional economic indicators on a regular (e.g., quarterly) basis. The key indicators could be selected by an institution's economics department or from a common-sense list that includes recent trends in industrial production levels, new housing starts, new unemployment claims, retail sales, consumer installment credit, the rate of inflation, manufacturers' orders, and inventory levels, among others. Using this information, lenders should answer the following questions:

- *Is the problem national or regional? If it is regional, which regions are affected and which are not?*
- *Is it confined to one or two major industries (e.g., farming, automobiles), or is it a general economic downturn affecting a broad category of industries?*
- *How steep is the downturn? How does this one compare with prior recessions?*
- *What is the government doing to handle the problem? Is it trying to stimulate the economy or is it intensifying the recession by fighting a perceived bigger problem such as inflation?*
- *How long is the recession expected to last and what are the signals to look for that the economy is turning around?*

2) Preparing an Action Plan

Management should prepare an action plan listing steps that *could* be taken in the event of a recession. A list could include:

FOR NEW ACCOUNTS
- *For a short while, stopping all major mail solicitations to the most seriously affected geographic regions.*
- *Eliminating selected occupations from mail lists if these are threatened in one region or another (e.g., real estate brokers, auto salesmen, defense workers).*

- *Tightening selection standards on new applications and mail solicitations in areas still being solicited.*

- *Reviewing scoring systems more frequently to determine if they are continuing to rank-order accounts as they did in the past. If they are still rank-ordering, increase the cutoff score to maintain an acceptable writeoff rate as currently projected; if the score is not rank-ordering accounts as expected, start developing a new score immediately using new criteria and/or determine whether a generic score will better meet your needs in the short run.*

- *Tightening debt-burden standards where used.*

- *Increasing the down payment requirements on secured products.*

- *Increasing the number of accounts screened with a second score (typically a generic, credit bureau score model).*

- *Assigning lower limits and shorter terms to all new accounts, and increasing them only on the basis of charge and payment history as behavior scores dictate.*

- *Allowing more high-side overrides for threatened occupations or where there are signs of excessive debt.*

For Existing Accounts in Affected Regions

- *Advancing collection activity either judgmentally or by score range to try and collect ahead of the competition.*

- *Giving collectors more flexibility to accept partial payments or lower monthly payments to accommodate debtors who have temporary problems.*

- *Raising the qualifying performance score level before extending any line increases, renewing lines, or offering new products to existing customers. Use new test and control groups to determine the impact of the revised score approval levels.*

- *Researching the performance of customers at the credit bureaus (as ranked by their behavior score) to identify those getting into trouble with other creditors. Research may indicate a need for the following actions:*

  = *Slowing down or stopping line increase programs for all but the most profitable or best customers.*

  = *Terminating lower-scoring customers. The basis for this termination could be derived from your own records or from the customer's performance with other lenders. While this adverse action must be explained to the customer (who will be unhappy if he is meeting the terms of his agreement with you), you have the right to terminate as long as you are legally consistent and you can demonstrate consistency in your policies.*

  = *Reducing credit lines if allowable under the terms of your contract and speeding up collection activity on lower-scoring accounts when appropriate.*

- *Increasing the attention paid to bankruptcy control, including the use of trained specialists and paralegals to suggest alternatives to bankruptcy and to identify fraudulent and excessive claims.*

- *For indirect relationships, reviewing informal indicators of dealer, broker, or merchant performance more frequently and in more detail (e.g., salespeople being laid off, store closings, increasing inventories). Try to terminate the higher-risk and undesirable relationships by allowing competition to take them over (if possible), particularly if there is any sign of intention to defraud. If the lender cannot get rid of the account, monitor it closely and provide financing with great care.*

- *For all accounts, providing strong support to the long-term, desirable accounts to help them get through the difficult times. This can represent a good opportunity to reinforce a long-term relationship.*

3) Implementing the Plan

The plan should be implemented whenever economic indicators make lenders sufficiently certain that a downturn is real. Do not wait for the pronouncement from Washington that a recession has begun; by then, it may be too late. For instance, the actual numbers later showed that the 1990–92 recession was officially announced the month that it ended. By the time the bureaucrats had admitted that the United States was in the midst of a recession, it was over.

4) Resuming Business

When the recession appears to be bottoming out—that is, when the monthly or quarterly figures are no longer going down (they may even be moving up slightly)—it may be a good idea to resume cautious solicitation of new accounts, particularly in the areas most affected by the recession. This action assumes that the government will be acting appropriately to stimulate the economy, that local and regional authorities are really working on the problems, that the problems can be solved, and that the downturn is only temporary. If these conditions exist, then the lender could be the first to go after new business in a quick window of opportunity to gain market share. This demands more courage than many are willing to muster, but those who went into the bad areas at the bottom of one recession—such as NationsBank (now merged with Bank of America), which moved into Texas with portfolio purchases and mailings when the Texas market had been devastated by a sharp drop in oil prices—have been rewarded.

Although the possibility always exists of a discontinuity in the U.S. economy— a recession so severe that no amount of stimulation can induce a quick turnaround —we all hope this will not occur. Does the past always predict the future? No one can say for certain. However, a look back over the last thirty years (the life span of

RECESSION SCORING

During a recession, one key question is: Does an application score system continue to rank-order accounts as predicted by the score developer or as it did in the past? If it doesn't, the lender would be justified in throwing out the scorecard during a time of economic hardship. If it does, the lender can at least continue to make informed decisions. Fair, Isaac has studied the impact of recessions on scorecard performance and concluded that a typical, validated card continues to rank-order accounts, but that applicant quality decreases at each score level. The concept is shown in the following exhibit:

EXHIBIT 14-4
Recession: Bad Rate by Score Range

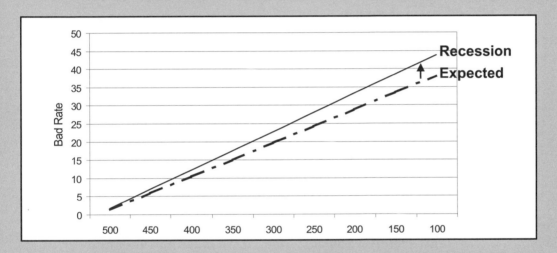

Gary Chandler, a former senior vice president at Management Decision Systems, came to the same conclusion. He noted that the number of high-risk scores (that is, applicants scoring over 800 on their bankruptcy score system) had nearly doubled from January 1990 to January 1991, but their models continue to rank-order accounts. (N.B. We apologize for the old statistics, but the recent recession is too new to be able to update the figures.)

Lenders have found that the net result of using the same scorecard during hard times and good times is a lower number of approved accounts during the hard times. This is because fewer people typically apply during a recession (most people use self-restraint when times are bad) and fewer achieve a passing score since the attributes typically scored will have changed.

Each lender should examine its own scorecard results more closely during a recession, using all appropriate tests (e.g., population stability, characteristic stability, actual performance, delinquency by score range, and so forth). If the scorecard is still rank-ordering accounts, raise the cutoff score to maintain an acceptable writeoff rate under the new conditions. However, lenders should realize that if they raise the cutoff score during the recession too sharply, they may be rejecting too many potentially good accounts just to eliminate a relatively small number of bad ones.

the modern consumer lending business) indicates that a national recession may not be the end of the world. In fact, it may represent an opportunity for the bold. And, to repeat, in my opinion, it is more important to be constantly addressing *regional* recessions through good management.

CONCLUSION

This brief chapter on recession ends our thoughts on managing consumer lending at the start of the twenty-first century. The business is fast changing, but we trust that our basic principles will be around for a few more years. In 1978, John Holder and I wrote a summary of ideas on good consumer lending practices that, interestingly, still hold true today. John and I were preparing for one of Citibank's new Consumer Lending Group's (the CSG) first "off-site" meetings on risk management at the Harriman Conference Center at Harrison, New York. We needed to create a "take-away" for the attendees. Sitting around the pool on a hot afternoon, we drafted the following *Ten Credit Commandments* (probably aided by a glass of wine), and I recently found a copy. Following is a slightly updated version of the original *Commandments*.

Ten Credit Commandments

1. *Credit is thy creed; neither create nor worship false idols, such as volume or growth, for their own sake.*
2. *Thou shalt consult with credit policy in accordance with credit laws.*
3. *Know thy products and regard their profits in the fullest detail.*
4. *Thou shalt use validated scores to the fullest extent of their abilities.*
5. *Be thou neither tardy nor inventive with thy MIS.*
6. *Be not ashamed of a product which turneth an honest dollar and a goodly return.*
7. *Thou mayest cast seeds on rocky and stony grounds but only in small numbers.*
8. *Thou shalt observe the movement of the actual numbers in comparison with thy forecast.*
9. *Thou mayest not covet the debtor's spouse, but canst take lawful possession of other assets.*
10. *Thou shalt develop realistic goals, which thy business should attain in the fullness of time.*

We wish you good luck in your career and hope that this book will help you to make a difference wherever you work.

DAVID LAWRENCE
ARLENE SOLOMON

Glossary

active account. An account with either a balance outstanding or some charge or payment activity within a designated time period, usually the prior year. An inactive account is one without any such activity.

adjustable rate mortgage (ARM). A mortgage whose interest rate varies up or down with a pre-selected index over the term of the loan. There is often a low introductory rate to attract customers.

affinity group. An association organized to provide services for a group of individuals who share an interest in the same hobby, profession, sports team, etc., or who have a commercial affiliation such as membership in a frequent flyer club.

amortization. The gradual reduction of a loan over time by making payments of principal (and interest). These payments can be regular or irregular depending on the terms of the loan.

annual percentage rate (APR). The cost of credit on a yearly basis expressed as a percentage of the outstanding balance owed.

application. A standard form required to be submitted along with a request for credit. It asks sufficient information on the applicant to enable the potential lender to make the credit decision. The length and complexity of an application varies by product.

application scoring. A scoring system designed to rank-order applications for credit, usually on the basis of risk. Application scores can also rank on the basis of profitability, anticipated revenue, etc.

appraisal. The value assigned by an evaluation expert to a physical asset, such as a house, that has been pledged as collateral for a loan. The appraisal typically forms the basis for the loan-to-value ratio on home mortgages.

ATMs (automated teller machines). Machines that handle many banking transactions without human intervention, including deposit taking, cash dispersal, account transfers, and so forth.

attribute. A classification or subcategory of a characteristic in a scoring system. For example, the characteristic *household income* might be classified into these attributes:

> $ Less than $15,000
>
> $ $15,000 – $24,999
>
> $ $25,000 – $50,000
>
> $ More than $50,000

attrition. A loss of active or inactive open accounts due to customers' voluntary termination of a credit relationship.

authorization. The process by which transactions such as credit card purchases and cash or credit line advances are approved by the lender. This (usually) highly automated review results in the transaction's being approved or declined, or the customer's being asked to call the issuing bank for further verification.

authorization scoring. A scoring system for rank-ordering transactions (cash or credit line advances, credit card purchases, etc.), usually on the basis of customer risk and the possibility of a fraudulent transaction. A transaction is fraudulent when an account is used, without permission, by someone other than the authorized user.

bad rate. The ratio, sometimes expressed as a percentage, of the number of bad accounts relative to the total number of accounts in the portfolio. (A bad account is usually defined as one that is unprofitable, frequently or severely delinquent, or is charged off.) Bad rate may also refer to the total dollar balance of bad accounts divided by the total dollar balance of all accounts, both good and bad.

balloon payment. The final payment on a loan that has not been fully amortized. It is usually significantly larger than the prior payments.

balance ratio. The ratio of the average balance among different accounts. The ratio is typically used to describe the average balance of accounts written off divided by the average balance of all accounts; it can also be used to describe the average balance of accounts in various stages of delinquency versus the average balance of all accounts.

bankruptcy. Protection granted by the courts to a borrower whose debts exceed his capacity to repay. There are three primary forms of consumer bankruptcy: Chapter 7, under which all unsecured debts are canceled, Chapter 13, whereby the debtor agrees to a formal plan to pay off a predetermined portion of his debts, and Chapter 11, which is similar to Chapter 13 but used by debtors with larger assets. Once a creditor receives a notice of bankruptcy, all collection activity must cease and the courts take over the distribution of the assets (if any). There are legal restrictions on how often a person can claim bankruptcy.

behavior scoring (also called **performance scoring**). A scoring system for rank-ordering accounts already on a lender's books, typically on the basis of internal data on your masterfile and other data. Behavior scores can rank customers' predicted behavior according to such factors as risk, desirability of offering line increases, probability of attrition, or likelihood of collecting past due amounts.

cap. A limit on the amount that the interest on a variable-rate loan can increase annually and over its lifetime.

characteristic. A variable used to calculate a score. A characteristic can be derived from any information used in developing the score, e.g., from the application, credit bureau reports, demographic data, and so forth. A characteristic from the application might be *household income*. One from the credit bureau might be *number of credit lines opened in the last six months*.

charge-off (also called **writeoff**). The balance owing on accounts the lending institution deems uncollectible. Most financial institutions charge off (or write off) accounts that have missed a predetermined number of payments (typically five to six). A charge-off also occurs when a borrower declares bankruptcy.

charge-off balance ratio. The average balance of accounts written off divided by the average balance of all accounts.

closing costs. Fees paid at a closing on a home mortgage. These can include attorney's fees, mortgage filing fees, accrued taxes, title search costs, insurance, and so forth.

cohort. See **vintage.**

confidence level. In statistics, the analyst's confidence that the conclusions reached in a test are correct and can be projected to the total portfolio. The size of the sample determines the confidence level: the larger the sample, the higher the confidence level. A sample size of 2,000 is usually adequate to ensure 95% confidence that test results would be the same if performed on the entire population.

collateral. Any item of value (e.g., an automobile, a home, a boat) legally pledged to secure a loan. The collateral may be repossessed in the event of nonpayment.

commission. A fee paid to a dealer or broker for referring business to a lending institution. The fee may be paid out immediately or over the term of the loan.

condominium. A legal arrangement between homeowners sharing common property, such as an apartment building or a cluster of homes or apartments. Under a condominium arrangement (as opposed to a **cooperative** arrangement, see below), each home buyer *owns* the property he lives in and shares expenses for the maintenance of the common property, such as lawns, pools, etc.

Consumer Credit Protection Act. Covered in the Federal Reserve Bank's Regulation B. The Act protects the rights of those applying for credit and the rights of borrowers who become delinquent. It also regulates access by lenders and others to an individual's credit bureau reports.

convenience account. A credit card account that pays the total balance owing within the allotted grace period every month.

cooperative. A legal arrangement between homeowners sharing common property, such as an apartment building or a cluster of homes or apartments. Under a cooperative arrangement (as opposed to a **condominum** arrangement, see above), each home owner owns a *share* of the total property, and common expenses (elevator maintenance, doormen, etc.) are divided according to the number of shares owned.

coupon (also called **response coupon**). A form included in a pre-approved credit offer to be returned to the lender by the prospect, indicating acceptance of the offer.

credit bureau. An organization that collects, files, and reports credit balances, repayment history, and total credit lines on all accounts reported to them. Credit bureaus compile individual reports, including personal histories such as current and past address, employment, marital status (where available) from data provided by, for example, lending institutions, retailers, doctors, and utilities. Credit bureaus also gather public information from courthouses and other sources on liens, divorce decrees, suits, bankruptcies, etc. Prospective or current lenders, insurers, employers, and others with legitimate business reasons may obtain these reports.

credit bureau characteristic. Information provided by a credit bureau that might be used as a variable in a scoring system, for example, *number of credit lines opened in the last six months.*

credit bureau inquiries. Requests for information from a credit bureau on current or prospective customers.

credit bureau trade. A record of credit lines or loans reported by lending institutions to the credit bureau. Trades may be *open*, meaning the account is currently active, or *closed*, in which case the historic performance of the account is reported.

credit cycle. The intellectual or conceptual model used to define the process of managing consumer credit products; steps include planning products, acquiring accounts, maintaining accounts, and managing collections and writeoffs. Management controls the credit cycle, using appropriate management information and decision tools.

credit history. An individual's current and past performance in obtaining and handling credit lines and loans. The information usually comes from credit bureau records or from a financial institution's own customer records.

credit line. The maximum amount of credit a customer may borrow on a revolving line at any particular time. Actual outstandings can be below this limit but should not be higher.

credit scoring. A process for rank-ordering credit applications or customers, using third-party (usually credit bureau) data, by the odds that they will perform in a particular way. Accounts or applications can be arrayed by their odds of being profitable, likely to respond, likely to become delinquent, or go to charge-off, etc. See also **application scoring** and **behavior scoring**.

cross-selling. Offering additional products to existing or new customers.

curing. The term applied to the process whereby a delinquent customer meeting his current obligations for a predetermined period (typically three or four months), but unable to catch up with his past missed payments, is brought back to a current state.

custom score. A scoring system designed for a specific lender's product(s) based on performance data from that lender's own portfolio (as opposed to generic scores, which are developed from performance data on the products of many lenders).

cutoff score. The score, calculated by a scoring system, at or above which one action is taken and below which another action is taken (e.g., accept all applications scoring above 640; reject those scoring below).

data mining. The term applied to the process of obtaining and analyzing large amounts of data, typically from many different sources, in order to understand better the target market, the customers, or the competition. The term originated in the 1990s with the monoline banks, which gathered data from many sources (credit bureaus, automobile records, catalog buyers, magazine lists, etc.) to prepare highly targeted offers for credit cards.

days past due. The number of days after the payment due date that an account remains unpaid. Delinquent accounts are often assigned to classifications or "buckets" by degree of delinquency, e.g., 1–29 days past due, 30–59 days past due, 60–89 days past due, up to the point at which accounts would be written off. The term is frequently abbreviated *dpd*.

debt burden. The estimated monthly payment on an individual's debt, or potential debt outstanding, as a percent of total or gross monthly income. Lending institutions frequently perform debt-burden calculations as part of the loan application process. Examples include the ratio of monthly payment on the loan being applied for as a percent of gross monthly income, or monthly payments due on all outstanding debt as a percent of gross monthly income.

debt consolidation. Using the proceeds of a new loan to pay off one or more existing loans. This is usually done when a customer has trouble meeting his existing obligations and is able to lower his monthly payments by consolidating existing loans with one loan at a more favorable term.

deductible. The amount deducted from any payment made by an insurance company for damages incurred on an insured product. For example, most people buy automobile collision insurance with a $500, a $1,000, or a larger deductible; this reduces the cost of the insurance significantly.

delinquency. The term for accounts where the contractual amount due is not paid as scheduled. A portfolio delinquency rate is typically expressed either as dollars past due as a percent of total outstandings or as total number of accounts past due as a percent of total number of accounts in the portfolio.

demographic data. Information available from the U.S. Census Bureau, magazine lists, automobile or housing sales, warranty registration cards, etc., on income, buying habits, and living styles (such as education and value of home) of individuals or households. Marketing companies assemble and summarize these data to provide lenders with useful information on potential or existing customers.

derogatories. Negative information found on a consumer's credit bureau records. Derogatories are usually rated as *Major Derogatories*, such as a bankruptcy or a delinquency in excess of ninety days, or *Minor Derogatories*, such as a thirty-day delinquency.

development sample. In scoring, a sample of accounts selected as representative of the total population of accounts to be analyzed. Samples are used to develop scoring systems to save the time and cost of analyzing total populations.

divergence. A measure used by some score developers to determine how accurately a characteristic or score can identify good and bad outcomes.

enhancements. Special services provided with or without charge to customers to encourage product usage and brand loyalty. These can include such diverse items as rental car insurance protection, free airline frequent flyer miles, coverage for lost or stolen goods, free or discounted merchandise, etc.

escrow. That portion of the monthly home mortgage payment set aside to cover the cost of insurance, property taxes, and other items that may be paid by the lender on behalf of the borrower.

exception (also called **policy exception**). A rule for rejecting an application based on general business policy. For example, a lender's policy may automatically reject any applicant for credit who has declared bankruptcy in the past, regardless of the likelihood of future default.

extension. The lengthening of the term of a loan because the customer has missed one or more payments during the course of the contract and can make these payments up only at the end.

Fannie Mae (Federal National Mortgage Association). One of the two publicly owned government-sponsored agencies (**Freddie Mac** is the other; see below) that buys packages of mortgages from lending institutions to hold or sell in the secondary market, thus providing liquidity to the lending institutions. To purchase the loans, these agencies are able to borrow money from the financial markets at favorable rates because they do not pay federal taxes and because there is an implied (but not clearly spelled out) guarantee that the government would not allow Fannie Mae or Freddie Mac to fail to pay their debts.

fragmented file. A file is called fragmented when a consumer has more than one credit bureau file, each with incomplete information. Fragmentation might occur due to a misspelled name, a different version of a name (John Jones vs. John R. Jones), or a recent move to a new address.

Freddie Mac (Federal Home Loan Mortgage Corporation). A second government-sponsored agency similar to Fannie Mae (see above).

Federal Reserve's Regulation B. See **Regulation B.**

first mortgage. A loan to buy a house, condominium, vacation home, etc., secured by a lien on the property. In the event of default on the loan, a first mortgage takes precedence over all other liens on the property.

floor-plan financing. Financing provided for an automotive, boat, recreational vehicle, or other dealer by a lender or the manufacturer's finance company so that the dealer can have units on hand to show potential customers. As each unit financed is sold at retail, the financier must be repaid. Sometimes also called *wholesale financing.*

foreclosure. The legal process required to gain possession of a house or property when a specified number of mortgage payments has been missed and the customer has not sold the house on his own.

generic scoring system. Scoring systems or models created by the major scoring companies and credit bureaus on the basis of random samples of national credit bureau files. Generic scores are particularly useful if current data to build a lender's own custom score are insufficient. Generic scoring systems can also be used in conjunction with custom scores to improve the credit decision.

good-bad odds. The ratio of goods to bads in a population or some subset of the population.

high-side override. A decision to ignore or override the scoring system and reject an applicant passing the cutoff score. Such action may be taken because an additional review discloses unfavorable information not taken into account by the scoring system.

holdout sample. The sample set aside for validating a scoring system after it has been developed. When developing a scoring system, the total sample is divided into two parts: a development sample used for analysis to create the scoring system, and a holdout sample set aside and used later for validation.

home-equity loan/line of credit. A loan or line of credit extended to a homeowner who has some equity or value remaining in the home after accounting for a first mortgage. The lender calculates this value by deducting the outstanding amount of any first mortgage from the current or appraised value of the home. Home-equity lending can take the form of an installment loan or a revolving line of credit.

inactive account. An account with either no balance outstanding or no transaction activity within a designated time period, usually the prior year.

index. The preselected base interest rate used to establish the price paid for a variable-rate loan over its lifetime. The lender sets the final customer rate by charging a number of percentage points (say, 1–10%) over a widely published cost-of-funds rate (e.g., the six-month Treasury Bill rate). The lender also establishes the timing of any changes and whether or not there is a cap or ceiling on the maximum.

indirect business. A term describing finance contracts sourced to a lender by a third party, typically applied to credit sales generated by automobile, boat dealers, etc., and to private label retailers or department store finance programs. Sometimes also called the *sales finance business*.

inquiry. A request to a credit bureau for information. Inquiries include both promotional and non-promotional inquiries. An inquiry is *promotional* if a creditor reviews a report without the prospect's prior request, as for pre-approving a credit offer. Promotional inquiries are not usually reported to other lending institutions. A *non-promotional* inquiry is posted to a credit report when a creditor reviews the report with the individual's permission, as when a person applies for credit or when an account is past due and the collections department reviews the report. Non-promotional inquiries are also made when a creditor reviews a credit bureau report for account monitoring purposes, e.g., to determine whether to increase or decrease a customer's line of credit.

installment loan. A loan scheduled to be repaid in a predetermined number of payments. The amount of the payment can vary if the loan is based on a variable-rate index, but the principal amortizes over time.

interchange income. Income that the credit card issuer and the merchant bank share on credit card purchases. The income, typically 1–5% of the amount charged, is deducted from the amount the merchant receives for the sale (the *merchant discount*, see below).

judgmental screening. Evaluating customer applications using rules based on lending officers' or experts' experience and judgment.

K-S test (Kolmogorov-Smirnov Test). A statistical test measuring how well a scoring system or statistical model separates desirable from undesirable accounts or prospects. The K-S test measure is calculated by subtracting the cumulative percent of undesirable accounts or prospects from the cumulative percent of desirable accounts or prospects, at various cutoff scores. The point where the absolute difference is greatest is the K-S measure. Higher K-S measures indicate stronger statistical separation.

late fee. A charge made by a lender for payments received after the stated due date.

leasing. A method of financing whereby an asset is leased or "rented" to a customer (vs. an outright purchase). The underlying ownership and title remain with the lessor (the financier); the lessee (the customer) has the use of and is responsible for insuring and maintaining the asset. Leases may be *open* or *closed ended*. With an open-end lease, the lessee is responsible for any difference between the residual value, that is, the calculated value of the unit when the lease ends, and the fair-market price of the goods. In a closed-end lease, the customer has the *option* of buying or *not* buying the goods at the residual price; if he does not wish to buy, the lessor must take the unit back and is responsible for any gain/loss on resale.

lessor. The legal owner of the property or goods being rented to someone else.

lessee. One who rents and uses the property or goods owned by someone else.

lien. A third-party claim on an individual's property or future earnings.

line increase. Raising the credit limit on an individual's revolving line of credit.

loan-to-value ratio. The ratio of the amount of a loan to the value of the property used as collateral. For example, an $80,000 home mortgage loan on a property valued at $100,000 would have an 80% loan-to-value ratio.

low-side override. A decision to ignore the scoring system and accept an applicant failing the cutoff score. Low-side overrides are often made because an additional review reveals information that is not taken into consideration in the scoring system, such as a longstanding relationship at a branch office.

mail solicitations. A method of acquiring new customers by direct mail. Prospective names are culled from existing databases, screened for risk and other variables, and the "survivors" are mailed an opportunity to either apply for credit, or are offered credit which can be accepted with some minimum qualifications (the latter is a pre-approved offer).

maturity. The term of a loan, usually expressed in years.

merchant bank. The bank which processes a merchant's credit card transactions, forwarding the transactions to the card associations for approval, and advancing money to the merchant within a prescribed settlement period. Also called **acquiring bank**.

merchant discount. The amount deducted from the total paid by the finance source (e.g., a MasterCard or Visa association bank, American Express, etc.) to the merchant or retail outlet for each credit sale (can range from 1–5% of the total dollar amount charged).

metrics (also called **MIS** or **management information**). The pieces of information or measurements to be monitored in order to understand whether a program is successful or not. A well-run consumer lending business will measure performance for every step of the account acquisition, account management, and collections process in order to understand profitability.

minimum payment. The minimum monthly payment of principal and interest contractually required to be paid to avoid becoming delinquent.

MIS or management information (see **metrics** above)

monoline. The term applied to a group of financial institutions which expanded their credit card portfolios rapidly during the late 1980s and the 1990s, primarily through the use of sophisticated, highly targeted, direct mail solicitations. These include small regional banks such as Capital One, First USA, Advanta, Providian, etc., which grew rapidly with national mailings and joined the Top Ten card issuers by the turn of the century.

multiple regression. A statistical modeling technique that uses several characteristics simultaneously to predict an outcome. In building a scoring system, multiple regression programs produce weights for each chosen attribute to derive an individual's score. Multiple regression is the most common modeling technique for deriving scores.

negative selection. The inability to attract good customers (either through bad product design, bad targeting, weak offering), which results in a lower percentage of goods (and therefore a higher percentage of bads) than should have occurred; the tendency for bad customers to be acquired easily while good customers are difficult to book.

neural nets (also called **neural networks**). Sophisticated scoring systems that use data-filtering techniques to constantly identify patterns in the data. Like scoring models (developed using multiple regression techniques), neural nets rank-order accounts.

odds. The likelihood of an event's occurring. For example, a loan portfolio with a 25% bad rate can also be said to have 3:1 good/bad odds or three goods for every one bad account.

outstandings. The total principal and any current or past due interest remaining to be paid on a loan at any given point in time. Sometimes also called **receivables** or *average net receivables (ANR)*.

over-limit accounts. A revolving credit account with a balance over the approved credit line. Minor over-limit amounts (e.g., less than 5–10% of the line) are usually authorized, but higher amounts are usually rejected at the point of sale. With a statistically validated and up-to-date behavior scoring system, lenders sometimes authorize an immediate line increase for high-scoring customers. The travel and entertainment cards (e.g., American Express, Diners, Carte Blanche) have no formally published spending limit, but they track charges carefully to avoid abuse.

override. A decision that reverses the action recommended by a scoring (or judgmental) system. For example, in an application scoring system, a low-side override would accept an applicant who scores below the scoring system's cutoff; a high-side override would reject an applicant who scores above the scoring system's cutoff. (See also **low-side** and **high-side overrides**).

partial payment. The payment of less than the scheduled amount contractually due on a loan. Typically, if the payment is at least 90% of the amount due, the account need not "age" to the next stage of delinquency; if less, it should.

performance scoring (also called **behavior scoring**). A scoring system for rank-ordering accounts already on a lender's books, typically on the basis of internal masterfile and other data. Performance scores rank customers' predicted behaviors according to such factors as risk, desirability of offering line increases, probability of attrition, or likelihood of collecting past due amounts.

points. 1. Values assigned to each attribute in a scoring system (also called **weights** or **regression weights**). Points are summed to calculate an individual's score. 2. An up-front charge paid by the borrower to the lending institution to cover the costs of processing and approving an application for a home mortgage. Points are usually expressed as a percent of the total loan (e.g., 2 points = 2% or $2,000 on a $100,000 loan application).

policy exception (see also **exception**). A rule for rejecting an application based on general business policy. For example, the lender may have a policy that automatically rejects any applicant for credit who has declared bankruptcy in the past, regardless of the likelihood of future default.

population. The total universe from which a sample is selected. The sample is typically only a small proportion of the population, but it must be representative of the whole.

portfolio. A group of consumer loan or credit outstandings acquired with standard terms and conditions. Analysis and control by portfolio(s) is the key to management of the consumer lending business. A portfolio can be further subdivided into "vintages" (i.e., similar accounts put on during the same time period). See also **vintage.**

prepayment. The early payout of the remaining outstanding balance of a loan. Sometimes there is a penalty for prepayment, particularly if it occurs in the first year of the contract term.

prepayment penalty. A charge imposed by a bank when a customer terminates a loan earlier than the contractual term.

principal. The total balance owing, excluding interest, at any point in time during the term of a loan.

private label business. The name applied to retailer or department store finance programs. Many small and large retailers use a third party (i.e., bank or finance company) to provide a full range of financing services. The retailer's name is on the charge card, but the accounts are owned and fully serviced by the financier.

private mortgage insurance (PMI). Insurance a lender requires that a customer purchase from a private insurance company to help protect the mortgage lender against default. This is typically required only when the down payment is less than 20%.

predatory lending. The term applied to lenders who take advantage of unsophisticated or ignorant consumers with limited or poor credit histories. Predatory lenders extend credit at very high rates of interest, impose large penalty fees for any violations, and collect delinquent accounts aggressively.

probability. The likelihood of an event's occurring; for example, the probability of heads when flipping a coin is .5, or one in two.

prohibited basis. A term used in the Federal Reserve Bank's Regulation B to indicate characteristics that may not be considered in a scoring system. Regulation B prohibits credit practices that discriminate on the basis of race, color, religion, national origin, sex, marital status, age, or source of income.

public record. Information such as bankruptcy, divorce, etc. recorded by the courts or other governmental agencies and available to the public. Credit bureaus collect this information and include it in reports as public record information.

"quick sale" price. The price estimated to be received for an asset such as a home if it must be sold immediately (usually estimated to be 10–20% less than the appraised value).

random sample. A sample selected to ensure no predisposition to pick one piece of information over another. The purpose of random sampling is to eliminate known bias from the resulting sample.

rank-ordering (also called *arraying*). Sequencing members of a population according to desirability. For example, a risk-scoring system would rank-order (array) the population in order of riskiness; a profit-scoring system would rank-order the population in order of profitability.

receivables. The total principal and any current or past due interest remaining to be paid on a loan at any given point in time. Sometimes also called **outstandings.**

recoveries. Money recovered from accounts already written off. This could result from additional internal or outside (agency or attorney) collection efforts. If funds are recovered through outside agencies or attorneys, the recoveries are reported net of the cost of collections. Writeoffs are typically reported net of recoveries.

regression weights (also called **score weights** or **points**). Values assigned to each attribute in a scoring system. Points are summed to calculate an individual's score.

Regulation B. The Federal Reserve Bank's regulation that specifies requirements for scoring systems used to evaluate the extension of credit. The Equal Credit Opportunity Act, as implemented in Regulation B, prohibits credit practices that discriminate on the basis of race, color, religion, national origin, sex, marital status, age, or source of income.

reject inference (also called **statistical inferencing**). A technique for extrapolating or projecting performance of rejected prospects through statistical or empirical methods.

repossession. The process of recovering an asset pledged to secure a loan. This begins only when the customer falls behind a predetermined number of payments and is unwilling or unable to sell the asset and satisfy the debt on his own.

residual value. The predetermined "buy" price or amount owing at the end of a lease.

response coupon (also called **coupon**). A form included in a pre-approved credit offer to be returned to the lender by the prospect, indicating acceptance of the offer.

response rate. The number of prospects who respond to an offer expressed as a percentage of the total number to whom the offer was made.

retention marketing. Marketing activities designed to persuade customers to continue a lending relationship with a lender.

return on assets (ROA). A measure of business performance calculated by dividing portfolio profits by portfolio outstandings or assets in total. The measure is usually annualized.

return on equity (ROE). A measure of business performance calculated by dividing portfolio profits by the share of portfolio assets represented by the ownership or equity interest. The measure is usually annualized.

revolving line. Credit extended with a ceiling (the "line" or "credit limit") that the customer can draw down (up to the limit) or pay off at his convenience. A minimum monthly repayment is typically required.

rewrites. A past due loan rewritten with lower monthly payments/more liberal terms to meet a customer's need for temporary relief from his regular obligations.

robust scorecard. A scorecard that is likely to remain valid even when the environment changes somewhat.

sample. A selected portion of a larger population. In most cases, the population is too large for statistical analysis so a sample is extracted to represent the total. Choosing a sample must be done carefully to ensure that the sample is a) large enough to be statistically significant and b) representative of all subpopulations in the total.

sales out of trust (SOT). Units that are floor-plan financed and sold by a dealer to a retail customer, but the loans are not paid off. The standard dealer agreement requires that a floor-plan unit be paid off as soon as it is sold.

satisfactory rating. The indication on a trade line at a credit bureau showing that the customer is paying or has paid his obligation(s) according to agreement.

score weights (also called **points** or **regression weights**). Values assigned to each attribute (e.g., *household income*) in a scoring system. Points are summed to calculate an individual's score.

scorecard. The listing of individual characteristics and weights used in calculating a score total. A scoring system may contain one or more scorecards.

scorecard validation (also called **validation**). A process of certifying that a scorecard performs satisfactorily.

scoring system. A family of scorecards that rank-orders accounts according to the user's requirements. A typical scoring system includes one scorecard for each statistically different subpopulation.

second mortgage. A loan made by a lender on a home for which there is already a first mortgage. In the event that the property is repossessed or sold, the first mortgage must be paid off before the second lender receives any funds.

secondary market. The name given to investors (Fannie Mae, Freddie Mac, the banks, insurance companies, pension funds, etc.) who buy packages of loans (mortgages, credit cards, auto loans, etc.) generated by the direct consumer lenders. The secondary markets provide liquidity to the direct lenders and an alternative source of funds versus their own depositors.

secured loan. A loan advanced usually to buy a specific asset. The asset is pledged against the loan and can be seized in the event of default to help satisfy the debt. The collateral can be any marketable asset.

securitization. Raising funds by selling a package of homogeneous loans to an investor(s) by a public or private offering. The receivables are placed in a trust and are administered and paid off over time in accordance with a clearly defined legal agreement. The trust may be administered in-house or by a third party.

settlement. An agreement to accept less than 100 cents on the dollar for any funds owed (typically seriously past due).

skip trace. The specialized process of trying to locate hard-to-find customers. Some of these missing customers may have intended to defraud by moving away; others could be missing due to an inadvertent mixup in name or address.

solicitation scoring. A scoring system designed to rank-order prospective customers for direct mail solicitation, based on information from credit bureau files and other sources. Solicitation scores typically rank-order prospects by risk, revenue predictors, and anticipated response rates.

spread. The difference between the total income received on an outstanding balance (interest plus all charges and fees) and the cost of funds.

statistical clustering. A statistical modeling program used to divide a sample into homogeneous or similar groups known as clusters. Individuals are grouped into clusters based on the values of selected characteristics which can then be analyzed and used to develop scoring models. (Also called *clustering routines*.)

statistical divergence. A measure used to estimate how well a scorecard separates goods from bads.

statistical inferencing (also called **reject inference**). A technique for extrapolating or projecting performance of rejected prospects through statistical or empirical methods.

statistical validity. Describes how well a score measures what it is designed to measure. When developing a score, there must be sufficient data (e.g., enough goods and bads) in order to accurately measure and assess the outcome.

subpopulation. A portion of a total population. For example, the population of auto loan customers can be divided into two or more subpopulations: those financing new cars, used cars, used cars over five years old, etc.

take-ones. Applications for credit placed at high-traffic retail outlets, designed to be picked up by people who might not otherwise seek credit.

trade. A loan, line of credit, or other consumer financial relationship as reported on a credit bureau report.

travel and entertainment cards (T&E). Charge cards (e.g., some American Express cards, Diners Club, Carte Blanche) without a formal spending limit, but the balance is required to be paid in full each month.

triage. The process of sorting anything from loan applications to accounts in collections into groups of items that can be treated similarly. For instance, loan applications can be triaged into those that are easiest to approve, easiest to decline, and all others. Accounts in collection can be triaged into those most likely to pay, least likely to pay, and all others.

underwriting. The process of reviewing, analyzing, and deciding whether to approve, reject, or modify an application for credit.

unsecured loan/line. A loan or line of credit advanced with no pledge of collateral, typically for any general purpose.

validation (also called **scorecard validation**). The process of certifying that a scorecard performs in a statistically satisfactory way.

variable (also called **characteristic**). A characteristic used to calculate a score. A variable can be derived from any information used in developing the score, e.g., from the application, credit bureau reports, demographic data, and so forth. A characteristic from the application might be *household income*. One from the credit bureau might be *number of credit lines opened in the last six months*.

variable-rate loans. Consumer loans with an interest rate or charges that can change periodically in relation to an index. See also **index**.

verification. The process of verifying that the customer applying for credit exists, and that information contained on the application is correct.

vintage. A block of accounts acquired during the same time period under standard terms and conditions. This could be one month's business, one quarter's, or accounts put on the books by one specific mailing. Sometimes also called *cohort*.

weights. Values assigned to each attribute in a scoring system. Points are summed to calculate an individual's score.

writeoff (also called **charge-off**). The dollar amount of funds advanced (principal plus accrued, unpaid interest) deemed uncollectible at a predetermined time of delinquency (e.g., after 180 days of delinquency on a credit card). A charge-off also occurs when a borrower declares bankruptcy. For accounting purposes, this amount is typically taken as a charge against reserves which have been established by ongoing charges against income. Writeoffs are reported gross and net of recoveries.

Index

Internal factors, planning processes and, 22–23
Internal mailing lists, 103
Internet marketing, 74, 75
  mortgage products and, 199
Introductory rates, special, 29
Isaac, Earl, 44

Jost, Allen, 70
JP Morgan Chase, 10, 34, 250
Judgmental screening systems, 82–85
  expert systems, 82–83
  limitations of, 84–85
  for portfolio managers, 54
Jumbo loans, 202

Kinney, Obie, 182–83
K-S (Kolmogorov-Smirnov) test, 62

Lagged reporting, 145–46, 241–42
Late fees, 216
  pricing, 29–31
Leasing, automobile, 185–87
Legal process, for mortgage products, 211
Letters of decline, 60, 94–95
Liability, of student cards, 76
Liability insurance, 178–79, 210–11
Lifestyle target markets, 25, 102–3, 104–5
Lifetime profitability analysis, 220–28
Line assignments, 24, 95–98, 108
  increasing, 127, 132
  initial, 96–98, 108
Living costs, debt-burden analysis and, 91
Loan Prospector, 202
Loan size
  automobiles, 176
  home mortgages, 201–2
Loan-to-value (LTV) ratios
  mortgage products, 204–6, 214
  vehicles, 176–77
Losses. See Writeoffs
Loss leaders, 219–20
Lost credit cards, 129, 130
Low-risk accounts, collection process, 140
Low-side overrides, 59
Low-usage, low-risk target markets, 26, 36–37
Lundy, Ed, 239

Mail campaigns. See Direct mail campaigns
Mailing lists, 103–5
  from external sources, 103–5
  from internal sources, 103
  screening, 107–8
Mail-intercept fraud, 112, 129, 130

Maintaining accounts. See Portfolio management
Management, 243–56
  of accounts. See Portfolio management
  creating a credit culture, 250
  functional, 243–44, 246–47
  positions and duties, 247–50
  predicting the future, 42
  principles of good, 10–18
  product, 243–45
  of risk. See Risk management
  strategies of, 21–22
  structures of, 243–47
Management information systems (MIS), 14–16, 233–42
  disaggregating data, 237–38
  graphical representation of data, 238
  indirect vehicle business and, 184–85
  lying with numbers, 240–42
  as principle of good management, 11, 14–16
  reporting trends, 234–35
  risk managers role in, 252
  standards or norms, 235–36
  summarizing data, 236
  telling a story, 238–40
  tracking mailings, 109–10
Manufacturers, automobile, 173–74, 182
Marketing, 72–76. See also Direct mail campaigns
  application process and, 78
  cross-selling, 26, 74, 128
  retention, 125–27
Market pricing. See Pricing
MBNA, 10, 31, 34, 74, 75
Metrics. See Management information systems
MetroMail, 103
MicroVision, 104
Migration reports, 144
Minimum monthly payments, 32–34, 37
MIS. See Management information systems
Mobile home financing, 171
Monitoring of scoring systems, 61–65
  report cards, 64–65
  statistical validation, 61–63
  warning reports, 63–64
Monoline companies, 9, 20–21, 100.
  See also specific companies
Monthly payments, minimum. See Minimum monthly payments
Mortgages. See Home mortgages; Second mortgages

Negative selection, 71–72
Net flow forecasts. See Roll rates
Net writeoffs, 144–45

Neural networks, 69–70
New technologies, introducing by risk managers, 251–52
NextCard, Inc., 75
Nonconforming loans, 195–96, 201, 204
Normal scoring errors, 60
Norms or standards, 235–36, 252

Objectives
  of direct mail campaigns, 95, 101
  of scoring systems, 47–48
Offering packages, 105–6
Open-ended loans. See Revolving products
Operating expenses, 114
Operations, application process and, 78
Operations managers, 248, 250
Originate and hold, 195
Originate and sell, 195–96
Overrides, scoring systems and, 58–60

Parent guarantees, of students, 76
Partial payments, 158
Payment extensions, 158
Payments
  minimum monthly, 32–34
  road map to, 150–51, 156
Percentage rates, determining, 32–34
Performance scoring. See Behavior scoring
Personal data, on applications, 78–79
Personal identification numbers (PINs), 131
Planning, 19–42
  background analysis, 22–23
  of direct mail campaigns, 101–5
  failures in, 19–20
  mortgage products, 198–201
  predicting the future and, 42
  as principle of good management, 10, 13–14
  of products, 23–42
    approval, 40–41
    definition of product, 23–24
    delivery, 41
    direct versus indirect, 25
    forecasting results, 38–39
    implementation and feedback, 41
    research and analysis, 26–27
    secured versus unsecured, 25
    target market and, 25–26, 35–38
    term/installment versus revolving, 24
    terms and conditions, 28–35
  for recessions, 264–68
  of scoring systems, 47–51
    behavior scoring, 117–20
    developers, 48–49
    good and bad accounts, 49–50

About the Authors

David Lawrence, President of D.B. Lawrence & Co., has more than thirty years' experience in the consumer lending business. Over nine of these years were at Citicorp, where he was the Senior Credit Officer of the consumer banking group and later its representative on the Credit Policy Committee. He created the bank's first training program for senior management on the consumer credit process and is the author of both the 1984 Citicorp publication *Risk and Reward—the Craft of Consumer Lending* and the 1992 Prentice Hall publication, *The Handbook of Consumer Lending*, a leading work on the management and control of the high volume consumer lending business. He was also Editor-in-Chief of *The Journal of Consumer Lending*.

Prior to joining Citicorp, David was with Ford Motor Company for 21 years. There he held a variety of positions which included launching and managing credit businesses in Australia, the Philippines, Japan, and Taiwan.

Arlene Solomon has extensive experience in consulting for a wide range of businesses. In addition to general consulting in organization and training issues, Arlene's company (Arlene Solomon Associates Inc.) designs and develops training and general communications programs. The work frequently involves collaboration with senior subject matter experts in complex areas, thus blending content and training expertise.

Arlene's firm has been involved in developing training courses for senior managers in planning and implementing principles of credit, marketing, advertising, and data processing. Her firm also develops courses in product knowledge and sales and general management.

For the last 15 years, David and Arlene have been developing and offering training and communications in the area of consumer lending.